The Confident Choir

D1563311

The Confident Choir

A Handbook for Leaders of Group Singing

Michael Bonshor

ROWMAN & LITTLEFIELD
Lanham • Boulder • New York • London

Published by Rowman & Littlefield
A wholly owned subsidiary of The Rowman & Littlefield Publishing Group, Inc.
4501 Forbes Boulevard, Suite 200, Lanham, Maryland 20706
www.rowman.com

Unit A, Whitacre Mews, 26-34 Stannary Street, London SE11 4AB

British Library Cataloguing in Publication Information Available

Library of Congress Cataloging-in-Publication Data

Names: Bonshor, Michael, author.
Title: The confident choir : a handbook for leaders of group singing / Michael Bonshor.
Description: Lanham : Rowman & Littlefield, [2018] | Includes bibliographical references and index.
Identifiers: LCCN 2017035627 (print) | LCCN 2017035670 (ebook) | ISBN 9781538102800 (electronic) | ISBN 9781538102787 (cloth : alk. paper) | ISBN 9781538102794 (pbk. : alk. paper)
Subjects: LCSH: Choral singing—Instruction and study. | Choral conducting.
Classification: LCC MT875 (ebook) | LCC MT875 .B66 2018 (print) | DDC 782.5/14—dc23 LC record available at https://lccn.loc.gov/2017035627

Printed in the United States of America

Contents

Preface   ix

Acknowledgements   xiii

Introduction: Singing Together   xv
    Amateur "Careers" in Group Singing   xvi
    The Highs and Lows of Singing   xviii
    Singers and Their Stories   xix
    Seeing the Bigger Picture   xx
    A Note on Terminology   xxiv

1   Conveying and Cultivating Confidence   1
    The Embodiment of Confidence   2
    Communicating Confidence   8
    The Cloak of Confidence   17
    The Conductor's Contribution   22
    Chapter Summary   28

2   Practice, Preparation, and Presentation   31
    Performance Anxiety and Motivation   32
    Musical Expression and Immersion   34
    Going with the Flow   36
    Practice and "Overlearning"   39
    Warming Up   42
    Repertoire Selection   44
    Keeping Up Appearances   47
    Practical Presentation   50
    It'll Be All Right on the Night!   52
    Chapter Summary   56

3 Choral Acoustics and Choir Configuration   57
    Here Comes the Science   58
    Hearing Each Other   60
    Closeness and Confidence   61
    Choir Formation and Communication   64
    Positioning the Performers within the Venue   67
    Individual Placement within the Choir   69
    From Rehearsal Room to Concert Venue   71
    Action Stations   75
    Chapter Summary   78

4 Collaboration and Communal Learning   81
    Community, Comradeship, and Camaraderie   82
    The Choral Team   84
    Trust, Support, and Reciprocal Peer Learning   87
    Role Models and Team Leaders   94
    Clashes and Conflicts   99
    The Choir as a Community of Practice   103
    Building Confident Choral CoPs   107
    Developing the Choral Community   109
    Chapter Summary   110

5 Conductors and Verbal Communication   113
    The Source of Feedback   114
    The Power of Praise   116
    Balancing the Amount of Positive and Negative Feedback 119
    Constructive Criticism   123
    Destructive Criticism   125
    Communication Style   129
    Individual Needs within the Choir   132
    Accounting for Choral Diversity   137
    Pause for Reflection   139
    Chapter Summary   142

6 Singer-Centered Choral Conducting   145
    Final Checklist for Conductors   149

Conclusion   153
    Facilitating Flow   154
    There Are Limits!   154
    Personal Reflections upon Professional Practice   155
    A Conductor's Mission Statement   156

Notes   157

Bibliography   171

Index   179

About the Author   187

Preface

I think it's amazing how a really good musical director can lift you onto a level you never thought for a minute that you could achieve, and that's such a fantastic feeling . . . just that there's somebody there that you're putting your confidence into.
—Dawn

The above quotation encapsulates the impact that a leader of group singing activities can have upon amateur performers. Dawn was one of the singers that I interviewed during a research project that was inspired by over three decades of working with people who sing together. As a conductor and singing teacher, I have met many singers like Dawn, who value the trust and rapport that can develop between a choir and their musical director. As a comparatively late-blooming researcher, I have made it my mission to find out how those of us who regularly wave our arms around in front of amateur singers can encourage them to have confidence in us as their conductors, and to develop confidence in themselves as performers.

This book is designed to be helpful to anyone who conducts, or wants to conduct, adult amateur choirs of any kind. It will also be of interest to anyone who participates in group singing activities, and students of group dynamics in choral performance. It includes a thorough exploration of some of the factors affecting confidence levels in amateur choral singers; it creates an accessible synthesis of some of the psychological models of confidence and relates them to the choral context; and it offers practical confidence-building strategies for conductors, teachers, community musicians and workshop leaders. Each chapter contains original research data, first-hand insights into the perspectives of choral singers, links to psychological and philosophical frameworks, and suggestions for the application of these concepts. There are also real-life case studies, practical exercises, hints and tips for conductors, and a series of handy checklists and reminders.

Some of this material is based on my own experience, acquired during a longstanding career of working with singers of all ages, abilities, and musical interests. However, much of the content is also derived from my more-recent empirical research career. Some of the findings have reflected my observations as a singer, teacher, and conductor; other results have been more unexpected and thought-provoking. My original research aims were to explore the lived experience of choral singers; to identify some of the main influences on their perceptions of their voices and performance ability; and to highlight some of the factors affecting their confidence as singers. The ultimate objective is to provide a set of useful recommendations for musical leaders with an interest in maximizing confidence in choral ensembles.

Throughout the text, precedence is given to the "voices" of the singers; we hear directly from them about their thoughts, opinions, perceptions, and feelings about the process of singing together. This book is about how amateur singers engage in group singing activities, and how conductors and other musical leaders can help them to optimize their enjoyment of choral participation. It focuses on the philosophy, pedagogy, and practice of developing confident and competent choral singers. The principal themes include verbal and nonverbal communication; group dynamics; collaboration and peer learning; musical leadership and group facilitation; practice and preparation; and environmental factors, such as the effects of acoustics on singers' perceptions of their own performances.

I hope that there will be something useful here for every leader of group singing activities, regardless of their background, training, or experience. There are probably as many routes to becoming a conductor of an amateur choir as there are individuals in this position. Some leaders of group singing may have studied conducting as part of their academic education, but there are also many excellent and charismatic self-made conductors who have received comparatively little formal training. Musicians often become choir conductors by accident rather than design, and the reasons for this are myriad. Some composers conduct because they prefer to lead performances of their own choral works rather than delegating this to a full-time professional conductor. Church organists and school music teachers are usually expected to conduct choirs, regardless of whether they have any desire for, or experience of, choral leadership. Rehearsal pianists are sometimes co-opted to the role of conductor to cover for absences, and some may subsequently develop their own career in choral conducting. Some singers end up conducting their own amateur groups due to a shortage of trained conductors, or perhaps due to a sense of vocation.

The evolution of a choral conductor has some parallels with the development of a singer. Conductors and singers work with their own physical, intellectual, and emotional resources, as well as with their musical knowledge and skills, and, of course, their unique voices. Also, as with dedicated vocal practice, much of the preparatory work of becoming a conductor is often carried out alone, with limited opportunities for obtaining constructive feedback before stepping out into the limelight. Moving from the discipline of studying scores and practicing gestures in splendid isolation to standing in front of a group of real live singers can be a daunting experience, for which it is almost impossible for many conductors of amateur groups to prepare. The reality of publicly honing the skills and mustering the resources required to lead a musical ensemble can be a sobering experience at times. Even for experienced conductors, the process of learning to fill this role never ends; I have found that the more I learn, the more I realize I need to learn! One of the purposes of this book is to provide support and guidance for anyone who finds themselves in this position.

Finding information about the mechanics of conducting is not difficult, and one can quickly learn how to use basic beat patterns, and gestures for synchronizing entries and endings, from a book or online resources. However, acquiring some of the more nebulous skills of coordinating a group of diverse adult singers is more complex, and it is harder to find guidance on this subject. This book aims to fill that gap by providing information on some of the extra-musical aspects of leading group singing activities, going beyond the intrinsic musical demands of choral performance and taking account of the social, psychological, and emotional elements of singing together. Learning to be a conductor is usually experiential and "on the job," which is, by definition, carried out in front of an "audience" from day one. Rehearsals themselves are a kind of performance for conductors, as they must appear to be on top of the situation, regardless of how they are feeling, and despite any personal or professional insecurities that they may secretly harbor. Although the main purpose of this book is to help conductors to encourage singers to develop choral confidence, a "confident choir" should include a confident conductor. I hope that this will be a by-product of reading and applying the material in the following chapters.

My goals are to help conductors to open a window on some of the subjective experiences of adult amateur choral singers; to place the singers' diverse musical, social, and emotional needs in the context of rehearsing and performing as communal learning experiences; and to develop a philosophical, pedagogical and practical approach that is designed to build choral confidence as well as performance quality. I also hope that all this will help conductors to enhance their own confidence as well as that of the singers they work with. Getting a handle on the collaborative, communicative, and configurational aspects of choral performance and rehearsal, as described in this book, is likely to underpin the conductor's work with a greater sense of security, and lead to increased satisfaction for everyone involved. Finally, for conductors who may feel that they and their choirs are already performing as confidently as possible, I hope that this book will still provide some stimulating ideas about the process of singing together.

Acknowledgements

With many thanks:

To my students for giving me perspective. With special thanks to Megan for helping me not to panic about my deadlines. When I told her I only had six weeks left in which to finish this book, she said, with the generous perspective on time that one still has at thirteen years old, "But that's *ages*! What are you so worried about?" And to Charlotte who, at a similar age, reminded me not to get above myself: "Just because you're doing a PhD doesn't mean you know everything about everything!"

To my choirs for providing me with a valuable "choral laboratory" while I was completing my research. Although my PhD thesis was based on a series of interviews and focus groups, it has been invaluable to have a front row seat for some of the interactions that were discussed. I also appreciated having so many opportunities to experiment with different approaches to learning and rehearsing, with tolerant groups of singers who were interested in my work and happy to engage with it.

To my research participants for being so generous with their time. Also, for being so forthcoming with details of their best and worst experiences of choral performance. And for their having the courage to reveal their inner-most feelings about singing, along with the major influences upon their confidence. This is a very personal subject, and I appreciate the honesty and openness of the interviewees. It was also very exciting and motivating for me to see the enthusiasm with which all focus-group participants and individual interviewees embraced these research sessions.

To all those who expressed an interest in my research and choral activities and encouraged me by confirming that my research explores important subjects for singers and conductors.

To my wife for her unwavering support. For her patience with me when I have woken her up and, with no preamble at all, launched into some convoluted question or idea about my work. For her calming influence when I felt frustrated by having so little free time to spend on my writing, due to other work commitments. For her high tolerance for reading and rereading my drafts, as well as for hearing about my work ad nauseam. For careful proofreading and reference-checking and for generally ensuring that my work made sense and was true to the research. I realized that she had probably done too much of this when she read a passage that I had drafted for my thesis and asked, "Is this in the data?" meaning, "I don't think it is!" And of course, she was right—I had gone off on a tangent for some reason.

To my PhD and MA supervisor, mentor, role model, and friend Professor Stephanie Pitts. For inspiring me to continue with my academic life alongside my teaching, performing, and conducting. And for providing endless practical help and moral support throughout my years of working with her.

To my esteemed colleague and faithful friend Professor Liz Mellor for being a thoughtful professional adviser and enthusiastic personal "cheerleader."

To everyone at Rowman & Littlefield who helped publish my work. With special thanks to Sarah Chapman, my first contact at the UK offices of Rowman & Littlefield, who enabled me to get this book started. And to my U.S. editor Natalie Mandziuk for making sure that this book got finished.

And finally, to Harley for keeping me grounded, as only a Parson Jack Russell can!

Introduction

Singing Together

The only thing better than singing is more singing.
—Ella Fitzgerald

Singing with other people is the most accessible form of amateur musical participation in many parts of the world. It requires no financial investment in expensive musical equipment, and the voice is the ultimate portable instrument as it accompanies us wherever we go. In 2015, Europa Cantat's "Singing Europe" survey discovered at least 37 million amateur singers who were regularly participating in some form of group singing activity.[1] This is the equivalent of the population of the sixteen largest European cities, which is a formidable statistic. Whether the group is a formal choral society, amateur musical theater company, church choir, auditioned chamber ensemble, open-access community choir, or informal close-harmony group, the many benefits of singing together are available to all those who participate. There is evidence that group singing activities can facilitate physiological improvements;[2] enhanced general health and well-being;[3] improved psychological well-being and mood enhancement;[4] social cohesion;[5] and community development.[6] These benefits are accessible to all of us, regardless of the quality of our vocal performance,[7] so group singing has transformative potential for everyone who takes part.

The news of this powerful tool for individual well-being and social change is becoming increasingly widespread through the popular media as well as the academic press, and the response has been a recent burgeoning of community choirs and singing groups with a therapeutic rationale. In the United Kingdom, the Alzheimer's Society has established "Singing for the

Brain" for people living with dementia, and Tenovus Cancer Care has set up a network of "Sing with Us" choirs for anyone affected by cancer. "A Choir in Every Care Home" has been initiated by the Baring Trust as a means of integrating social care, music, and healthcare, while research at the Sidney de Haan Center has demonstrated the benefits of group singing for mental health service users and people with respiratory conditions. Workplace choirs are also becoming increasingly commonplace; even Westminster has its own Parliament Choir, which allows Members of Parliament and Peers to leave rehearsals when they need to place their votes.

Despite the growing evidence of the benefits of group singing activities, and extensive participation by amateur singers, there are very few written records of their experiences and perceptions of practice and performance. In the current culture of honoring celebrity, it is comparatively easy to find autobiographies and biographies of professional soloists[8] and well-known maestros,[9] and there have been innumerable interviews in the media with superstar conductors and solo performers in every genre. In contrast to this proliferation of literature on the relative minority of elite musicians, we very rarely hear about the experiences or perceptions of the amateur singers who swell the ranks of every local choral society, church choir, operatic society, community choir, male voice choir, and amateur chamber choir throughout the Western world. While amateur choral singers are ever-present in a wide variety of performance settings and make a valuable contribution to our musical culture, they are simultaneously under-represented in most academic and popular publications.

When I added a research career to my professional portfolio, I decided to focus on the world of these hitherto neglected stalwarts of our cultural life because I had worked with them for so long. Accordingly, I carried out a series of in-depth interviews with adult amateur singers, the content of which forms the basis of this book. The interview format was designed to offer an unprecedented opportunity for these musical participants to give voice to their opinions, perceptions, and feelings about their experience of collective singing; to offer interested observers a unique insight into the world of amateur choral performance; and to create a "conductors' toolbox" for building confident choirs.

AMATEUR "CAREERS" IN GROUP SINGING

My interest in amateur group singing activities started during my teens and helped to provide a firm foundation for my professional musical life. A fascination with singing was sparked by members of a local Gilbert and Sullivan society who visited my primary school and demonstrated how much fun can be had from singing together. Until that point, I had enthusiastically played my cornet in the school orchestra, but I had been a resolute choir avoider. After watching extracts from *Ruddigore*, *Iolanthe*, *The Pirates of Penzance*, and *HMS Pinafore*, I was hooked. I borrowed opera scores from the library and entertained myself (and no doubt annoyed everyone else) by constantly thumping them out on the piano. Very little finesse was involved but I was having a whale of a time. One day a teacher caught me playing the act 1 finale from *The Mikado* and performing all the chorus parts and solos— I especially enjoyed being Katisha! My teacher said, "I know you think you're funny, but actually that's rather good. Why don't you join the operatic society and learn how to do it properly?" And so, this seemingly trivial obsession became the center of my musical and social world for a while.

Learning to sing, act, and even dance (which I had never considered before) with a group of supportive adults set me on the road to a life-long musical career. Shortly after joining the company, I was offered solo roles, and I decided that I had better get my voice trained if I was going to do a decent job of singing in public. After that there was no stopping me. I sang in as many performances as I could and started earning money as a rehearsal pianist. My singing teachers at college mentored me, taught me how to teach, and recommended students to me when I was ready to start passing on my skills. Giving singing lessons helped me to survive financially through my college years and, fortunately for me, I discovered that I loved teaching just as much as performing.

After an early career as a professional singer with a couple of international contracts under my belt, I stashed away my suitcases and decided to concentrate on teaching and conducting. Through these professional activities I have been privileged to meet many committed singers and conductors of all ages and abilities and with a wide range of musical interests and individual perspectives on performance. An average teaching day can include working with a "Queen of the Night," a "Broadway Baby," an Elvis impersonator, and a "Sweet Transsexual from Transylvania." My work with amateur and professional groups of singers has been equally varied, ranging from auditioned chamber choirs and musical theater companies to open-access community choirs, choral societies, and informal singing groups of all shapes and sizes.

Having worked with so many dedicated amateur singers over the years, I was delighted to encounter the term "career amateur."[10] This phrase was coined by sociologist Robert Stebbins, and it reflects that fact that amateur singers commonly invest a great deal of their time, energy, and resources in their singing activities, sometimes to the exclusion of other hobbies and interests. For these performers, singing becomes "serious leisure,"[11] and although they receive no professional fees for their singing, they are strongly committed to performing to as high a standard as possible. Some amateur singers may take their singing less seriously and prioritize social aspects over musical attainment; others are novices who are just starting out and who will admit that they have a lot to learn. However, I have met many amateur singers who have acquired a wide range of musical and vocal skills, technical knowledge, and performance experience. For the purposes of this book, the definition of an adult "amateur singer" covers all participants in group singing activities of any kind.

THE HIGHS AND LOWS OF SINGING

Whenever I meet a singer, they always want to tell me about how much they love singing, the performances they have enjoyed, and the choirs that they belong to. They are often very proud of their performance record and excitedly tell me the highlights of their group singing activities. This happens whether we meet in a singing lesson, during a rehearsal, at a performance, or in the pub. Sometimes, though, they also want to tell me about less positive aspects of performing as a singer. For some people, their enjoyment of singing is tempered by a lack of confidence, which may manifest itself in a very mild and manageable form or, in more extreme cases, as performance "nerves" or even "stage fright." In countless singing lessons, we have spent almost as much time on confidence-building work as on musical and technical aspects of vocal performance.

Musical performance anxiety (MPA) is a well-known problem among musicians, with up to 79 percent of professional instrumentalists experiencing such severe anxiety that it impairs their performance.[12] Symptoms can include shaking, increased heart rate, shortness of breath, dry mouth, memory slips, and inhibited performance due to the fear of making mistakes.[13] All this can seriously interfere with the quality and enjoyment of vocal performance, whether the singers are seasoned professionals or amateur performers, and regardless of age and experience. Despite this, adult amateur singers have generally been neglected in performance anxiety research, with most studies focusing on professional instrumentalists[14] and full-time music students.[15] When MPA among adult singers has been examined, the emphasis has tended to be on professional soloists,[16] and participants in choral research have usually been drawn from professional or semiprofessional ensembles.[17]

In response to this shortage of empirical research on MPA among adult amateur singers, I initiated a research project of my own.[18] Through this, I discovered that although mild performance anxiety is experienced by some adult amateur singers, very few of them experience the debilitating physiological and psychological symptoms of severe MPA described by some professional musicians and full-time music students.[19] However, I also confirmed that more general confidence issues are a common concern for amateur singers, with the result that their enjoyment of performing is often impaired and their participation in choral activities is sometimes limited to some extent. This supported some of the following observations that I had made while working with choirs and individual singers.

Some singers do not feel sufficiently confident to join an auditioned choir, or to volunteer for a solo; others feel daunted by the idea of joining a very large singing group or, conversely, worry about feeling exposed in a small ensemble. Some unconfident singers may "hide" in the back row of a large community choir when, in fact, they have unfulfilled ambitions to extend their performance experience to other vocal genres or types of ensemble. Other singers even report a dread of public performance, despite their enthusiasm for rehearsing and their profound enjoyment of singing with other people. This is a pity, especially bearing in mind the well-established benefits of group singing activities. I have therefore made it my mission to carry out a detailed exploration of the subject of confidence among adult amateur choral singers by examining their experiences and perceptions of rehearsing and performing.[20]

SINGERS AND THEIR STORIES

Having had over thirty-five years of listening to singers talk about their feelings about performing, as well as listening to them learn and perform their repertoire, it was natural for me to choose a life-story approach for my research. Every student wants to tell me at least part of their personal life history, which helps to put their vocal development in context. This is almost inevitable in private singing lessons, as the voice is so inextricably bound up with the singer's feelings and experiences. Their physical, emotional, and psychological well-being constantly affects their vocal production, and their personal perceptions affect their subjective view of their own vocal quality. When singers need to express their feelings about whatever is happening in their lives, they can achieve a form of catharsis through their singing. However, they sometimes need to verbally "let off steam," or "vent," before they can concentrate on their singing, especially if they are having a tough time emotionally.

These quiet moments when singers tell me what is affecting them on a personal level are always very instructive and often help me to help them move forward vocally. I therefore designed a set of interviews to record a "vocal confidence life history" because this seemed to be the obvious route to finding out about the factors affecting confidence levels in amateur singers. I then carried out three focus group interviews involving a total of eighteen adult amateur singers, followed by sixteen individual interviews. Each interview and focus group lasted approximately 2 hours, so a total of over 40 hours of recordings were obtained, which took a further 350 hours to transcribe and analyze. This was well worth the effort, as the interviewees provided a wealth of rich data based on their individual contributions to the world of amateur choral performance. It also gave me the opportunity to represent the "voices" of the singers rather than focusing on the role of the conductor who, as the traditional figurehead of the choir, has tended to be featured more often in the media.

Each of the thirty-four participants had experience in a variety of types of choral singing (see figure 1), including church choirs, choral societies, chamber choirs, and operatic societies. The majority also had experience in performing with several different conductors: over half of the participants in the individual interviews had sung with more than ten choral conductors (see figure 2). The interviewees were all experienced choral singers (see figure 3): most participants had over five years of choral experience, and twenty-three of them had over fifteen years of experience. Between them, the interviewees had accumulated over eight hundred years of choral singing experience.

Geographically, the participants' experience was similarly broad, with many of the singers being well-traveled and having experience in performing with choirs in several locations. The combined experience of participants included singing with choral ensembles throughout the United Kingdom, including Wales, Cornwall, Devon, Lancashire, Yorkshire, Rutland, Leicestershire, Nottinghamshire, Lincolnshire, Surrey, and Hampshire. Despite their keen interest in choral singing and their vast practical experience, however, only two of the thirty-four participants had continued their musical education beyond secondary school, and most reported receiving very little formal musical training during their school years.

SEEING THE BIGGER PICTURE

The largest commercially available jigsaw puzzle in the world has 32,256 pieces and measures almost 6 x 18 feet. For me, embarking on this research project felt like tackling such a complicated jigsaw puzzle without being able to see the final picture. Another analogy that frequently occurred to me was that it was rather like working with a paper bag over my head! This was partly because of my qualitative approach: all the findings of a qualitative project emerge directly from the participants' contributions to the research rather than from any hypotheses formulated in advance by the researcher. This emergent strategy obviously makes the entire process very unpredictable.

There are also unlikely to be many reassuring statistics, which, in quantitative research projects, can be used to dramatically prove or disprove a theoretical hunch. The strength of qualitative data, such as a recorded conversation with a participant, lies in the content rather than the numbers. One

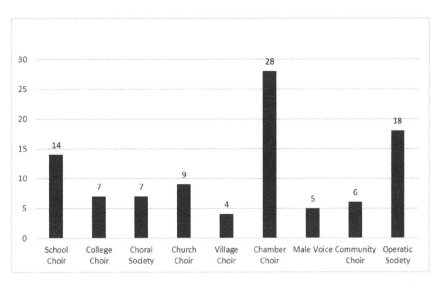

Figure 1. Types of Group Singing Activities. Michael J. Bonshor, 2014, "Confidence and the Choral Singer: The Effects of Choir Configuration, Collaboration and Communication."

expressive and succinct interview quotation can be just as powerful as a set of statistics, especially when we are exploring unquantifiable aspects of human experience such as personal feelings and subjective perceptions. This is especially relevant when talking about singers' feelings about their voices and their own confidence levels, which are very intimate aspects of their lives.

The main point of qualitative research is to gather detailed, in-depth material about the "lived experience" of the participants and to honor them as the experts on their own lives.[21] The usual method is to formulate open questions, to ask the questions in a nondirective way, to give plenty of space for the answers—and then to wait and see! This emergent process can initially lead to uncertainty and ambiguity, which can occasionally be disconcerting and frustrating for the researcher. However, for the same reasons, this approach can also be both stimulating and rewarding. Sometimes completely new findings emerge from a qualitative study, either contradicting assumptions that we thought were common knowledge or providing us with fresh insights or information that we had not previously considered. On the other hand, sometimes, once the data has been analyzed and interpreted, assumptions that seem like common sense are confirmed as fact. This is very useful if factual support or contextual information are required to help with solving a problem.

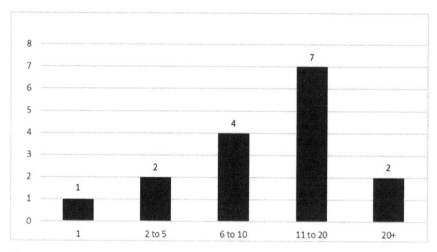

Figure 2. Number of Conductors. Michael J. Bonshor, 2014, "Confidence and the Choral Singer: The Effects of Choir Configuration, Collaboration and Communication."

In this book, there are some examples of truisms about choral singing that have been confirmed by my research as well as examples of data that contradict these perceived truisms and provide food for thought. The results have brought me full circle, in some ways: my practical experience in working with singers originally inspired my research interests, and my research has contributed to a practical approach to building choral confidence. In the following chapters, the outcome will be presented, largely in the words of the singers I interviewed, and their words will underpin the practical, philosophical, and pedagogical approaches I suggest for building a confident choir.

In the following chapters, I will also present the main themes as they spontaneously arose during the interviews. These themes are used to illustrate existing psychological frameworks relating to confidence-building and to demonstrate how these frameworks can be directly applied to the experience of performing as an adult amateur choral singer. Each theme is then used as the basis for suggesting practical strategies for confidence-building in the context of a wide range of group singing activities.

In chapter 1, the singers give their own definitions of confidence and describe attributes of singers who are perceived as confident performers. These attributes are largely described in relation to physical appearance, body language, posture, and gesture. Chapter 2 examines the importance of thorough practice and preparation and the impact that personal and group presentation can have upon confidence. Practical guidance is provided on practice and preparation strategies, including rehearsal techniques, repertoire choice, memorization, and approaches to learning.

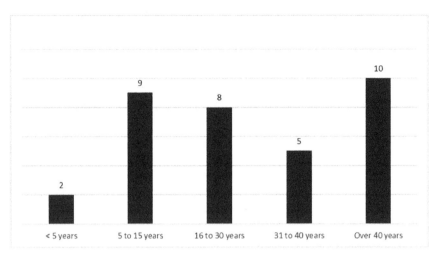

Figure 3. Amount of Group Singing Experience. Michael J. Bonshor, 2014, "Confidence and the Choral Singer: The Effects of Choir Configuration, Collaboration and Communication."

Chapter 3 introduces the concept of choir configuration, which encompasses choir layout, the position of the choir within the venue, the position of the singer within the choir, and the spacing between the singers. These aspects of configuration all affect the acoustic ambience for the singers, their perception of their own and others' vocal performances, and their confidence levels. The practical implications of these acoustic and configurational factors are considered in detail. In chapter 4, the singers discuss the importance of community, comradeship, and cohesion as confidence-building factors in rehearsal and performance. They also highlight the positive effects of collaborative learning and peer feedback. Guidance is provided on developing a supportive environment based on a facilitative approach to multidirectional learning. Examples of practical team-building exercises are included, which will help to "jump start" choral bonding and to invigorate existing inter-singer support networks.

When we reach chapter 5, the spotlight finally shines on the conductor, with the singers' evaluations of their conductor's communication style and how this can affect the choir's confidence levels during rehearsals and performances. This is a significant reversal of the traditional position in amateur choirs, where the feedback has more often been experienced as flowing in the opposite direction. The roles of constructive criticism and praise, goal setting, and communication style are explored, and practical recommendations are provided for optimizing choral confidence through meaningful and effective feedback. Chapter 6 draws together some of the main themes to suggest a philosophical, pedagogical, and practical model for musical facilitators working with adult amateur choral singers.

A NOTE ON TERMINOLOGY

Throughout the rest of this book, I use the terms "choir," "choral singing," and "conductor" as a form of shorthand for the musical activities and roles under discussion. This terminology, however, is not intended to limit the scope of the book to formal, "choral" contexts. The word "choir" is obviously less cumbersome than the term "group singing activity," and I have used the two terms interchangeably. For me, the word "choir" describes any group of people who sing together, and "choral singing" stands for any kind of coordinated group singing. The diversity of adult amateur singers, choirs, and their conductors is an important facet of choral participation, which will be considered in the following chapters. Within this text, choral leadership will be reframed as group facilitation, with an emphasis on collaborative learning. However, it is usually more convenient to use the word "conductor" than "facilitator of group singing activities," which is my preferred term for the role.

Chapter One

Conveying and Cultivating Confidence

Health is the greatest possession.
Contentment is the greatest treasure.
Confidence is the greatest friend.
—Lao Tzu

While the first two elements of Lao Tzu's triumvirate of "health, content-ment, and confidence" have either evaded me or favored me at various times, it is the third component that has constantly fascinated me. As a Boy Scout, I confidently bored my long-suffering mother with all the practical applica-tions of bowline knots, sheet bends, and clove hitches. However, when dem-onstrating this for an achievement award, I could not avoid fumbling, drop-ping the rope, or forgetting what I was doing and ending up in a hopeless tangle. When our scoutmaster realized that my problem was with my test anxiety rather than my ability, he said, "I wish I could manufacture confi-dence and bottle it. Then you could put it on like aftershave!" This started me on a lifetime of wondering what exactly confidence is, how we recognize it in other people and ourselves, and, most importantly of all, how it might be cultivated and conveyed.

The word "confidence" comes from the Latin "fidere," which means "to trust." Self-confidence is trust in oneself, and this is reflected in most diction-ary definitions, which describe a "belief in one's own abilities"[1] or "a feeling of self-assurance arising from an appreciation of one's own abilities or qual-ities."[2] In the field of social-cognitive psychology, confidence-related issues are usually defined and explored within Albert Bandura's self-efficacy theo-ry.[3] This is "concerned with judgments of how well one can execute courses of action required to deal with prospective situations."[4] The following defini-tion of perceived self-efficacy is particularly appropriate to the challenges of learning complex choral works and participating in public choral perfor-

1

mances: "the belief in one's competence to tackle difficult or novel tasks and to cope with adversity in specific demanding situations."[5] As there are obvious parallels between the psychological concept of self-efficacy and the dictionary definitions of confidence, I will use these two terms interchangeably, with "self-efficacy" functioning as a technical description of the more widely understood concept of self-confidence.[6]

Sadly, the idea of bottling self-confidence and wearing it like an aftershave is still in the realm of wishful thinking, or maybe science fiction. However, Albert Bandura distilled the essence of self-efficacy in his analysis of its key features. He also successfully applied his findings to the treatment of patients with severe phobias by gradually increasing their exposure to a perceived threat. For example, his program of systematic desensitization helped ophidiophobics deal with their fear of snakes.[7] Fortunately, there are usually no snakes involved in choral singing, but repeated exposure to performance can similarly reduce music performance anxiety (MPA) for many musicians.[8] There are exceptions to this though, as some extremely experienced instrumentalists, singers, and actors suffer from performance anxiety.[9] For example, repeated exposure did not seem to alleviate Adele's tendency to vomit due to her anxiety about singing in public;[10] and Laurence Olivier's late-onset stage fright struck after many years of maintaining a high-profile career.[11] However, cases such as these are very extreme and usually occur in high-pressure, professional performance situations[12] rather than being prevalent in the arguably less pressurized world of amateur choral music.[13]

The most striking feature of self-efficacy is that it is malleable and subject to change.[14] This means that efficacy perceptions can respond to a program of adjustment, which can have confidence-boosting effects. Bandura outlined three main strategies for changing self-efficacy perceptions: participant modeling (direct personal experience); vicarious experience (modeling by others); and exhortative approaches (verbal persuasion).[15] Participant modeling is usually the most constructive method of altering self-efficacy, while modeling by others is most effective if the models are similar to the observer. The impact of verbal persuasion or encouragement depends upon the individual's perception of the credibility and trustworthiness of the person delivering the encouragement.[16] Some of the applications of these strategies, in the context of group singing activities, will be presented during the rest of this book.

THE EMBODIMENT OF CONFIDENCE

It is down to body language a lot of the time—the way you stand and the way you look. (Irene)

My own continuing search for the essence of confidence inspired one of my first interview questions: "Please tell me how you might describe a confident performer. How do you think they might behave and perform?" I hoped that the answers might provide a definition of confident performance in the singer's own words, which would be directly relevant to amateur choral singing, and which might suggest practical strategies to help singers cultivate and convey confidence. In response to this question, all three focus groups and thirteen of the individual interviewees immediately initiated lengthy discussions about various aspects of nonverbal communication. These included body language, personal appearance, collective presentation, and physical elements of performance that indicate confidence. Their responses reflect the nature of the voice as an embodied instrument,[17] with no external instrument forming a barrier between the singer and the audience.

The internal, embodied nature of the vocal instrument means that singers need to be very aware of their physiology and their physical position in the performance arena. They must also be very aware of their physical appearance in relation to each other, the conductor, and the audience. The singers I interviewed saw body language as the most significant physical manifestation of confidence and felt that good "posture . . . how they stand and present themselves" (Ross) was a fundamental part of this:

> Actually, I have an image of somebody being a bit taller, you know. You stand upright [demonstrates] and hold yourself taller. (Matt)

These two singers were not alone in having specific expectations about the main elements of confident body language:

> If somebody's sort of standing like that [demonstrates hunched posture] then they don't look confident. (Liz)

Some singers reported that they use positive body language to reinforce their confidence when performing, usually by "standing up a bit straighter and trying to smile" (Miriam). This is a powerful tool because, as well as demonstrating how someone is feeling, posture and gesture often have deterministic effects on emotions and thought processes. For example, tilting the head upward can induce a sense of pride,[18] and hunched postures generally elicit feelings of depression and helplessness.[19] Body posture also affects self-evaluation, or "thought confidence."[20] During a scientific experiment, participants were asked to note their best and worst qualities while sitting in a "confident posture" (defined by the researchers as maintaining an erect spine and expanded chest) or in a "doubtful posture" (slouching with a curved spine). The experimenters found that adopting confident postures activated feelings of confidence and that the converse was also true.[21] This suggests that reminding singers to establish and maintain a confident posture can create a positive feedback loop, which will help them improve their performance and feel more confident.

As well as playing the dual role of conveying confidence to the audience while simultaneously creating the sensation of confidence in the singer, good posture also counteracts some of the physiological symptoms of low self-efficacy. This is because we partly make judgments about our own capabilities based on our subjective interpretations of our perceived physiological state.[22] In challenging situations, such as singing in public performances, high emotional and physiological arousal occurs. The production of adrenaline increases, which precipitates somatic symptoms such as increased heartbeat and faster respiration. Some singers report "my knees are knocking, my hands are shaking" (Leanne) or "I get a terribly dry mouth. And my teeth stick to my lips!" (Joyce). These symptoms are often interpreted as signs of stress, which then have an impact on performance quality and the singer's enjoyment of the experience.

People who are particularly vulnerable to this anxiety arousal sometimes become so preoccupied with their physiological symptoms that they are distracted from the demands of the task. This is especially likely when they interpret these symptoms as a sign of either a threatening situation or their perceived inadequacy to rise to the challenge. Consequently, their performance quality suffers[23] and self-confidence drops. Strategies for dealing with this include helping singers to reinterpret their physiological arousal markers, reframing them as excitement or alertness rather than anxiety or nervousness. For example, Tim's approach to his faster heart rate, sweatiness, and "slightly dry mouth" was to tell himself, "It's nothing to worry about. In fact, it's something that's *good*." "So, when it happens I think, '*Yes*! I'm ready.'" Adopting a positive interpretation of their "symptoms" helps to reduce the singers' concern about their physiological state and allows them to focus on their performance. Clive felt that raised adrenaline is a natural reaction to appearing in front of an audience and that it provides the heightened awareness necessary for performing effectively:

> You're bound to get a few butterflies. If you don't get a little bit of nervousness then you're not going to do yourself justice.

Positive experiences can also help counteract the negative effects of high anxiety arousal. Participating in successful performances increases the likelihood of engaging in similar activities. These experiences build competence and confidence so that more effort continues to be invested in the activity. More improvements then take place due to increased effort, perseverance, and experience. This creates an upward spiral of task mastery, self-efficacy, effort, and successful performance. Providing plenty of opportunities for satisfying performances, which are artistically successful and emotionally fulfilling, is one way of helping to build confidence in choral singers:

> The more of it you do, the more confident you get. I think that's the main thing. And the more confident you get, the better you get, so the more you want to do. (Barry)

For inexperienced groups of singers, informal performances can help to build their confidence. With my open-access community choirs, I have arranged end-of-term "show and tell" sessions in which they perform their new songs to their family and friends. Tickets are not available to the general public (in fact, the concerts are so informal that we don't usually even have tickets), and the audience consists solely of supportive significant others who have been invited by the singers.

Acquiring a back catalog of positive performance experiences takes time, but there are strategies that can make a difference in confidence levels almost immediately. Since body language has so many effects on how singers feel while performing, starting rehearsals with some postural work and physical warm-ups can be transformative. Conductors can usefully lead their choirs in the following exercises.

Postural Exercises

- Review the basic stance for singing: relaxed but poised; calm but ready for action. Feet should be a shoulder-width apart for stability, with equal pressure upon the toes, heels, and balls of the feet so that you are neither leaning forward nor leaning back.
- Locked knees tend to bring the abdomen over the toes, which limits the expansion of the abdominal muscles when a singer is trying to breathe deeply. Relaxed, slightly bent knees bring the hips in line with the heels and allow freer expansion. Try squatting slightly, with knees bent, and then slowly straighten the legs until the point just before the knees would usually lock.
- Imagine you are carrying a heavy bucketful of water in each hand, and picture the heaviness of your arms so that the shoulders open out and relax. Keep hands open and relaxed rather than clenching your fists to hold the imaginary "bucket."
- To counteract the slight "downwards" feeling created by the relaxed knees and heavy arms, imagine that you have a piece of string attached to the top of your head. This "string" is attached to the ceiling, and gently pulls the

spine upright. The spine must only be as straight as is comfortable for each individual singer.

- Encourage singers to maintain a relaxed but poised posture when sitting as well as standing:

   1. The soles of the feet should be placed flat on the floor, approximately a shoulder-width apart.
   2. The tendency to slump can be counteracted by sitting toward the front edge of the seat so that the edge is felt about halfway along the muscles in the singer's bottom. Slumping when sitting in this position is quite uncomfortable, so an upright posture is more likely to be maintained.

Relaxation Exercises

Practice the following physical warm-ups with your choir:

- Try a few backward shoulder rolls, followed by an equal number of forward shoulder rolls, to loosen any tension in the shoulders.
- Shrug and sigh: as you breathe in, bring your shoulders up to your ears. When you breathe out, sigh heavily as you let your shoulders drop back down again.
- Repeat some circular "front crawl" and "back crawl" movements with each arm. Imagine your arms moving through water rather than air so that they feel heavy and relaxed.
- Swivel your waist from side to side, with your arms swinging by your sides. Let your arms become very heavy, and allow them to swing freely until they feel as if they no longer belong to you. Imagine how a puppet in the British TV series *Thunderbirds* moves, and try to replicate that.

As well as trying to adopt positive body language, many choral singers describe "taking deep breaths and standing quiet" (Miriam) to help themselves relax and feel more confident. Combining deep, slow breathing with a relaxed but poised posture can help give the impression of confidence. It can also alleviate the physiological symptoms of raised adrenaline by slowing down the respiration and heart rate:

> I take time to . . . [demonstrates] deep breathe. I sort of stand there and do that quietly and that helps tremendously. (Joyce)

If this strategy is practiced consistently, it becomes second nature; and the calming effects will not only help with the demands of choral performance but can be transferred into everyday situations. For example, when I was telephoning everyone to let them know that my wife was critically ill, one of my voice students was with me and said, "I couldn't work out how you were staying so calm, and then I realized you were doing your singing breathing!" I was not consciously doing this to keep my emotions under control, but clearly a lifetime of breathing for singing as well as survival has provided some useful habits.

It is not easy to check that every member of a choir is breathing in a relaxed way when they are singing. Rehearsals rarely allow time for the necessary individual attention, and in larger choirs this would be impossible. Also, some choral singers may resent taking time out from practicing their repertoire to work on breath control and vocal technique in any detail. However, it is worth adding a few simple breathing exercises to the warm-up routine. Joining the singers in the following exercises will help them breathe for relaxation and confidence as well as for musical phrasing and support. Doing this will also help the conductor and the singers to take a few moments to release any tensions that otherwise might be carried over into the rehearsal.

Exercises for Calming the Breath

- Adopt the confident "singing stance," then sigh exaggeratedly. Place your hands palms down on your abdomen between the sternum and the navel, to register the movement there.
- With the hands in the same position, try panting to create more energetic movement in the same area.
- Breathe in slowly, feeling some expansion between the sternum and the navel. Exhale violently, as if blowing out one hundred candles on a birthday cake.
- Inhale slowly, feeling the gentle abdominal expansion, and relax as you exhale. Take a few deep, calming breaths in and out, at a steady pace.
- Count out loud while the singers carry out this exercise: breathe in for 4 counts, hold the breath for 4 counts, and breathe out for 8 counts. Repeat several times without stopping. The number of counts can be proportionately increased with practice.
- Repeat the above exercise without the "holding the breath" stage.
- Stretch your arms up in the air, raising your hands above your head until the palms are touching overhead. While in this position, give a heavy sigh to empty your lungs as much as possible then breathe in very slowly, being aware of the expansion below your sternum, around your middle, and into your ribcage. When you are fully expanded, start to exhale slowly while slowly bringing your arms back down to your side. While doing this, keep your palms down, and stretch your arms out to the sides so that

each arm describes a semicircle on its way back to the side of your body. Imagine that your arms are moving through water rather than air. Pace it so that you are full of air when your arms are above your head and you are not "empty" until your hands reach thigh level. Everyone should do this at their own pace rather than trying to synchronize movements.

- Do these exercises while sitting as well as standing to ensure that deep, relaxed breathing is maintained in both positions.

COMMUNICATING CONFIDENCE

Many singers agreed with Tim, an interviewee who said that smiling is the most obvious sign of confidence. Naomi explained that smiling can reflect singers' confidence in their level of preparation and in their belief that they can achieve a successful performance. Pamela's description of smiling at the audience as an expression of pleasure in response to their attendance suggests a useful tactic for performers. A positive approach to the presence of the audience is likely to make it easier to adopt a welcoming smile, endowing the singers with a more confident appearance:

> It's a case of smiling at somebody before you sing. You see them looking at you, so you smile because you're pleased they're there. (Pamela)

A relaxed, happy appearance makes the performance more enjoyable for the audience to watch. It indicates that the singers are confident about their part in the event and creates a sense of positive expectation that is shared by the audience and the choir. This is another example of an upward spiral encompassing embodied confidence, increased task mastery, and enhanced self-efficacy. A confident appearance provokes a positive audience response, which encourages the singers to perform to the best of their ability. During an increasingly self-assured and competent performance, the singers' confidence continues to grow and spurs them on to achieve even more and to enjoy their success.

This association between nonverbal communication and emotion has a long history. Charles Darwin believed that the intensity of emotion is directly linked to its physical manifestation. He proposed that facial expressions reflected from other individuals can have a profound impact on the subjective experience of emotion. The explanation for this reciprocity was based on Darwin's own observations of instinctive empathy:

> When a child cries or laughs, he knows in a general manner what he is doing and what he feels; so that a very small exertion of reason would tell him what crying and laughing meant in others. [24]

The physical portrayal of an emotion has powerful repercussions even if, at first, the emotion is not genuinely experienced. When participants in an experiment were instructed to deliberately replicate facial expressions, the majority reported a subjective physical change, and physiological reactions were confirmed by measurements of EEG activity. They also began to experience the simulated emotion.[25] Further research on "embodied cognition" (the interconnectedness of physical and psychological states) has confirmed that manipulating one's facial expression can subjectively affect internal emotional states.[26] Strack, Martin, and Stepper demonstrated that holding a pen horizontally between one's lips to ensure contraction of the *zygomaticus major* (the "smile muscle") can induce or intensify positive feelings such as pleasure and amusement.[27] The converse was also true: holding the pen in a way that inhibited zygomatic contraction (i.e., pursing one's lips around the end of the pen so that smiling was not possible) resulted in less positive emotional states.

These effects of facial feedback are caused by self-perception mechanisms,[28] which means that we use our own facial expressions to derive information about our emotions and attitudes. The experience of smiling usually results in a subjective perception of increased positive feelings, while frowning increases subjective perceptions of negative emotions. In simple terms, smiling can make us feel happier, and frowning can make us feel worried! Physiological responses to assuming a specific facial expression contribute to these subjective emotional experiences even if we are unaware of having assumed the expression in the first place.[29]

There is neurological evidence of a "central, hard-wired connection between the motor cortex and other areas of the brain involved in directing the physiological changes which occur during emotion."[30] Functional magnetic resonance imaging (fMRI) investigations have confirmed that the subjective experience of deliberately adopting emotional facial expressions results in activity in the same areas of the brain that would be activated when the emotion is actually experienced.[31] This can have a powerful impact on choral performances involving the expression or simulation of emotions. It also suggests the strategy of adopting positive facial expressions as a means of conveying and cultivating positive feelings when singing. Preparatory smiling can also be used before starting to conduct or sing to encourage positive facial feedback responses among the performers.

At this point, a brief caveat is advisable about smiling while singing, as I have observed many conductors exhorting choirs to smile, regardless of the repertoire and performance context. A smile exaggerates the lateral and upward movement of the zygomatic major, which lifts and stretches the lips, creating a very infectious positive facial expression.[32] However, this does not necessarily optimize vocal tone. Pulling the lips back into a wide smile can tighten the jaw and "overbrighten" the voice,[33] while too much lateral lip movement at higher pitches can result in "shrillness."[34] Furthermore, a bright smile is not always appropriate to the repertoire or mood of the song.

I have found that there are several alternative ways of adding brightness to the sound and emotional warmth to the facial expression during choral performance. One option is to suggest using an excited or surprised expression rather than a wide smile. These facial expressions involve raising the eye brows slightly, which will help to counteract the tendency to frown during challenging passages. They also involve raising the cheek muscles and dropping the jaw slightly, which will improve the tone. This is usually preferable to constricting the sound by tightening the mouth. The defining characteristic of a genuine "Duchenne" smile[35] (which involves muscle movements throughout the face rather than only the mouth) is the contraction of the *orbicularis oculi, pars lateral*; in other words, gently raising the cheek muscles under the eyes. This action alone will often be sufficient to brighten the tone while simultaneously softening the facial expression to provide an impression of general positive regard. A useful term for this has been coined by Tyra Banks: when she wants fashion models to just "smile with their eyes," she asks them to use their smiling eyes, or "smeyes"!

Smiling Exercises

- Ask the choir to try to sing a happy song without smiling, then with smeyes. What differences do they notice between the two renditions?
- Ask the choir to sing a sad song while smiling, then with smeyes. What differences do they notice between these two renditions?
- Ask the singers to look around and smile at as many people as they can. Then ask them to sing a serious song while picturing how it felt to share those smiles.

As well as assuming happy and relaxed facial expressions, many singers felt that moving in a confident and relaxed way helps to set up positive expectations from the audience:

> A confident performer is someone who looks really happy and relaxed when they are doing it. Like they have always done it . . . if they come into the room or onto the stage with a big smile and walk with confidence. (Leanne)

To help your choir develop a relaxed approach to walking on stage, join them in doing the following exercises. However, it should be noted that the point of these exercises is to continue to breathe deeply and calmly while moving steadily, rather than providing a cardio session!

- While walking in place, inhale for 8 steps, hold the breath for 8 steps, and then exhale for 16 steps. Repeat this several times without stopping. The number of steps can be reduced or increased as necessary. For example, try a pattern of 4:4:8 for beginners or extend to 10:10:20 (and so on) if they are Olympic breathers.
- Repeat the above exercise without the "holding the breath" stage.
- Practice walking confidently while singing, using "walking songs" to inject some kinetic energy. "Si Si Si," "I'm Gonna Be (500 Miles)," or "These Boots Are Made for Walking" are popular choices for this exercise. You could also have fun moving assertively to songs like "I'm Gonna Wash That Man Right Out of My Hair"!

The singers' emphasis on the importance of facial expression and body language naturally led to a detailed consideration of audience interaction:

> I think a confident performer stands and looks at the audience or looks up . . . It takes a lot for you to get yourself to the stage where you dare look at people's faces and look at their reaction. (Barbara)

Confidence was inferred from observing singers communicating expressively with the audience:

> [This soprano is] very confident . . . She's very open, she's very forward, and she just goes for it, whether she gets it right or not . . . Her whole body language is very open, and she'll turn to the audience and sing. (Joyce)

Matt had been impressed by a solo singer who physically engaged with the audience, as well as being able to make eye contact with them. He saw this as the epitome of confident performance:

> Looking in people's eyes rather than looking over their heads or avoiding eye contact. Something like that will, for me, be a confident singer. And someone who's not singing from the words, who's not singing it rote would be a confident sign for me. Someone who's quite happy to move around. [There's an alto], you know, very confident singer—never has any words. She'll come round an audience and sing, sit on people's laps, mess up their hair and all that sort of stuff.

This level of interaction is not usually a requirement for choral singers (and it would be an unusual performance if choral singers behaved so flirtatiously!), but Matt interpreted it as a physical demonstration of the self-confidence that he coveted.

Reading between the lines, I think the interviewees were talking about that almost indefinable but highly prized quality, "stage presence." I have heard performers of all genres and styles discussing those who have it and those who don't. There is widespread agreement that it is an essential ingredient in "star quality" but less agreement about how to achieve it. When I was very young, I would sometimes be told that I naturally "had it" and at other times, confusingly, I would be told that I "needed to work on my stage presence." When my "presence" was strong, I knew that I was performing well, and when it escaped me, I was painfully aware that my performances were substandard and that my confidence suffered. However, I was not certain what I was doing differently. To me, it seemed to be an elusive, fickle, and temperamental will-o'-the-wisp—an element that I could neither capture securely nor rely upon. In my teens, I spent a lot of time watching other performers and trying to work out what this thing could be and how it worked. With some frustration at times, I wondered, "Is it something you can learn? Can you turn it on and off? And how?!"

Again, I resorted to my dictionary, which was surprisingly unhelpful this time. It told me that "presence" is "the state or condition of being present"— which seemed self-evident.[36] It also told me that "presence" is "a person's appearance or bearing, especially when imposing," which was closer to what I needed to know. However, I still couldn't work out what the main components were or how to acquire them. Fortunately, as Anna in *The King and I* found, "if you become a teacher, by your pupils you'll be taught."[37] Decades of helping other people to sing and perform has led to some flashes of insight about presence, partly through analyzing my students' body language and helping them to adjust it to convey confidence. Maintaining a relaxed but poised posture, using deep breathing for relaxation as well as for developing lung capacity, and adopting positive facial expressions all contribute to creating a confident appearance, which may be interpreted as stage presence. However, this is not the whole story; even with all of this in place, there may be something missing. That "something" is establishing a connection with the audience, and eye contact is one of the key factors.

In an ideal performance, presence can create feelings of intimacy; if we are fully present with people, we can experience knowledge of each other through our physical and emotional presence, our breath, our voice, and our eyes.[38] As singers, we can create the illusion of intimacy with our audiences by making eye contact as well as by sharing our voices with them. This is what Patsy Rodenburg, a leading voice and acting coach, calls "second circle presence," and I have found some useful ways of applying second circle principles to choral performance to increase audience engagement, convey competence, and instill a sense of confidence. Second circle presence can help singers convince the audience that they are experiencing something special. Eye contact plays a very important part in establishing this rapport and, sometimes, a hint of indefinable charisma. In second circle performances, singers look directly and openly at the audience so that a sense of sharing an emotional connection is established. Conversely, first circle singers and third circle singers tend not to truly engage with anyone other than themselves, and their misdirected or unengaged eye contact gives this away to their audience.

In first circle performances, the singer's focus is inward-looking and self-absorbed. This reduces their perception of everything outside themselves, including fellow performers, the conductor, and the audience. The first circle singer's demeanor is introspective and withdrawn, and there is a lack of eye contact with the audience and fellow performers. Psychological manifestations include feeling uninvolved, insignificant, or self-conscious. These feelings, and the singer's physical responses to these feelings, reduce the impact of the performance and diminish self-confidence. On the other hand, third circle performances go to the opposite extreme with an outward-looking approach that uses an impersonal and superficial energy to attract attention. In third circle vocal performances, eye contact is not direct. Third circle singers may look through, or over the top of, the audience rather than directly at them. This impersonal lack of eye contact means that the singer does not fully acknowledge the audience's presence, create a sense of intimacy, or allow any genuine communication. Third circle choral performance might, on the surface, appear to be more outgoing, but it does not create real presence, rapport, or confidence.

If Rodenburg's second circle principles of eye contact are applied to choirs, the singers will be more focused on their audience, and their performances will become a reciprocal exchange. There will be a sense of giving and receiving as the performance becomes a two-way communication between the singer and the audience. In second circle singing, we are fully present, which means being in the moment, feeling alert, and communicating fully with other people around us, including the audience, our fellow singers, and the conductor. Really looking at the audience helps performers to notice and respond to their reactions and to set up a virtuous circle of authentic interactions. In second circle choral performance, we are aware of our role as part of the audience's experience of the event as well as our own personal contribution to the choral sound and the overall impression that the choir is making. We maintain our relaxed but poised posture, breathe deeply, and direct our performance toward our audience, while remembering to make genuine eye contact. All this helps us communicate expressively and convey confidence. Here are some exercises that I have developed for conductors and singers to do together.

Exercises for Encouraging Eye Contact

- Breathe calmly together while making eye contact. In small groups, use eye contact to coordinate slow, relaxed, synchronized breathing. Cultivate a welcoming, open, and direct gaze without staring at one person for so long that it becomes overpowering. Imagine that you are looking at someone that you like a lot, even if this is not the case! This creates an open expression, with slightly "smiling" eyes.
- Arrange the singers in circles so that they can sing rounds to each other while making eye contact.
- Divide the choir into two halves so that they can sing call-and-response or partner songs (such as "Swing Low, Sweet Chariot" with "When the Saints") to each other while making eye contact across the wider group.
- Encourage singers to focus on their listeners. Learning songs that are easy to memorize (perhaps with a limited number of words) aurally can reduce singers' fascination with the printed page and free them to make eye contact with each other, the audience, and the conductor.

The nonverbal communication of choral singers has a strong impact upon audience expectations and responses. This can have a reciprocal effect, creating a positive feedback loop that affects the quality of the performance and the singers' perception of their own competence and confidence. The same kind of reciprocity was also evident when interviewees talked about the impact of the emotional state of their fellow singers. Sometimes this has a positive effect, if they are conveying confidence and a relaxed state through their body language. However, negative effects are also common. The transmission of performance "nerves" between singers can reduce the confidence of individuals and adversely affect the mood and performance of the whole choir:

> I was next to somebody who had their folder open, was going over the words, and was asking me if I knew the words, and they didn't know the words, so the more I thought about it, and the more they were getting worked up, the more I got worked up! (Naomi)

Matt talked about "catching" confidence from the singers around him, and the "infectiousness" of nerves: "I think their confidence level must affect yours 'cause if they're not confident, they'll waver in their singing, and if they're wavering then it makes me waver." Phoebe even experienced what seemed like a physical transmission of a co-performer's emotional state: "[Soprano's] just terrified! I mean, standing next to her in concerts is a nightmare 'cause you can feel it off her—it's like palpable! This aura 'round her of nervousness." She graphically described how quickly this can spread through a choir:

> When [some singers] get into an actual performance situation, they seem to get really outwardly nervous. It actually bounces off everybody, and before you actually then start singing, everyone's on tenterhooks. And they weren't previously. They were quite relaxed and calm. But they feed off the energies of these people that are nervous. And you find yourself getting nervous when you weren't before!

This empathic reaction is known as the "chameleon effect": the "non-conscious mimicry of the postures, mannerisms, facial expressions, and other behaviors of one's interaction partners, such that one's behavior passively and unintentionally changes to match that of others in one's current social environment."[39] The natural tendency to mimic other people's nonverbal behavior often leads us to share some elements of their emotional state.[40] Perceiving similar body language in others fosters empathy and rapport, plays an important part in social bonding, and has an impact on cohesion and cooperation in musical ensembles. This partly explains the "emotional contagion"[41] that can accompany performing with other people, as perceptions of physical expressions of emotion induce mimicry. This, in turn, provides a source of facial feedback about the individual's own emotional state and results in the sharing of emotion. The reciprocal ability to infect those around us with an emotion and to catch the emotions of others is rooted in the "mirror neuron" system, which helps us to learn from other people by copying their behavior:

> Every time we are looking at someone performing an action, the same motor circuits that are recruited when we ourselves perform that action are concurrently activated.[42]

In its extreme form, emotional contagion can become a kind of "mass anxiety hysteria" that is "spread by visual contact."[43] In the 2014 film *The Falling*, one schoolgirl has fainting fits in reaction to stress, and before long, there is an epidemic of swooning throughout the school. Outside the film industry, this type of phenomenon has been recorded in marching bands,[44] train stations,[45] and convents[46] as well as in classrooms.[47] Although these cases demonstrate the power of emotional contagion, I am glad to report that I have never witnessed mass hysteria in a choral performance or rehearsal! In fact, emotional contagion during musical performance can be very useful, as it reinforces emotional states related to musical interpretation and expression. For choral singers, the sharing of their body language and feelings can act as a reminder of dynamics and other aspects of expressive performance. It also transmits a wide range of extra-musical feelings such as anticipation or apprehension, excitement or apathy, self-confidence or self-doubt.

The combined processes of emotional contagion and the chameleon effect mean that the nonverbal communication of singers has a strong influence upon the emotional state of those around them as well as an impact upon their own mood and emotions. It is therefore important to remind singers frequently to monitor their own body language and to make sure it is as positive as possible. The following checklist can be used by conductors to help their choirs to experience, share, and transmit positive feelings:

Embodying Confidence: A Checklist for Singers

1. Are your feet a shoulder-width apart?
2. Is your body weight distributed evenly between your toes, heels, and the balls of your feet?
3. Are your knees relaxed, i.e., slightly bent rather than locked?
4. Are your hips over your heels rather than over your toes?
5. Are your arms feeling relaxed and heavy by your side?
6. Are your shoulders and neck relaxed?
7. Is your spine as straight as is comfortable for you?
8. Can you feel any unnecessary tension anywhere? If so, try releasing the tension as you breathe out slowly.
9. Have you remembered to attach an imaginary piece of string to the top of your head so that you feel as if you are suspended from the ceiling like a puppet?
10. Are you remembering to expand and relax as you breathe in?
11. Are you smiling with your eyes?
12. Are you making eye contact with the conductor, your fellow singers, and/or the audience as appropriate?
13. Are you including the whole audience in your gaze whenever possible?
14. When making eye contact, are you looking directly at the person rather than through them or over them?
15. Are you able to look over your sheet music so that you can watch the conductor and engage with the audience?
16. Are you able to see the conductor from where you are standing?
17. Are you looking at the audience as if they are people that you like and are delighted to see?
18. Are you remaining focused on your posture and your breathing throughout the performance?

19. Are you remembering to take a few calm, deep breaths whenever you have a chance; for example, during introductions and while other sections are singing?
20. Are you paying attention to other aspects of your nonverbal communication such as your facial expression and gesture? (If you are singing from memory and therefore have no printed music to hold, think about what you are doing with your hands!)

THE CLOAK OF CONFIDENCE

In *The King and I*, when Anna Leonowens and her son are apprehensively traveling to meet the formidable King of Siam, they keep up their spirits by whistling cheerfully and concluding that "you may be as brave as you make believe you are." Similarly, many research participants suggested that "striking a careless pose, even when you're "shivering in your shoes,"[48] can help you perceive yourself as more confident. All three focus groups and eight of the individual interviewees wondered whether the appearance of confidence is always genuine. There were lengthy discussions about whether the presentation of confidence can be manufactured not only to persuade the audience of the performer's competence and assuredness but also to boost the singer's own sense of self-efficacy. In other words, a *The King and I* approach to choral confidence-building could mean that "when I fool the people I fear I fool myself as well."[49] Conversations between participants in the first focus group were particularly revealing, with several singers disclosing their own strategies of assuming a confident physical appearance. It was admitted that the adopted attitude of self-confidence is not always genuinely felt, but it can be very liberating and empowering in the performance arena:

Irene: You tend to think [confident singers] are very outgoing people but that could just be a mask that once they're in front of people, dressed differently, doing a different job, then they're somebody else. It's an act.

Una: It's like when you do a part on the stage isn't it?

Irene: You are being that person and not being yourself.

Dawn: That makes a big difference. You can do an awful lot of hiding behind a part that you probably wouldn't do.

Una: People who do perform well, they don't show any nerves—they probably are nervous but they probably don't show it outwardly, and that makes you feel really confident.

Doreen: You've got to put on a different face.

During the third focus group, the singers talked to each other about their own appearance of confidence, and revelations were made about the reality behind this:

Ross: It's the presence they seem to bring . . . They don't look as if they're worried, they're not shaking . . .

Doug: And most people are nervous, aren't they? Some are a lot better at not showing it.

Gordon: It's all about being a swan above the surface, never mind what's going on below the surface. You've got to keep the swan in front of the audience. And as long as you can do that, then you'll exude that air of confidence.

The image of a swan paddling madly under the water while floating gracefully on the surface captures the illusory world of the performer. Cultivating the appearance of confidence is part of creating an identity as an effective performer, whether the confidence is genuine or a facade. Several interviewees suggested "looking like you know what you are doing, even if you don't" (Barbara) as a strategy for creating confident performances:

When [confident singers] are in a situation where they're not confident, they look like they're being confident . . . which is good 'cause obviously a lot of how people in the audience perceive things is actually about what you look like—it's not actually by . . . what noise you're making. You can cover a hell of a lot up just by looking like you know what you're doing. (Phoebe)

All this suggests a strategy for building confidence: using the acting ability of singers to portray confidence on stage. During choral performance, the pretense of confidence can morph into a genuine emotion just as it did in the empirical experiments on facial feedback.[50] Since physical posture and facial expression can produce as well as reflect positive feelings, we can use our body language to prepare ourselves physiologically and psychologically to cope with challenging social circumstances[51] and public performances. The ability to "fake it until you make it" can enhance confidence as well as performance quality in risk-taking or stressful situations such as public speaking or job interviews.[52] There is also a relationship between assuming the open and expansive postures associated with power and authority and the subjective experience of relative power for individuals adopting these postures.[53] This experience of power has a significant beneficial effect: it reduces anxiety, fear, and stress hormone levels.[54] "Power postures," even when not indicative of genuine dominance, can have a similar impact on physiology, behavior, psychology, and subjective feelings, including

> elevation of the dominance hormone testosterone, reduction of the stress hormone cortisol, and increases in behaviorally demonstrated risk tolerance and feelings of power.[55]

As well as maximizing the effects of positive body language during performance, incorporating positive postural practice into performance preparation is beneficial. Adjusting our nonverbal behavior prior to an evaluative social situation can help us prepare psychologically and emotionally for the challenges of the event. Preparatory power posing is an effective performance-boosting tool even when the audience has not seen these nonverbal behavioral displays.[56] Consequently, attending to posture and facial expression immediately before a choral performance, as well as during the event, can have several positive effects. First, it enhances the singer's subjective perception of their own self-confidence as well as their appearance of confidence. Secondly, it can improve their performance, which will enhance their sense of task mastery or competence, and it will therefore add to their feelings of confidence. Third, it can help to cultivate the elusive quality of stage presence during performance.[57]

Exercises for Power Performances

- Have the choir raise their arms above their head into a *V* shape with their legs spread widely apart so that they resemble starfish. Amy Cuddy called this pose "The Performer" as a tribute to Mick Jagger.[58] Ask them to imagine soaking up tumultuous applause in this position.
- If your singers seem fidgety or edgy, do some jumping jacks together to release some kinetic energy. Obviously, the appropriateness of this exercise will depend on the general fitness of the singers, so use it with discretion. It is also best to do this before you go on stage rather than when you are in public!
- Ask the choir to model exaggerated power postures. Try impersonating your favorite flamboyant opera singer or super hero. How does it feel to sing as Wonder Woman or Batman? How about a Ninja Turtle?
- Tell the singers to model more relaxed postures while maintaining the main elements of the power posture. Remind them to keep their arms relaxed, their spine straight, and their feet about a shoulder-width apart. Have them take a few gentle breaths in that position—and then sing!
- Have the choir practice walking confidently into the performance area while remembering positive feelings from the power posture exercises. If

you can't rehearse in the performance venue, create a rehearsal space that is a similar shape and size to the performing area at the venue and practice confident movements in that space.

- "Busk" through an almost-performance-ready piece without stopping to comment or correct errors. Encourage the singers to keep singing while maintaining positive facial expressions and confident posture, no matter what happens!

- Special reminder: Keep checking your own posture to ensure that your example reminds the singers to sit, stand, and move confidently.

For some singers, faking confidence until they "make it" is taken a step further as they adopt a stage personality as a strategy to increase their confidence. Alex Newell's male-female transgender character in *Glee* (Wade "Unique" Adams) uses her singing to give her the confidence to express her female identity:

> I tend to hide behind my status of being a diva; it's easy for me to embrace that part of me and seek confidence by being a bit outrageous at times.

This exact circumstance did not apply to any of the participants in my interviews. However, Gordon similarly compared his past experience as a nervous performer with his present self-confidence, which had come from putting on his "performance persona":

> Somebody came up to me and said, "You should go into the talent competition," but I just didn't have the nerve because I was, and still am, a very shy person. Then I couldn't do it—now I do it just like that [snaps fingers]. I turn into somebody else when I go on stage.

Andrew observed the charismatic effect that adopting a stage persona can have, while recognizing that the confident outside shell may sometimes conceal a nervous interior:

> I'm not saying they're like that when they come off the stage, but when they're on the stage they have this persona, this charisma that actually portrays somebody that knows what they're doing, is good at what they do.

Several singers suggested that the appearance of confidence can be almost as important as genuine confidence in many different performance scenarios. They provided imaginative depictions of confidence as a metaphorical item of clothing that performers may decide to wear. Pearl talked about putting on her "mask" of confidence, while Doreen used her "stage hat" as a metaphor for giving the impression of self-confidence. Nina was very clear that confidence often has to be put on, in the sense of being worn as an empowering facade:

> I have to fake confidence in a lot of scenarios, and it's the cloak they put on just before they do it. 'Cause you can be a wreck just before you go on, or whatever, before you do something, but you think, "Okay. Confidence hat goes on!" It's like Beyonce's Sasha Fierce, or whatever she calls her.

She went on to explain how even world-famous superstars have their own ways of putting on their performance persona so that this can almost seem to become a separate part of their personality. These personifications of confidence can act as a more adventurous alter ego, enabling performers to adopt onstage behavior that contrasts with their everyday life.

> Well, ordinarily she's Beyonce, and then just before she goes on stage, it's like she goes "Bring it! I've got to give a performance." So it's not her, it's Sasha Fierce, and she goes on stage, and she does all the wild things, and then belts it out and dances around, does all of that. And then she comes off stage and she's Beyonce again.

Exercises for Creating a Confident Choral Persona

- Rehearse a song in different, maybe even inappropriate, styles. Ask the choir to adopt different characters while they are singing. How about singing "Do You Hear the People Sing" in the style of Ethel Merman? Or "O Come All Ye Faithful" in the style of Shirley Bassey? Encourage them to make eye contact with each other and sing as flamboyantly as possible. Then ask them to sing "as themselves" but to remember how it felt when they were pretending to be someone else.
- Ask the singers to try the following: Think of someone you perceive as a confident performer, either someone you know or someone you have seen on stage. Picture their body language and how they behave when they are singing. Now imagine that you are that person, and adopt his or her confident body language while you sing. While you are doing this, remember to think about your posture, your facial expression, and your eye contact with the conductor and the audience.

THE CONDUCTOR'S CONTRIBUTION

[Conductors] have got to have the sort of personality that, when I get on that stage, they look relaxed, and confident. (Naomi)

Emotional contagion between conductors and singers, as well as between fellow singers, can have a strong effect on choral confidence. Tim introduced the negative effects of working with an unconfident musical director and worried about his conductor's apparent lack of experience in the role:

I just got the impression it was the first time he'd done an adult [amateur] operetta, and therefore he was feeling his way . . . so probably his appearance of being uncertain decreased people's confidence.

Frank, however, suggested that a conductor's own nervousness can be in evidence despite extensive experience. This nervous appearance spreads a sense of unease among the singers, with predictably negative effects upon morale and confidence levels:

I like them to be calm . . . I've noticed [my conductor gets] a bit nervous sometimes. And I've thought "God, he's done so much, and yet . . . you see the nerves" . . . and I think sometimes we pick that up . . . so we're quite tense as well, and then it's sort of a vicious circle of winding each other up!

Many other interviewees talked about the impact on individual and collective confidence if a conductor is perceived as anxious or uncertain. Naomi, a very experienced alto, was emphatic about the consequences of displaying physical evidence of performance nerves:

If I had somebody that was doing this [shaking] that would not give me a lot of confidence . . . I'd be a nervous wreck! [laughs]. There's no way I could sing in a choir with somebody [who's] a quivering wreck, or slightly nervous— No!—I couldn't cope with that. I have to have somebody in front of me that is confident.

As well as the problems arising from visible nervousness, other forms of negative body language from conductors can reduce the singers' confidence. Phoebe described the phenomenon of some conductors insisting on being attended to while being apparently unaware that their facial expression and general demeanor discouraged eye contact from the singers:

Sometimes there's been situations where—maybe because that particular part of that music is particularly tricky, or there's some sort of language issues or whatever—and you're not looking as much as you should do . . . this kind of like [frowns threateningly] . . . this kind of thing. You feel like you're with a schoolteacher. And they're pointing at their eyes and looking at you and glaring at you. And again, that throws you and completely undermines you. And it makes you look stupid! . . . [The singers] don't want to be looking up because they're frightened of what they see so they just look down.

Unsurprisingly, choral singers like Joyce want conductors "to look at me and smile, just to give me confidence":

Certainly, standing there and looking at people and smiling, as they're singing, really helps. If it looks like they're pleased, that certainly helps. (Phoebe)

The way in which a conductor uses body language and eye contact can make a significant difference in the emotions experienced by a choir during rehearsals and performances. In my work as an examiner for trainee choral conductors, I have observed three main types of nonverbal communication, which are described in the representational case studies below.

Conducting Case Study 1: Glenn

Glenn was a kit drummer who had no interest in becoming a choral conductor, did not like choral music, and could not see the point of learning to conduct vocal ensembles. He was bored by the music chosen for the assessment, and he did not like the sound that the chamber choir were making. He just wanted the assessment to be over so that he could get back to his soundproof studio and practice for his next gig. How did I know this? Well, apart from the fact that five minutes into his exam he asked, "How much longer have I got to do this?" there were a few other clues. First, his conducting gestures were virtually all below the music stand, as if he couldn't be bothered to lift his arms. Second, he stood hunched over the music and maintained a stolidly sullen expression. Third, he rarely looked at the singers, confining his gaze to the score or the floor. He did not engage with the singers and they did not engage with him. They quickly sensed his lack of interest and lost interest themselves. The vocal performance was lackluster, and the singers were disappointed and demoralized. Their confidence visibly sagged, along with their body language, which reflected Glenn's dismissive nonverbal communication.

Conducting Case Study 2: Mimi

Mimi was a trained classical singer, and she arrived in full "performance mode" with a complicated coiffeur, full stage make-up, stagey attire, and a very operatic demeanor. All of this meant that the session was immediately energized: the choir perked up as soon as she took to the podium. She spoke very assertively and expressively, and her face and gestures were very animated. However, it quickly became clear that this was a performance for Mimi rather than a rehearsal for the choir. She was more concerned with the impression she was making than with genuinely communicating with the singers. How did I know this? Well, her gestures and facial expressions were very flamboyant, but they did not reflect the mood of the music. Mimi's arm movements were very high, above the singers' heads, and extravagant, even in pianissimo passages. Her eyes were very bright, and her gaze swept around the room, but it never settled on any of the singers; in fact, she was mainly looking above the choir in a way that became quite disconcerting and alienating. It was obvious that she was not fully aware of what the singers were doing, whether they were enjoying the rehearsal, or whether they needed any help with anything. Mimi's neglect of the choir was almost as complete as Glenn's, although it manifested itself differently. At face value, she was apparently an engaged and enthusiastic conductor, but she was not engaged with anyone except herself. The choir initially responded well to her energy, and the singing was quite uplifting at times, but something was lacking. I think that something was genuine communication between the conductor and the choir, and the singers seemed to lose their commitment once it became obvious that they were just part of their conductor's own personal performance.

Conducting Case Study 3: Rachel

Rachel was a first-study violinist. She was not a trained or particularly accomplished singer, but she enjoyed working with choirs, and she loved the end result once the choir were harmonizing together. Her priority was to enable the singers to perform competently and confidently. How did I know this? Well, Rachel focused on the choir throughout the rehearsal. She listened attentively while she did some troubleshooting with the timing and pitching of notes, and she watched the singers carefully to see if anyone needed extra help with anything. Her patterning was clear and easy to follow, and her arm movements mainly took place in the area between the top of her music stand and the top of her head. Her gestures were open and expansive in a way that felt inclusive: she seemed to be welcoming the singers and inviting the choir to perform. Rachel looked at the choir during most of the session, as she was familiar with the music and needed to glance at it only occasionally. She encompassed the whole of the choir in her gaze, whenever possible, and gave eye contact to each section as she worked on their notes. She also looked and smiled at singers whenever they made a musical entry. The singers responded by watching her carefully and responding to the gestures that indicated changes in musical dynamics, and, by the end of this rehearsal, they were singing accurately and expressively. Rachel's body language was very positive, with an upright but relaxed posture, and an open stance. The choir's appearance reflected this, and their confidence appeared to soar during the rousing performance that rounded off the session.

These case studies show some of the ways in which a conductor's nonverbal communication can have a major impact upon choral performance quality and upon the singers' emotions and mood. It is important for conductors to communicate with the choir through every aspect of their body language in a clear, genuine, and inclusive way. For a conductor, this includes giving the singers his or her full attention, embracing them with an open and empathic gaze, and physically conveying confidence without becoming so flamboyant that the performance becomes conductor-centered rather than singer-centered. These are key factors in bolstering the confidence of a choir, which can create a further virtuous circle of perceived confidence, improved performance, enhanced task mastery, and self-efficacy:

> If [conductors look] confident, it's bound to make you feel confident. It inspires you, doesn't it? (Clive)

The fact that singers' confidence levels are clearly affected by the conductor's body language, as well as by their own facial feedback and the emotional contagion between fellow choir members, suggests a few practical strategies. For example, confidence-boosting power postures,[59] if convincingly modeled by the conductor, will be reciprocated by the choir; the chameleon effect then ensures that the beneficial results of assuming positive body language are shared among the singers. Positive facial expressions also encourage the sharing of positive emotions between the choir and the conductor, as well as among the singers. The conductor's contribution to choral confidence therefore includes modeling confident posture, body language, stage deportment, and facial expression so that the choir reciprocates by performing in a relaxed but poised manner. As a conductor, I find it helpful to remember that "what *they* see is what *you* get."[60] The sound emanating from the singers reflects the posture, expression, conducting style, and gesture that they see in the choral director:

> If the sound coming back to you is not what you want, you must be willing to accept that the sound is a mirror image of your conducting.[61]

Although the aims of this book do not include providing specific guidance on conducting gestures, it is worth noting that conductors' movements have a strong influence upon the choir's musical performance, bodily sensations, and emotional state. Tense conducting gestures convey physical and vocal tension to the singers,[62] while conductors who model an expansive posture can help singers to keep their ribcage expanded, with beneficial effects for breath control and vocal production.[63] The conductor's facial expressions can also affect choral tone,[64] and the conductor's general demeanor has a strong impact on the appearance of the choir:

> The correct basic posture for a choral conductor is identical to what we seek to develop in the singers.[65]

The tendency among singers to replicate the conductor's body language and facial expressions means that the conductor should embody the "sort of sound he would like to make if only he could sing all the parts at once."[66] If the conductor can lead by example, even if not feeling genuinely confident, and express (or mimic) confidence through nonverbal communication, he or she will help the singers to mirror his or her positive body language. This will help create positive feelings, improve performance, increase the singers' sense of task mastery, and enhance perceived self-efficacy. As a by-product of the conductor's modeling of relaxed but poised body language and positive facial expressions, and the singers' mirroring of this, there are likely to be improvements in vocal production and tone, which will enhance the singers' confidence in their own performance.

Using the following exercises and checklist will not guarantee that a choir will always perform confidently, but it will hopefully help conductors fulfill some of the items on Frank's wish list for "a conductor that's good, clear, concise, friendly, doesn't get uptight themselves, and just sort of calm. Clear and consistent. And just encourages people to do their bit, by watching them, you know."

Exercises for Empowering Conductors

- Practice making eye contact with the singers. Include the whole choir in your gaze, and make eye contact with vocal sections whenever they have a musical entry or a "big moment."
- Try bringing in sections without moving your limbs—rely on facial expressions only!
- Make sure your gaze is directed at the singers rather than through them or over their heads.
- Don't be shy about briefly making eye contact with individual singers who are looking at you.

- Remember to smile at the singers whenever they have a challenging section to perform, an exposed musical entry, or a particularly long note to hold.
- Practice preparatory power postures and preparatory smiling before starting to conduct. This will encourage the choir to do the same.
- Encourage singers to use bright expressions, smiling with their eyes while avoiding the tightness that can arise when smiling widely with the lips. Use your smeyes!
- Raise awareness of body language and its impact on performance and confidence; practice modeling different postures and asking the singers to copy you.
- If possible, position the choir in a large semicircle. This will enable the singers to see each other as well as the conductor so that they can mirror each other's body language and facial expressions.
- Practice conducting in front of a mirror to check that your own posture is relaxed but poised, that your facial expressions are encouraging, and that your gestures express the mood of the music rather than any insecurities or tensions you may have.

The following checklist is designed to help conductors use nonverbal communication as a confidence-building tool for themselves and their choirs.

Modeling Confidence: Checklist for Conductors

1. Have you scheduled a gentle, pre-performance physical warm-up with the singers (whenever possible)?
2. Have you remembered to include pre-performance power posturing and brief physical activities to release tension and build confidence?
3. Have you checked your own posture?
4. Are you physically relaxed but poised, calm but alert?
5. Can you feel any unnecessary tension anywhere? If so, try releasing the tension as you breathe out slowly and smile at the singers.
6. Are you remembering to breathe with the singers when possible? Don't forget to expand and relax every time you breathe in.
7. Are you smiling with your eyes?
8. Are you making eye contact with the singers?
9. When making eye contact, are you looking directly at the singers rather than through them or over their heads?
10. Are you including the whole choir in your gaze whenever possible?
11. Are you able to look over your sheet music so that you can engage with the singers?
12. Are you remembering to smile at the singers whenever they have a musical entry, a challenging section, or a long note to hold?

13. Have you checked that all the singers can see you from where they are standing?
14. Are you looking at the singers with warmth as if they are people that you like? If this is difficult for some reason, imagine that you are looking at people who fall into that category!
15. Are you paying attention to your own posture and breathing?
16. Are you remembering to take a few calm deep breaths whenever you have a chance; for example, between songs and in instrumental introductions?
17. Are you paying attention to your own facial expression and other aspects of your nonverbal communication?
18. Are your gestures appropriate to the music? Make sure they convey the mood that you wish the choir to express rather than indicating your own mood!
19. Are your gestures clear and large enough for your choir to see easily?
20. Are your movements fluid and relaxed? If there is any unnecessary tension, try to reduce this. Practicing conducting in front of a mirror may not be popular, as it clearly reveals any imperfections in posture, gesture, and facial expression. However, this can help us start to address any shortcomings that we may have so that we can convey and cultivate confidence in our choirs.

CHAPTER SUMMARY

- Many singers who participated in my research defined the portrayal and perception of self-confidence in terms of nonverbal communication. This included posture, body language, deportment, facial expression, eye contact, expressive performance, and engagement with the audience.
- There was widespread recognition of the contagious effects of nonverbal communication and its potential to influence confidence, both positively and negatively.
- Modeling confident posture, body language, and facial expression by choir members and musical leaders can cultivate as well as convey confidence.
- Being able to see the other singers (when possible) and the conductor is helpful for sharing positive nonverbal communication.
- Preparation should therefore include close attention to the nonverbal communication of the choir as well as thorough musical rehearsal.

Nonverbal communication has a significant effect upon confidence in the sphere of amateur choral performance. This has practical implications for physical preparation in rehearsals, and for postural and expressive modeling (by conductors as well as singers) in performance. The singers' emphasis on posture may also partly explain the reported use of the Alexander technique as a successful strategy in the management of music performance anxiety.[67] This technique is a system of aligning bodily posture to maximize clavicular and thoracic relaxation, chest expansion, and tension-free vocal production, and it has clear parallels to the body language necessary for competent and confident choral performance.

The importance for choral singers of factors related to body language, facial expression, and posture is doubtlessly connected with their subjective experience of themselves as an embodied instrument. The voice is an integral part of their physiology, and their performance is inextricably linked to their physique and neuropsychobiological condition.[68] This complex relationship between the singer, their "instrument," and their feelings about performance, combined with the fact that they have no external instrument to physically separate them from the audience or "towards which they can project their feelings and attention,"[69] can lead to an intense focus on physical, appearance-related aspects of performance. This will be further explored in the next chapter.

Modeling confident postures and facial expressions can clearly be an effective tool in building self-efficacy among choral singers. Even if the subjective emotion is not initially genuine, the adoption of positive body language by conductors and singers can contribute to the portrayal and sensation of self-confidence. Positive nonverbal communication should therefore be strongly encouraged in choir rehearsals and performances to ensure that postural and facial feedback are used to their greatest advantage. Physical warm-ups that include paying attention to body language and expression will help with this. Positioning singers, where possible, so that they can see each other's facial expression will also be helpful, as well as ensuring that all singers have an unimpeded view of the conductor's positive body language.

Chapter Two

Practice, Preparation, and Presentation

Start by doing what's necessary; then do what's possible; and suddenly you
are doing the impossible.
—Saint Francis of Assisi

In 1993, when appearing on the concert platform after a long absence, Barbra
Streisand sang the opening words to "As If We Never Said Goodbye" from
Sunset Boulevard, aptly beginning, "I don't know why I'm frightened."[1]
Despite her reputation as one of the best-selling recording artists of all time,
and her highly acclaimed career in film and television, Streisand was well
acquainted with performance anxiety. Due to severe stage fright she had
withdrawn from live public concert performances for over twenty years, and
she openly acknowledged this during her much-celebrated return to the
stage.[2]

So far, I have mainly concentrated on the positive aspects of choral confidence-building rather than focusing on the more debilitating anxiety states
experienced by some performers. However, I include a brief discussion of
music performance anxiety (MPA) here, as this is sometimes experienced by
amateur singers[3] as well as professionals like Streisand. Performers of all
kinds are often in a situation that can be perceived as threatening, usually not
physically, but certainly psychologically and emotionally. This sense of vulnerability is a natural reaction to stepping into the public arena and potentially exposing our flaws as well as our skills. There are complex neuropsychobiological responses to this perceived threat, but the three main reactions are
popularly defined as "flight, fight or freeze."[4] These "alarm responses" have
been essential in evolutionary terms,[5] as they can help people to react appropriately to physical danger. These days, however, they are also triggered by
numerous scenarios with a social aspect, including "fear of humiliation or
disgrace."[6]

Alarm reflexes may be useful when trying to avoid being captured by predators, but they can be "deleterious to the very delicate and intricate motor and intellectual activity involved in musical performance,"[7] and they are clearly of limited practical use in the choral context. With an audience keen to hear their performance, singers are unlikely to flee the venue. Some of this nervous energy can be usefully channeled into the performance once the choir arrives on stage. However, it would be undesirable to activate the fight option while waiting in the wings! The freeze response often results in a kind of paralysis before the performance; during performances, it manifests itself in a "deer in the headlights" expression on the faces of some singers.

Many strategies for managing music performance anxiety have been explored, including cognitive behavioral therapy (CBT), desensitization, Alexander technique,[8] mental skills training, and physical exercise.[9] One of the earliest approaches was suggested by Paderewski, who recommended that performance anxiety could be reduced through carrying out in-depth harmonic analysis of the music.[10] It would be unrealistic to suggest that this tactic should generally be included in amateur choral rehearsals, but getting to know the music as thoroughly as possible is still a vital part of confidence-building for choirs. Detailed preparation is not a panacea, but it can contribute to a healthier relationship with the performer's natural anxiety about placing themselves in the public gaze. In the following sections, there will be an exploration of the role of practice and preparation in reducing performance anxiety and increasing choral confidence.

PERFORMANCE ANXIETY AND MOTIVATION

When suppressing their instincts to fly, fight, or freeze, singers may experience a range of indicators of MPA as a performance approaches. Among the most common physical symptoms are increased heart rate, dry mouth, excessive sweating, muscle tension, and breathing difficulties.[11] Cognitive symptoms may include negative or distracting thoughts, while behavioral disturbances, such as the avoidance of practice, may also occur.[12] The manifestations of MPA vary from person to person, but a participant in my earlier research described some of the common effects for singers:

> I just basically, sort of, tighten up, I suppose . . . I get sweaty palms and start to choke . . . when I tighten up it's sort of my throat—everything else seems to go loose and wobbly. I've got no control over it! . . . At the audition I felt my voice was wavering: it just generally didn't have the support like it could have. (Jonathan)[13]

The onset of MPA also varies from performer to performer; it may commence minutes, hours, or even weeks before a scheduled performance.[14] The anxiety that begins immediately before a performance is usually caused by an adrenaline rush, which is designed to enable us to cope with challenging situations.[15] Adrenaline can provide the energy and attentional focus to perform well, and the more worrying physiological effects tend to diminish once the performance starts. Reinterpreting some of the symptoms of anxiety (such as butterflies in the tummy, shaking, or sweating) as signs of excitement[16] can help to give this reaction a positive makeover so that we can welcome it as an energizing response to the demands of performance.

Early onset anxiety, however, can sometimes be more difficult to deal with. In my teens, I often experienced a rush of dread about two weeks before a performance. This usually resulted in two weeks of virtual hell as I vacillated between a vague sense of impending doom and moments of abject panic. When I started asking myself what these emotions were trying to tell me, I realized that I didn't feel adequately prepared for part of the performance. Like many people, I was avoiding handling the things that worried me the most. Avoidance is a form of self-sabotage, as not practicing the hard stuff limits our competence and confidence. The avoidance of practice is sometimes used as an excuse for inferior performance, and the whole rehearsal period is then haunted by low expectations. This sets up a destructive cycle of anxiety, avoidance, unsatisfying performances, and diminishing confidence.

Using my fear to identify what I needed to practice helped me to tackle the most anxiety-inducing areas of my performance. Forcing myself to practice these problem passages provided a constructive focus for my nervous energy rather than leaving me frozen with fear. It helped to soothe my nerves and left me feeling better prepared and more confident. I eventually embraced my performance anxiety as a helpful friend who prompts me to look at what I need to address rather than as a saboteur looming over me like a paralyzing nightmare. Now, when my stomach metaphorically turns to blancmange, I ask myself, "What have I neglected?" The answer is usually something like "You haven't sorted out the scary bit in the middle of that piece of music!"

Although Barbra Streisand's experience of performance anxiety was, at times, crippling, she eventually overcame it sufficiently to resume touring, and she continues to perform live to sell-out audiences well into her eighth decade. Her philosophical approach to the emotional and psychological challenges of performance is thought-provoking:

> Doubt can motivate you, so don't be afraid of it. Confidence and doubt are at two ends of the scale, and you need both. They balance each other out.

My interpretation of Streisand's advice is that self-doubt can motivate us by indicating that it's time to do more practice! However, practice is unlikely to "make perfect" in this context because perfection is not usually a realistic target in the demanding world of the performing arts. Every musical experience probably includes some aspect with which the performer is dissatisfied, even if they have gifted the audience with an enjoyable and impressive performance. Since musical perfection is so frustratingly unattainable for most performers, extreme perfectionism is not usually a helpful personality trait. In fact, it can be one of the roots of severe MPA. This is because perfectionism is generally associated with higher anxiety, lower confidence, less goal satisfaction, and "a failure (rather than a success) orientation to one's performances."[17] This can be mitigated by being forgiving of one's own limitations and learning to accept when a performance is "good enough." On the other hand, a modicum of self-doubt can sometimes motivate performers to prepare in a way that can increase competence and develop confidence.

In chapter 1, the interviewees' descriptions of confident singers were centered around nonverbal communication, including posture and body language, smiling and making eye contact, and performing expressively. Some singers also explained that thorough preparation is a prerequisite for being able to employ positive body language during a performance:

> They smile as well 'cause they're confident, and they know "We can do this now. We can actually do this on our own." And yeah, it's the whole posture, I think. (Phoebe)

In the following sections, the singers describe how practice and preparation, including working on practical aspects of group presentation, help to build their belief in their own ability.

MUSICAL EXPRESSION AND IMMERSION

> [You're] in control . . . You're on top of your breathing. You're on top of your notes. You're on top of your interpretation. You're understanding the music. There are some pieces of music where you know the notes, and you sing it and that's fine, and there are other pieces of music which are part of you, which is quite different. (Harry)

Learning the words, melody, and harmonies for songs is usually the most obvious part of practice and preparation. Harry also included breath control, phrasing, interpretation, and musical understanding. He described the significant difference between singing music that has been superficially learned and performances that are almost second nature because the music has become so ingrained.

Total familiarity with the music helps the singers to know that the performance is well within their capabilities. It helps them to relax enough to enjoy the experience, perform confidently and expressively, and share their enjoyment with the audience. Naomi suggested that being able to make eye contact with the audience gives more than a superficial impression of self-confidence; it also indicates a confidence-boosting level of familiarity with the text and the music, which allows the singers to be fully involved in the performance:

> I can always tell with the basses . . . once they've got it, they're different, they're a lot more relaxed, and they give it everything. I don't mean loud, but they're straight in, and they're not down here in the books, they're actually looking up, because they know that's the note [they're] singing. If they're not so confident, their body language changes, and they're tentative and not so sure.

Andrew felt that confident singers were identifiable by their capacity to interpret the music and communicate the meaning of the song, and by their complete involvement in the music:

> There is this confidence . . . They tell a story. They're in the zone, they're into that part, and this charisma comes across, blended with the quality of the voice and the song they're singing.

As well as being an indication of confidence and competence, this absorption in the music can, in itself, be confidence-building. Colin's concentration on the music prevented him from dwelling on the audience's reaction and distracted him from any anxieties about his performance:

> I think it's being in the song as well. It's being in the zone. If you're so engrossed in the song itself that you're singing, then that produces confidence as well because you're just involved in the story or the tune or whatever. It produces confidence because you know what you're doing.

Harry's total immersion in the music may account for his self-identification as a confident choral singer. He recommended putting the music first rather than worrying about anyone's opinion of his performance:

You are a servant of the music. You are the servant of the person who's composed this beautiful piece of music, whoever it may be. And the last thing you are doing is saying, "Hey, look at me!" That's not what it's about, to me.

Ursula described herself as a less confident singer, but she similarly found that total concentration on the music counteracted any potential distractions and helped her to enjoy performing:

I think that when I'm actually doing the singing, that's where I am. Just in the singing at the time . . . I think it is this idea that once I'm singing that's all I'm doing, and I really don't see or hear or notice anything else that's going on around me . . . Actually, even when I know I've got the wrong note, that's not noticing what's going on around me, that's just me and my singing.

GOING WITH THE FLOW

What's nice would be to feel that you're not just singing the number, following all the signposts or whatever, but to really feel that you're telling the story . . . You've got to add that little bit of *je ne sais quoi*, that color. (Frank)

As we saw in chapter 1, when evaluating confidence in other performers, many singers focus on the physical embodiment of confidence, including positive body language, expressive nonverbal communication, direct eye contact, engagement with the audience, and evidence of an emotional connection with the music. In the previous section, some participants also described alleviating their own anxieties and increasing their self-confidence by immersing themselves in the performance, becoming absorbed in the music, involving themselves in the emotional interpretation, and enjoying the sense of occasion. Several of the interviewees described this total absorption in their choral singing as "being in the zone," a phrase that will no doubt be familiar to many sports enthusiasts. This concept was developed by the Hungarian psychologist Csikszentmihalyi in his exploration of "peak performance," or "flow":

A sense that one's skills are adequate to cope with the challenges at hand, in a goal-directed, rule-bound action system that provides clear clues as to how well one is performing. Concentration is so intense that there is no attention left over to think about anything irrelevant, or to worry about problems. Self-consciousness disappears, and the sense of time becomes distorted. [18]

In choral performance, the main conditions for creating a state of flow are a focused approach that excludes all distraction, and engagement in a musical task in which the main challenges are matched to the singer's skill level. Singers who achieve a flow state experience a loss of self-consciousness and an increase in self-confidence because they focus on enjoying the performance rather than feeling anxious or worrying about the impression that they are making on the audience.

Several participants made the obvious but salient point that thorough preparation is a prerequisite for enjoying their own choral performances. Without sufficient grounding in all the technical and musical aspects of performance, it is difficult to interpret and express the music confidently. Equally, without thorough preparation, singers will be anxious about less familiar aspects of the performance and will be unable to relax and achieve total immersion. Clive explained that working on expression, interpretation, and communication on top of learning the notes and lyrics can help the singer to feel more confident:

> You're telling a little story really, aren't you? That's what you're doing. And I think that's another thing—as someone who sings, you sing words, and perhaps you've heard it before, and then sometimes you think to yourself, "My goodness, I didn't realize what that was actually about." Until you've actually sung it. And if you've done it a few times, I think you tend to put it over better in that sense . . . It makes it a bit more confidence building.

Singers in the focus groups felt that total immersion can only be achieved when the choir is so well-drilled in the words and the music that they can move to a higher level of interpretation:

> Matt: It's a bit like it's second nature, really. You don't have to think about the words—they just come out . . .

> Colin: You're so well-rehearsed that you're just in the performance.

> Ross: You then go from just singing something to actually performing something.

Don perfectly summarized the virtuous cycle of thorough preparation, feeling prepared for performance, and enjoyment of the experience:

> I guess that's one way you can talk about a confident singer. Whatever the level they're at, they know what they're singing, they know they're getting it right, and they're enjoying what they're doing.

Ross was one of several singers who made analogies between the level of preparation required for work-related "performances," such as presentations and sales pitches, and the amount of practice necessary for confident choral performances:

> We used to say, as project managers, "Failing to plan is planning to fail" . . .
> that preparation, being prepared, gives you the confidence to do it.

In his focus group, Colin entertained everyone with his well-grounded guide to successful performance, regardless of the context:

> In sales, we used to call it "The Five *P*s: Poor planning is piss-poor presenta-
> tion!" [laughter] . . . If you didn't do your preparation, then your presentation
> was going to be crap. And seven-eighths of performance is preparation. And
> one-eighth is performance. And it doesn't make any difference if that's a
> presentation or singing in front of an audience.

In the following section, a more extensive set of rehearsal strategies will be provided, but here are some preliminary suggestions for laying the musical foundations of a secure performance.

"Note-Bashing" Strategies

There is no magical way to make this sexy, but it is essential groundwork, especially in choirs where sight-singing skills are limited. Some of the following strategies will help to maintain interest while allowing useful musical repetition. Not all of these strategies will need to be used for every song and every choir, but they may provide some useful additions to the rehearsal process.

- Recite unfamiliar, complex, or foreign words, or very fast lyrics before singing them.
- If songs have complex or syncopated rhythms, explore the rhythmic patterns through clapping exercises.
- Practice singing the melody with open vowel sounds or nonsense syllables before singing the words.
- Try singing the words without the consonants.
- Give everyone a chance to sing the melody—in whichever octave they prefer!
- Give each vocal section the opportunity to concentrate on singing their line without the other parts. Then ask them to repeat their line while singers in the other vocal sections hum along to acclimatize everyone to the harmony.
- Practice each harmony line with the melody.

- Rehearse all the harmony parts together without the tune.
- Try different voice combinations together. Work out which parts are helpful to each other and practice those together. Work out which voice parts might distract each other—due to difficult intervals between the two parts, for example—and practice those together.
- Practice short sections, then extend the sections and incorporate them into the song. Don't spend too long on one voice part before giving the other singers a chance to practice.
- Try what I usually call "backward chaining." Start by practicing the last (say) 4 bars of a section, then add the penultimate 4 bars, then the 4 bars before that, and so on. Keep working back toward the beginning of the section until everyone is ready to perform it in the right order.
- Work in detail on one of the more challenging passages. Now connect it to the preceding passage. Then connect it to the succeeding passage. Do this until the section flows smoothly. Finally, integrate it into the rest of the song.
- Practice transitions from one section of a song to the next. Pay special attention to connecting passages, repeats, first and second time bars, codas, key changes, and tempo variations.
- Ask relatively confident choirs to "busk" through a new song—busking is a less intimidating concept than sight singing for many singers! Only stop if the performance falls apart. Do not provide a detailed critique at this stage, but use the rendition as a starting point for troubleshooting and examining some of the more complex passages.

PRACTICE AND "OVERLEARNING"

> Excellence is an art won by training and habituation . . . we are what we repeatedly do. Excellence then is not an act but a habit.
> —Aristotle

All focus groups and interviewees valued meticulous rehearsal as an integral part of creating a fluent and confident performance. Ross felt that non-singers are sometimes unaware that choral excellence largely depends upon hard work and application:

> When people have spent all that time, the preparation, the effort, and everything else, then it looks easy, and [other people] think, "Ooh, I couldn't possibly do that." They haven't seen that they've been practicing.

Similarly, Gordon attributed his vocal attainment to effort and determination:

If I had a pound for every time somebody has come up to me and said, "I couldn't possibly go on stage and do what you're doing" . . . Everybody can . . . You're not just given a song and you stand up and sing it. You practice and you practice and you practice and you practice. And that's what rehearsals are all about.

This dedicated approach to practice is sometimes described as "overlearning": "the continued training of a skill after performance improvement has plateaued."[19] Non-musicians are sometimes surprised that musicians keep practicing pieces of music long after they can play them fluently, and sometimes even after they have delivered ostensibly flawless performances. The concept of overlearning was originally established by Hermann Ebbinghaus, the psychologist who also popularized the idea of a learning curve.[20] Overlearning can help people to remember what they have learned and to retain skills that they have acquired. Overlearners stabilize their expertise, fixing it firmly within their repertoire of skills and knowledge. In comparison, those who stop learning as soon as they have mastered a skill are more vulnerable to distraction and interference from subsequent tasks.[21] In choral singing, overlearning is therefore likely to be a major factor in facilitating flow states, with their confidence-building characteristics of concentration, immersion, and loss of self-consciousness.[22]

The singers I interviewed mentioned numerous aspects of choral performance that they needed to practice thoroughly, including note-bashing, memorization, word learning, and familiarity with lyrics, especially for songs in foreign languages. Tim's self-confidence fluctuated according to his level of musical preparation:

My confidence depended on how well I knew the music. If I knew I knew the music, my confidence was fine. If I knew I was going to struggle with some bits of the music, my confidence would decrease.

During her interview, Dawn relived some painful memories of the adverse effects of under-preparation:

The [operatic society] did a show where we were totally under-rehearsed and it was just awful. I went on the first night not knowing it and I went on the last night not knowing it, and I swore I would never, ever have that again. That was just awful. You cringed at the, you know, the thought of it.

Colin felt that he needed to be so well prepared that he automatically went into "performance mode." Once he was "thinking performance," he felt ready to focus on interpreting the music, entertaining the audience, and performing confidently. Likewise, Phoebe felt that after learning their music thoroughly, singers can concentrate on immersing themselves in the communicative aspects of their performance:

> [A confident singer is] somebody that, even if they do need to refer to the music or whatever, they tend to be able to look up and over. They have a good connection with the person conducting. They have, or try and get a connection with the audience. They're not afraid to have good diction and open their mouths and be expressive. I think, to me, that's what I would say is being a confident singer.

Practice seems an obvious, if unglamorous, factor in confident choral performance. There are unlikely to be any exciting definitions, but here is a useful one: practice is the "repeated performance or systematic exercise for the purpose of learning or acquiring proficiency."[23] It is also essential, even for accomplished performers, in maintaining their expertise and fluency. Among musicians, Paderewski's epigram about practice is legendary:

> If I don't practice for one day, I know it. If I don't practice for two days, the critics know it. If I don't practice for three days, the audience knows it.

Other purposes of practice include improving technique, building stamina, learning and memorizing music, developing interpretative and expressive elements of the music, and making cognitive and practical preparations for the demands of public performance. The following rehearsal strategies can contribute to thorough choral preparation.

Rehearsal Strategies

- Once note-bashing is complete, rehearse the whole song—and when it goes well, try not to rest on your laurels. Do it again immediately to consolidate. Ask the singers to think about what they were doing when it went well and to try to repeat that consciously.
- Develop expressive and interpretative skills by asking the singers to respond to the written dynamics—then try diverging from the printed instructions and ask the singers to respond with whatever volume or tempo you indicate, regardless of what is on the page.
- Help the singers remember words and communicate expressively by exploring the meaning of the lyrics.

- Develop memorization skills by learning some simple songs or short extracts by ear. This encourages instant memorization by releasing the singers from any habitual overreliance on the printed page.
- Use lyric sheets or posters to remind singers of the words as an interim measure between reading the music and performing entirely from memory. They can then be weaned off the visual cues.
- Remember to familiarize the singers with musical introductions and instrumental sections.
- Practice finding starting notes from instrumental or other vocal parts. Check that entries are secure after introductory passages, instrumental sections, or breaks from singing while other vocal sections perform.
- When starting some songs, it may be helpful to provide the first interval for some parts rather than just a single note at the beginning of the piece.
- For a cappella work, help the choir to get used to whichever source will be used for the starting notes because singers may react differently to a pitch pipe, tuning fork, voice, keyboard, string or wind instrument, electronic tone, and so forth.
- There is no shame in asking each part to hum their starting notes before beginning a song, especially in unaccompanied music. Some singers worry that this may make them appear to be less competent, but it is better to be prepared than to have a rocky start to a song.
- Don't forget to look at the singers' faces! Does anyone look worried during any part of the song? This can be a prompt to check whether words, notes, or any other musical component is causing insecurity at this point.
- In the short term, try to design each rehearsal in a way that builds on and extends the choir's existing skills. In the longer term, try to do the same over the whole term or rehearsal period so that the singers can see how much progress they are making within a structured learning program.

WARMING UP

One of the most important stages of each practice session and performance is a preparatory warm-up routine. Physical and vocal warm-ups are a vital part of developing choral technique as well as essential for preparing the voice—as an embodied instrument—for peak performance. In rehearsals, gentle warm-ups can be used to coax the voice into the optimum condition for singing, just as an athlete or dancer would stretch before physical exertion. Singers often recognize the significance of having a thorough warm-up, and Matt noted the emotional and vocal benefits:

> You have a warm-up and it sounds good and it makes you smile, you know . . .
> It does make you smile and set you up for a good lesson or a good perfor-

mance, I think . . . So I think it is important. And it's enjoyable. It builds confidence. (Matt)

Frank saw vocal warm-ups as part of a comforting pre-performance routine that could help to reduce anxiety:

> I like to prepare, to be warmed up. Having got into the habit now—the operatics never used to do it, and now everyone asks for it . . . [to] try and get rid of the nerves, and just calm down and just sort of get prepared.

Familiar warm-ups can help the singers to relax, switch off from the distractions of their everyday lives, focus on the forthcoming event, and become familiar with the acoustics of the venue. A thorough vocal warm-up can reassure them that their voices are working well and that they are as ready as they can be for the performance. This routine gives the choir a few last moments of preparation time with their conductor and provides a valuable opportunity for some attention and encouragement from him or her before the performance starts.

Nick delivered an important caveat on this subject though, as he had experienced some warm-ups that were not useful for the singers. He felt that his musical director was lacking in knowledge about what made for an effective warm-up. He also felt that the exercises were childish and delivered in a patronizing way, which was unsuitable for adult singers:

> I didn't really care for the warm-ups . . . it seemed to be a little bit of an egotistical thing for the conductor, doing everything the same every time. It wasn't warming up people's voices, it was doing stupid little ditties and how fast you can sing it and "Let's miss out the third word" and . . . stupid. It didn't warm your voice up at all! It's "Look at me—how clever can I be?! 'Cause I can play this song and sing this song, and I'm gonna make you do it!" . . . They were games—they weren't warming you up. It was just rubbish! Very frustrating.

He then described a simple warm-up routine that he felt would be more helpful vocally:

> I think it would be just to start with something that is fairly narrow, or compact, in terms of its range, its pitching, but then just builds, so it is fairly medium in terms of its loudness and restricted to a small, narrow band of pitches. And then it just builds and gets bigger and bigger and bigger. And louder. That's how I think is the best way. So it just expands the volume, and the pitching of it as well.

The following is a set of basic principles for developing a vocal warm-up routine.

Warm-Up Suggestions

Start with a reminder of the "relaxed but poised posture" for singing, a few gentle stretches, and some basic breathing exercises (see chapter 1). Using a limited range, which is likely to be accessible to most adult singers (and asking them to choose the most comfortable octave), try the following vocal exercises:

- Humming short scale passages (perhaps only three or four notes) with gently closed lips, on a "mmm" sound, then repeat on a "nnn" or "nng" sound, with lips slightly open.
- Extend the scale passages slightly (five or six notes) and perform them on open vowel sounds.
- Extend the exercises into longer scales, melodic phrases, broken chords, or arpeggios to suit the range of the singers.
- Add consonants to create nonsense syllables as the voices become "warmer."
- Sing simple words with open vowel sounds, just using scales or broken chords at first.
- Add gentle crescendos and diminuendos.
- Use basic songs with words or phrases from foreign languages to focus on open vowel sounds. I often use arpeggios with simple phrases such as *io t'amo, je t'aime*, and *ich liebe dich*. There's nothing nicer than hearing a whole choir sing "I love you"!
- Sing a round or call-and-response song with a limited range so that everyone can complete the warm-up routine comfortably.
- Extend the warm-up into some of the music that the choir is learning, perhaps by quietly humming passages from a song they learned the previous week, or by singing a familiar section to open vowels or nonsense syllables. Then add the words.
- Pick out the more challenging phrases in one of the choir's well-rehearsed songs and apply some of the above warm-up techniques to these sections. The warm-up will now have segued into the musical rehearsal.

REPERTOIRE SELECTION

An important prerequisite for achieving a state of flow is matching the skills of the participants to the challenges of the activity.[24] This is partly achieved by thorough rehearsal so that the singers feel as well prepared as possible to meet the demands of performance. The selection of appropriate music is also a crucial factor that requires a realistic evaluation of the skills and aims of the singers as well as a wide knowledge of the repertoire. For the conductor, repertoire selection is a key part of the preparation before rehearsals even start, and taking time to think carefully about this can prevent serious setbacks in the learning process. Practicing a song that is unsuitable for the choir can waste rehearsal time and have a negative impact on confidence within the group. It can be demoralizing for the singers and the conductor if a poorly chosen song is either performed badly or ends up being abandoned.

Many of the singers that I interviewed associated confident, enjoyable choral performances with repertoire that is challenging enough to engage their interest, while being sufficiently well prepared and familiar to allow a successful, assured performance. Inappropriate repertoire may sometimes be selected if the conductor prioritizes his or her own musical targets over the emotional, psychological, or vocal well-being of the choir. When this happens, the singers' enjoyment is often diminished, absorption in the music is reduced, flow is difficult to achieve, and confidence suffers. The complex neuropsychobiological needs of the singer,[25] therefore, need to be considered, as well as the achievement goals of the conductor and the choir. Problems can sometimes arise if the singers have unrealistic expectations, perhaps putting pressure on a conductor to rehearse repertoire that is overambitious for the developmental stage of the choir. In this case, it can be challenging to select repertoire that will be musically satisfying for the singers, provide a stimulating experience, and set performance goals that are simultaneously exciting and comfortably achievable in the time available.

Nick felt that considering the singers' enjoyment was paramount when choosing choral repertoire. He described a "virtuous circle" of liking the song, singing it well, knowing that the performance is good, and enjoying the experience. All this helps the singers to perform more confidently. Nick also described the opposite scenario, where more unattainable repertoire, or less enjoyable music, has a negative effect on task mastery and self-efficacy:

> It's that virtuous circle thing, you know. You like something, you sing it better, you get a kick from it, you sing it better the next time, and everybody's smiling and it's all getting better and better and better. Whereas, you've got one that you don't like, or is less easy to sing, then you are definitely more nervous singing it . . . And you're more critical of yourself. It just takes longer and longer . . . And it may be something that you never get to like and you never really think you sing it that well, possibly. But I think definitely the ones that you like are easier to sing.

On the other hand, Naomi explained that she found that musical complexity acted as a useful distraction from her nerves. Having to concentrate on demanding repertoire helped her to become immersed in the music rather than think about other elements of the performance such as the presence or opinion of the audience, which had contributed to her previous anxieties about choral performance. This interviewee was one of only two participants in this study who had studied music at tertiary level, so her appreciation of increased complexity may not be widespread among amateur singers. However, it is a reminder that choosing engaging repertoire that is of a suitable standard for the choir can have a positive effect on the confidence of the singers:

> The more complex it is the more I enjoy it 'cause it makes me think more . . . and this is going to sound really weird, but because it's more complex, and because it's a challenge, I look forward to the concert because I think, "Right. Nerves under control. You can do this." . . . It takes away the fear . . . because I'm thinking exactly what I'm doing, and I never even think about the audience at all.

Choosing Repertoire

- Think about the musical and vocal skill levels of the singers. Are they technically, musically, and vocally ready for this music? If not, what extra training or support might they need? Is there another, more accessible song, that would fulfill a similar function in your concert program? With more advanced choirs, are they being challenged sufficiently by the musical demands of the repertoire but without risk of vocal fatigue?
- Get to know the comfortable ranges for the singers. Bear this in mind when choosing songs and be prepared to substitute or re-allocate notes where necessary. Try rearranging harmonies so that the overall effect is preserved while taking some of the pressure off the singers.
- Look at the tessitura as well as the range of each vocal line. Sometimes the overall range of a song may not be unusually wide, but it may contain long passages that are all toward one extreme of the singers' range. A very high or low tessitura may be tiring for some singers and should be avoided.
- Check where singers will obtain their starting notes from, and which vocal lines or sections of the accompaniment will give useful cues for entries. If the arrangement of a song is overcomplicated, or poorly designed for amateur choral performance, starting notes may be hard for some singers to find.
- Try arranging music for your own choir so that you can account for their unique strengths and weaknesses. My choirs have been excited to premiere my custom-made arrangements; it makes them feel special to know that I have taken the time to write something especially for them and to know that the music is unique to this ensemble. When the music has been

arranged specifically for a group, choral "magic" can happen: the choir sounds good, the singers know they sound good, and they feel good about that.

• Don't try to be too clever. Writing a complex arrangement may show off your musical expertise, but it may also have the opposite effect if the result is not sympathetic to the human voice. The fact that a combination of notes can be played on a keyboard does not mean that it will be easy or pleasant to sing. Overcomplex arrangements sometimes sound clumsy and are not fun to perform, while simple but well-sung arrangements that fit a choir's capabilities will be enjoyed by audiences and singers alike. My advice to myself when arranging music for groups of performers at any level is KISS—Keep It Simple, Stupid! This reminds me that using over-complicated arrangements will frustrate and dishearten the singers who are trying to perform the music.

KEEPING UP APPEARANCES

> I think your own personal appearance counts for a lot. I know, when I've got my performance outfit on, and ready, I think, "Yes, I'm fine." If I had to go on in any old, rough clothes, because something had happened, and I had to sing, and I wasn't properly dressed, I would feel very unconfident because I'd feel as though I was picking myself out for people to say, "Ooh, look at her!" (Pamela)

When asked, "What do you do to help to increase your confidence before or during a performance?" many choral singers talked about their own individual preparation. For them, this included paying attention to details of their personal appearance such as clothing, hairstyle, make-up, and jewelry. Naomi's meticulous preparation was typical:

> In my mind, I have to be totally regimented . . . and it's a routine of gotta be there on time, I've got to look right, so I've got my uniform, and that's all in one place so I'm not scratching around trying to find the earrings or the necklace, so that's all in one place. Make-up, hair, everything—and then I'm ready.

Male singers were equally emphatic about the importance of personal grooming. Andrew felt that paying attention to his appearance made a vital contribution to his self-confidence and performance experience:

> I enjoy the concerts. I really do. I enjoy dressing up, when I put the bow tie on—I really do. And I enjoy doing a good job. It's as simple as that, really.

Audience reactions to the appearance of the choir helped Frank to feel more confident about performing:

> You go and say to somebody, "What did you think?" And they'll say, "Oh, yeah. And you all looked really smart too." And it makes you think, "Ooh, yeah." 'Cause I think it looks good. It looks really good. I know [evening dress] is a bit sort of traditional, but it looks good.

Barry also derived confidence from knowing that the presentation of the whole choir made a good impression:

> You've got to feel confident that you look right as well . . . In the choir, if you're all dressed the same, like in a uniform, it looks brilliant, when you've got a choir all wearing the same outfit. So, I suppose that's a sort of first impression. People sum a lot up with first impressions, and if you look good that helps. It helps your confidence.

As well as the positive effects of having confidence in their appearance, singers also emphasized the importance of physical comfort. Frank felt that he needed to be comfortable as well as smart to reduce any unnecessary distractions when performing:

> I'm tending to focus on one narrow aspect, that is the comfort . . . Maybe I'm like the princess and the pea—maybe I'm a bit too sensitive about these things [laughs]. I even like to feel right in the suit that I've got. I don't like . . . Well, nobody likes being too hot or too cold. As long as you feel good about it, I think you give a better performance.

Some singers had idiosyncratic preferences for their appearance when performing, including wearing specific items of clothing, jewelry, or other accessories. Clive, for example, favored wearing an older pair of spectacles rather than his latest prescription lenses:

> I tend to wear a different pair of glasses . . . I have got a pair . . . and I don't know why, but I just feel more confident singing in them . . . I just feel happier if I've got them on. If I haven't got them on I think, "Oh my God, I've got my wrong glasses on!"

For many singers, all the components of their appearance, including choir uniform and personal grooming, were an integral part of stepping into the role of "choral singer" for the performance:

> Obviously, if we're all wearing a uniform, and you do your hair . . . It's like going on stage really. I know nobody's looking at me, but you do those preparation things. You don't roll up looking any old how! (Celia)

Frank often featured in a local operatic society's annual productions, and he compared choral singing with "getting into character" for a leading role:

> When you're stood up for a choir performance, if you're dressed nicely, and you've got all your music, and you've got all your folders all the right color, and the same, that's a little bit like being in character, isn't it? . . . When you're in the suit, you feel like you're in a choir, sort of thing. And the same with the male voice choir, we dress in lounge suits, but . . . it's getting the feeling right. Even the fact that I clean my shoes . . . I always think if you look the part, you'll be the part, to some extent.

For Frank, the uniform appearance of the choir helped to create a sense of group identity and belonging, which had a positive effect on individual and collective confidence. It may also have the effect of distancing the individual from their everyday life and focusing their mind on the task at hand, with positive effects on performance quality. In a recent experimental study, teaching assistants in smart, formal clothes were perceived as more intelligent than their casually dressed peers, and people wearing white lab coats scored higher in tests requiring a lot of concentration. The researchers concluded that "the clothes we wear have power not only over others, but also over ourselves."[26]

In chapter 1, I suggested that choral singers evaluate confidence in terms of body language partly because of the voice's status as an embodied instrument. Because the singer has no external instrument separating him from the audience, or to focus on during the performance, the voice is intimately connected with the singer's physical condition. For these reasons, singers and their audiences often focus on appearance-related aspects of performance such as clothing and personal grooming. Uniformity of choir presentation can contribute to a sense of belonging, and this can facilitate confidence-inducing states of flow. The singers that I interviewed consistently reported deriving confidence from their sense of the choir as a community, and this will be discussed in more detail in chapter 4. However, the following principles for collective preparation can help the choir to feel that they are presenting themselves as a well-polished, cohesive team.

Adding Polish

- The first question to consider is how "uniform" a choir uniform needs to be. This will depend on the nature, function, and composition of the choir.
- Try to keep the choir uniform simple, easy to obtain and replace, and affordable.
- Sometimes the simplest uniforms are the most effective and easiest to coordinate. For example, in my female choir, they chose a black base ensemble (loose trousers and tops) with matching accessories (such as scarves or jewelry, depending upon the occasion) in an accent color.
- Consider whether the chosen uniform is suitable and obtainable for all shapes and sizes, and whether it will be acceptable to all singers across the age range of the choir.
- Think about whether the style will date quickly or whether it is likely to remain appealing for the foreseeable future.
- Ask yourself if your choir's current uniform is something that the choir is proud to wear. If not, what needs to change?
- Matching music folders can add an extra touch of coordination and class to a choir's appearance.
- Music stands can be used to reduce the hazards of balancing piles of sheet music and books during performances.
- Appointing a uniform monitor can help to maintain standards. The monitor can take responsibility for checking that everyone has the items of clothing that they need, and perhaps for storing matching accessories that belong to the choir.
- A choir handbook could be provided with information about uniform requirements and ground rules on group presentation and performance arrangements.
- Hold a literal dress rehearsal before performances to give singers the opportunity to check that all their uniform requirements are in order.
- Consider whether it would be appropriate for the conductor to wear the same uniform as the choir to demonstrate solidarity, or whether he or she should be distinguished by wearing something different. The answer to this question will obviously vary from choir to choir, and from conductor to conductor.

PRACTICAL PRESENTATION

Other aspects of group presentation include posture and deportment, the position of the choir in the venue, and the placement of individual singers within the choir. Phoebe suggested that planning these practical elements of performance can help singers feel that they look "right," and it can help them feel comfortable and more confident:

> I think some attention . . . I think that would give people more confidence—that you go on, you mean business, you know where you should be standing and how you should be standing . . . You go on stage, you have time to organize yourself, prepare yourself. Are you standing right? Are you standing in the right formation? Has everybody got enough space? Rather than all huddling up like this [hunches shoulders] and folders like that [demonstrates holding music tightly to the body].

She illustrated this with her negative experiences of performing with a chamber choir in a nearby city:

> I always feel that we're a bit of a rag-tag bunch. We are not organized, we're not . . . and some of that can help with nerves and confidence because . . . it makes you feel skittled before you've even started singing. You don't feel prepared. It's a bit like going out to work but you've not got your shirt and tie on, or you've not got your handbag. You're half-cocked.

Frank compared some of the poorly prepared performances with his male voice choir to the detailed preparation he was accustomed to in musical theater productions:

> It was quite a huddle last time we went, and this time I thought it was much better organized . . . Sometimes I think, "Why didn't somebody have a look at this before, and work this out?" You wouldn't go charging onto the stage in act 1 of a musical without having done a lot of preparation, and a tech rehearsal, and you know where everything is. And sometimes, with the male voice choir . . . I've thought, "Why don't we spend a little bit of time—get there a bit earlier—and work out something that everyone's happy with?"

As a seasoned male voice choir member, Andrew also appreciated the importance of working on the physical and practical elements of choral presentation:

> There was a lot of discipline there, in that male voice choir. But I thought there was a bit of that on Saturday . . . When we came off, we came off in a line. So I quite like that disciplined side of it, without it being too OTT [over the top], rather than just strolling on. I saw [a community choir] doing it at the Baptist Church . . . and it looked awful. They just came in from the sides, and they were just scrambling on the stage, and whatever. And I think [the male voice choir] did the same. And I thought, "Well, this doesn't look right to me."

Singers talked at length about the importance of rehearsing physical entries and exits, the problems of being located differently due to the size and shape of performance venues, and the need to be able to trust other singers to remember their positions and movements in relation to their fellow performers. For some singers, these extra-musical concerns can take precedence over music-related considerations, and lack of attention to these details creates an unwelcome distraction. Limited opportunities to rehearse in the concert venue can compound the confidence issues relating to some of these practicalities:

> So I know I need to be here at this time, and I need to be there quickly, but there's four people standing there, going, "Oh, are we going on or off?" Then I feel really tense about it 'cause I think it looks awful . . . I think we should be fairly confident about what we're singing by the time we reach a performance, but what we're not confident about is actually getting on the stage . . . getting off the stage. (Barbara)

Singers used words such as "upsetting," "daunting," and "worrying" to indicate the emotional insecurity that can arise from these logistical challenges, especially when insufficient preparation has taken place.

IT'LL BE ALL RIGHT ON THE NIGHT!

> Organization? It's just about keeping everybody happy, really. (Pamela)

Along with many other singers, Pamela stressed the importance of including the practical elements of group presentation in concert planning and preparation. She felt that there was room for improvement in her chamber choir:

> I think if you know where you're going to be sitting, particularly with a small group, it helps, because sometimes you may be in a different venue for a rehearsal, so you might be a bit late getting there, and so if you can just move into a position properly, you know, instead of having to go into a side cupboard and collect a chair and carry it across and put it on the end of a row somewhere.

Angela painted a similar picture of her relatively chaotic experiences of choral society dress rehearsals. She felt that these could run more smoothly with better advance planning and attention to practical organization:

> You get [shorter] people, coming late, who are stuck at the back and can't see. And that's a big beef. We keep saying, "Put the smaller people at the front." And there are people who love to be on the front row—they are there, very much! . . . It's the most amazingly ridiculous situation to be in. It really is. For goodness' sake!

Although relatively few singers had serious concerns about the standard of musical rehearsal in their choirs, several would have preferred a more proactive approach toward coordinating stage entries and exits and toward positioning the choir effectively in the performing area. Andrew gave an example of a strategy that some choirs use to help with planning dress rehearsals and performances:

> In the male voice choir, we used to have a marshal . . . like a sergeant-major. And before performances he would suss out the area where we were standing . . . We would come in . . . and then stand in our positions, and he would stand in front, and go like that [mimes checking the spacing between people] before we started, and then, when we left, he'd come and say, "Right," and we'd lead off.

Naomi described the sense of security that she derived from a well-organized dress rehearsal in which positions, and physical entries and exits, were thoroughly rehearsed. She appreciated the discipline of this part of the preparation:

> I like it the way it's organized . . . You [the conductor] put us in positions, and we know exactly what we're doing. We go through it, and then in the evening we know where we're sitting, we know what we're doing, and I like that. I know where we have to sit, so when we've finished we come off, this is where we go. And I like it very rigid like that.

The complex relationships between choir position, performance venues, acoustics, and choral confidence will be examined in more detail in chapter 3. In the meantime, the following preliminary suggestions will help choirs and conductors plan successful, confidence-building dress rehearsals.

The Finishing Touches

- Pay a site visit to the venue in advance of the event and get to know the performance area.
- Try to hold at least one rehearsal in the venue to give the singers chance to acclimatize to the space and acoustics.

- Plan seating positions for all singers. Don't forget to consider the needs of any singers with physical disabilities or limitations.
- Make sure that all singers have adequate room to stand and sit comfortably.
- If the singers are using sheet music, check that they have enough elbow room to hold their books or folders.
- Give the singers opportunities to practice making smart stage entries and exits.
- Decide when the choir will stand and sit, and practice doing this in a neat and timely manner.
- Appoint a choir marshal to position the singers in the performing space and to check that the choir is as well presented as possible.
- Check where outdoor clothing and bags can be stored to minimize clutter in the performing area.
- Provide clear travel directions and parking information.

Bringing It All Together

> How you go on stage, and whether you've got music covers, and what you're wearing, and all that stuff. Oh, they [the chamber choir] spend hours . . . The women go, "What are we going to wear?" [laughs]. "Clothes!" Actually, it was a big step forward when [the previous conductor] managed to get the women not to wear their brogues! (Harry)

Although these concerns may seem superficial compared with the technical and musical challenges of polishing a choral performance, they are deeply rooted in the singer's psyche. Many extra-musical aspects of vocal performance, including dress and behavioral conventions, are derived from traditional social and ceremonial rituals.[27] These conventions persist partly due to habit, custom, and practice. However, they often acquire significance for the participants that is retained even when the original function of the behavior has been forgotten.[28] Some of the ceremonial elements of traditional ritualistic behavior have gradually become established as an integral part of musical performance. Examples of these ritualistic elements in Western art music include adherence to a formal dress code; the way in which musicians and singers enter and leave the performing area; and performance etiquette, such as publicly acknowledging fellow performers.[29] Audience behavior is also subject to conventions, such as maintaining silence during a performance and applauding at certain points. While the formality of many Western classical performances adds to the sense of occasion for the audience and performers, it may also be partly responsible for the sense of pressure and self-consciousness that some musicians and singers experience:

Singing to oneself . . . is likely to be perceived differently from singing on the concert stage in front of a paying audience. The former is private and personal, relaxed and unselfconscious. In contrast, public singing involves a greater sense of "performance," of implied "correctness" against some perceived expectation of what counts as "appropriate" musical behavior.[30]

Conversely, for some singers, conforming to these social and performance conventions may add to their sense of self-confidence because the instinct to conform, and the discomfort arising from failing to do so, is very deep-seated.[31] Dress and stage behavior, as well as personal attractiveness, often have an influence on the evaluation of musical performance.[32] The effects of concert dress and physical appearance have been found to have a significant effect on perceptions of female classical soloists' musical abilities in a range of genres.[33] It has therefore been suggested that audiences have strong, culturally defined expectations of appropriate costume and behavior for performers, which is related to the musical genre. Dress and stage deportment that are perceived as inappropriate to the occasion have a detrimental effect on audience perceptions of performers' musical abilities. Performance quality ratings in high school solo vocal performances are affected by stage deportment and attire, and there is some awareness among school children of the impact of these extra-musical factors.[34] Music students similarly realize that evaluations of their performance are likely to be affected not only by their vocal skill and interpretation of the repertoire, but also by their physical image, personal grooming, expressive performance elements, and body language.[35]

The adult amateur choral singers that I interviewed agreed that personal grooming and group presentation affect the audience's evaluation of their performance quality. They were instinctively aware that a well-presented choir can raise the audience's expectations of the singers, which can have a positive impact on the reception of their performance. An encouraging audience response can then inspire the singers to perform more confidently. The singers also felt that feeling comfortable and well-presented helped them to concentrate on performing well. Extraneous distractions, such as concerns about the appearance or comfort of a choir uniform, or anxieties about staging and group presentation, can interfere with achieving flow, so that singers are less immersed in the performance, experience fewer positive emotions, become more self-conscious, and lose confidence. Preparatory time should therefore be allowed for paying attention to collective presentation as well as to musical practice. If a uniform monitor and choir marshal are appointed, the responsibility for auditing collective presentation can be shared between these roles.

CHAPTER SUMMARY

Flow, as a source of confidence, cannot be experienced if there are too many distractions from the task.[36] Some singers report that musical and practical preparation is not always adequate to allow them to develop the fluency required for total immersion in the music and enjoyment of the performance. This may be the case if too little time has been spent on learning the words or music, if scant attention has been paid to expression and interpretation, or if group presentation has not been considered during preparation and practice.

Studies of ritualistic pre-performance behavior in sport have shown that some players attach an almost superstitious significance to their preparatory routines.[37] Adhering to these routines can increase their sense of control over challenging situations[38] and help them deal with stress and anxiety.[39] Many choral singers also have pre-performance rituals, and these often focus on attending to their own appearance and the general presentation of the choir. For singers, the emphasis on the significance of appearance-related factors is probably connected to their enculturation into the social and cultural norms of performance etiquette. They also have an instinctive awareness that audience expectations and evaluations are affected by extra-musical factors such as a choir's collective appearance and stage deportment. Finally, and most obviously, choral singers benefit from the inherent sense of self-confidence that arises simply from the knowledge that they are well-prepared and looking their best.

In sum,

• The ability to become immersed in the music, to perform expressively, and to enjoy the performance is confidence-building for choral singers.
• A confidence-boosting level of engagement and immersion is only possible with thorough preparation and practice.
• Distractions can preclude immersion in the music and enjoyment of the performance. These distractions can include insecurities about stage entries and exits, about deportment and clothing, and about positioning within the performance space.
• Confidence-building preparation includes attention to the physical comfort and collective presentation of the choir as well as thorough musical rehearsal and practical preparation.

Chapter Three

Choral Acoustics and Choir Configuration

If I had to describe a choir to a visitor from another universe, I would probably come up with something like this:

> A collection of living human bodies with built-in instruments called "voices" that operate in a synchronized way within a variety of physical environments.

This definition is very literal and somewhat clumsy, and it neglects to mention any of the musical, aesthetic, or expressive qualities of choral performance. However, it does convey the main characteristics of group singing activities as a bemused intergalactic traveller might see them. It also summarizes the interactions between the individual voice, the collective performance, and the environment. In this chapter, these interactions will be explored in a way that will be helpful to human "bodyminds"[1] rather than for the benefit of alien observers.

Because the vocal instrument is located within and integral to the body of the singer, the voice reacts to a wide range of physiological, neurological, and psychological stimuli that are inextricably linked and constantly interacting during performance. Similarly, the singer is located within his or her physical environment and is physiologically, psychologically, and emotionally affected by the conditions of this environment. These situational factors include effects on physical comfort, such as warmth and light; the influence of the humidity or dryness of the atmosphere on vocal production; the effects of room acoustics, which are principally governed by levels of reverberation or absorbency;[2] and the influence of choral acoustics. The latter refers to the way in which multiple voices interact acoustically during group singing, and this subject was usually raised by interviewees when I asked, "Are there any particular circumstances in rehearsals or performances that have an effect on your confidence?" When answering this question, singers often talked about the interaction between acoustics and the physical layout of the choir within the rehearsal room or performance venue. This chapter will therefore focus on constructive approaches to the acoustic challenges of "many people singing together and hearing each other in a room."[3]

The sound of a choir changes in response to several situational factors, including choir formation or layout. This may vary according to whether the singers are arranged in, for example, a single semicircle, sectional blocks of specific voice parts, or mixed-voice arrangements in which no singer is adjacent to another of the same voice part. Further situational variables include the spacing or distance between the singers, and voice placement, which refers to the position of individual singers within the choir. I have grouped all these positional factors under the heading Choir Configuration, and the main discussion of this is framed around the singers' own words. There is, however, one more thing that I feel I should do before presenting the singers' thoughts and perceptions. Because choral acoustics play a leading role in this chapter, there follows a very brief introduction to the main concepts.

HERE COMES THE SCIENCE

Making sense of all the sensory signals available during a choral performance presents an "unusual challenge to the auditory system" of a singer.[4] It is therefore not surprising that many of the singers that I interviewed mentioned that acoustic factors often affected their confidence. The likelihood of successfully meeting the acoustic demands of choral performance is largely dependent upon the functioning of the singer's preferred self-to-other ratio (SOR). This is the ratio between the sound-pressure level (SPL) of two main elements—namely, feedback and reference.[5] The relationship between these two elements can affect a choral singer's perception and enjoyment of their own vocal performance.

The feedback is the sound of the singer's own voice, which is made up of three components. First, there is direct airborne sound, which is diffracted around the singer's head from their mouth to their ears. Second, there is reflected airborne sound, which is returned to the singer's ears after interacting with environmental acoustics. Third, there is bone-conducted sound, which is heard internally by the singer, and which is independent of room acoustics.[6] We hear bone-conducted sound from inside our body rather than having it conveyed from the outside world into our eardrums.[7] This gives us a unique perspective on our own voice, which is quite different from what our listeners hear, and it complicates the acoustic situation for all singers.

The reference is the sound of the rest of the choir. The SPL of the reference is made up of two components. There is a direct component, which is derived from the neighboring singers in the choir, and a reverberated component, which is derived from the room reflections of the sound of the whole choir. These ingredients of the reference enrich the choral sound, but they also compound the complexity of interpreting subjective vocal feedback. The interaction of all the elements of the reference and feedback means that in choral performances, there are likely to be difficulties in hearing oneself and others accurately. Predictably, this has an impact upon the singers' perception of their own voices, upon the security of their intonation, and upon their confidence in their own performance.

The preferred SOR of individual singers can be affected by several variables, including the number of singers in the choir, their location in relation to other singers, the volume of their voices compared to that of the singers around them, and the level of room reverberation or absorption.[8] Despite individual variations in preferred SOR, the choral singers participating in earlier research generally preferred an SOR that allowed them to hear their own voices above that of neighboring performers.[9] In the next section, it will become apparent that the amateur choral singers I interviewed would rather hear the other singers than their own voices. The differences between my results and earlier findings may partly be because my research examined the effect of choir configuration on singers' subjectively perceived confidence levels,[10] while earlier research often focused on the effects of choir configuration on the choral sound from the point of view of independent listeners, audience members, or conductors.[11]

The differences in opinion between the amateur singers and earlier research participants are not likely due to lack of experience among the singers I interviewed, as most interviewees had sung for many years in several types and sizes of choral ensemble. However, these differences in preferred SOR may be related to levels of training. The participants in other studies of choral acoustics and choir configuration have usually been highly trained singers, often university- or conservatoire-level musicians who are voice majors.[12] In contrast, although the participants in my research were very competent and dedicated amateur choral singers, most had received comparatively little formal musical training. This may partly explain their self-professed reliance on hearing other singers for musical cues and moral support (see chapter 4).[13] Their preference for hearing other singers rather than themselves may also reflect the fact that amateur singers are likely to have different priorities than full-time voice students who often self-identify as vocal soloists in training.[14]

Finally, my qualitative methodology elicited detailed information from the singers about their subjective, emotional state, including their confidence level, in relation to choir formation, position, and spacing. Most earlier studies have concentrated on listeners' opinions rather than on the subjective perceptions and emotional experiences of the singers. When singers have previously been asked about their reactions to configurational factors,[15] the questions tended to be limited to their evaluation of the sound that they made in different configurations rather than an exploration of their emotional or psychological responses. The open questions that I asked allowed the singers to talk about their subjective experiences of rehearsing and performing and to discuss the way that they felt about a wide range of aspects of their choral life. The answers that they gave reflected this focus on their personal experience in group singing activities.

HEARING EACH OTHER

It's important to me, for my confidence, that I *hear*—that I can hear the other sections. (Andrew)

All three focus groups and the majority of the individual interviewees introduced concerns about various aspects of choral acoustics and choir configuration. Many participants talked at length about the importance of being able to hear each other, the influence of choir configuration on this, and the effect that this could have on their self-confidence during performance. Phoebe helpfully summarized her perception of the complex interaction between different performance environments, being able to hear her fellow performers, and her self-confidence when singing in public:

Certainly, the dynamics of the hall, in terms of the acoustics and things like that, do really affect me and how I feel I'm performing. So, certain halls that have not got brilliant acoustic capabilities, they seem to make me feel that I can't hear what's happening very well. So I don't particularly like that.

Nick was similarly emotionally and cognitively affected by situational factors and stressed the importance of being able to hear the rest of the choir:

If you can't hear people, then you don't know whether you should be singing it louder or whether you need to pipe down, or be quiet, and try and listen to them a bit more. So I think the acoustics and the ambience of the place really affects [my confidence].

Frank's account of his choir's reaction to a difficult performance situation shows a range of emotional responses. Some singers may be frustrated if their meticulous preparation is counteracted by the acoustic shortcomings of the venue; others may show their annoyance by fidgeting and talking among themselves:

> People tend to get a bit niggly, and shift and you know . . . "This isn't very
> good, is it? How are we going to hear that?" And mutter, mutter, mutter, you
> know [laughs]. If you don't feel, you know, good karma, it's very rattling . . .
> Maybe we should be more professional than that and sort of deal with whatev-
> er we've got, but you just feel that you've done all this work, you've got this
> all off pat, and then you can't hear the sopranos or whatever.

The final sentence expresses the disappointment and dissatisfaction that can
be experienced by an amateur choir when the singers cannot hear each other
clearly. This negatively affects their perception of their own performance
quality, which can lead to a deterioration in performance quality and precipi-
tate a dramatic loss of confidence:

> If we're not positioned where you can hear people . . . I've been in quite a few
> churches especially with the male voice choir, and a couple of times with [the
> chamber choir] where, if you're not in the position that you feel happy with, it
> can just crumble. (Frank)

The fact that amateur choral singers prioritize their need to hear each other
over their need to hear themselves is one of the main ways in which these
performers differ from the full-time music students and professionally
trained singers who have featured in other related research. Earlier studies
found that "on average one's own voice needs to be about 6dB stronger than
the rest of the choir. In most rooms, this implies a fairly spread-out formation."[16] By contrast, in the next section, amateur singers will explain their
preferences for a more tightly knit configuration.

CLOSENESS AND CONFIDENCE

> It's a lot, lot better if we're all close together and can all hear each other . . .
> you can hear each other. And that gives you confidence as well. (Joyce)

The amateur singers I interviewed frequently made a direct association between their confidence levels, their ability to hear the other singers, and the
amount of physical space between choir members. They felt that closer spacing between singers helped them to hear other sections of the choir as well as
their immediate neighbors, which then helped them feel more confident.
Celia used the word "configuration" when describing her preferred spacing
within the choir:

> I'm more comfortable with a more compact configuration, rather than
> stretched thin . . . I think it's easier to sing with other people. I can hear what's
> going on, on each side of me, and I can hear the other parts.

Some singers, like Clive below, reported negative experiences when they felt
physically distant from the other members of this choir. This was often
associated with feelings of isolation, which adversely affected their experience of performing together:

> It was awful really, because we were too far apart. We weren't together—we
> didn't feel together. And because you couldn't hear what the other parts were
> singing, it was very, very difficult . . . At the end of it I felt as if I was going
> through the motions. I didn't feel as though I was singing with the rest of them.

The sense of isolation arising from relatively wide spacing between choir
members can lead to feelings of exposure and insecurity. Pamela felt worried
when she couldn't hear the rest of the choir: "You feel as if you're doing a
solo for the whole performance." Naomi contrasted two different situations
that highlighted the importance of inter-singer spacing for her:

> It was okay [earlier when the other choir was] there because then we were all
> squashed up, but [later] I felt there was quite a gap between [a fellow alto] and
> me . . . Where I've got people either side of me that are squashing me, that's
> when I feel comfortable.

Frank described the uncertainties arising when a combination of wider spacing and unsympathetic room acoustics made it difficult to hear the other
singers:

> In [a church] one time, we had a pretty bad concert. It was a big [church], and
> because we were so far apart, and the acoustics in there . . . That's what's
> obviously the problem, because you can't hear people. It's the acoustics and
> positioning.

In the above scenario, the position and layout of the choir, as well as the
inter-singer spacing, were partly determined by the size and shape of the
venue. Several singers described acoustic disadvantages when there was a
separation between the vocal parts due to singing in church choir stalls. A
dislike of this position was relatively common:

> Somehow the sound doesn't transmit in the same way, so it is a bit disconcerting, but I actually prefer to sing out to the [audience]—not across the church but down. (Angela)

While the layout of the performance area in some halls and churches can make it difficult for the singers to get close enough to hear each other well, the most unpopular events were open-air performances. Singing outside brings its own acoustic challenges, which are unsympathetic to singers trying to project their voices, and these were frequently mentioned. Some of the complications of open-air choral events include feeling as if one's voice is being carried away on the breeze; competing with ambient noise from weather, traffic, or passersby; and competing with distractions created by other activities, especially if the performance is part of a garden party, summer fair, or other celebration such as a wedding reception or birthday party. In the third focus group, there was a lively discussion of one of these occasions:

> Owen: I think the other time that sapped our confidence was when we sang outside.
>
> Matt: And we couldn't hear each other.
>
> Owen: We couldn't hear anything! . . .
>
> Doug: Nobody could hear anything.
>
> Matt: I think we were all just singing louder and louder 'cause we thought they couldn't hear us . . .
>
> Owen: We didn't feel too good that day!
>
> Author: Was it that you couldn't hear yourself or couldn't hear the others?
>
> Several at once: We couldn't hear the others.
>
> Doug: It was as if you were singing a solo.
>
> Owen: You didn't know whether you were in tune or not.

Again, participants felt that standing closer together helped them to hear each other in these situations:

> If we're somewhere like in the open air, it's really difficult to hear everybody unless we're really, really close together. (Joyce)

Andrew suggested that when a choir is performing in the open air, some of the acoustic problems may be counteracted by placing the singers more closely together than might be usual in other environments:

> The only problem we had was outdoors when you can't hear it—that's the biggest danger. So [maybe] there needs to be a tighter formation outside.

In earlier studies, the spacing between singers was similarly agreed to be the main influence on their SOR, and a wider spacing was favored because it helped the singers hear themselves above the other performers:

> The farther apart the singers are standing (especially from their own section colleagues), the greater the SOR, and the easier it will be for them to hear their own voices—and conversely, the harder it will be for them to hear the others. [17]

In contrast to the preferences of the undergraduate and professional choir members who have previously been studied, the amateur singers I interviewed always prioritized hearing their fellow performers, especially the singers in their own vocal section. They felt that this was facilitated by closer inter-singer spacing, which they therefore consistently preferred.

CHOIR FORMATION AND COMMUNICATION

> It's quite important to be able to hear your colleagues. And if you're in an awkward formation, you know, or the sound goes up into the ceiling, or you can't hear them, then that really does affect . . . your singing and therefore affects your confidence as well. (Nick)

Like Nick, singers often used the word "formation" to describe the layout of the choir within the venue. It was generally felt that choral formation could interact with room acoustics and affect the singers' ability to hear each other, which then affected their self-confidence. Nick liked his choir "to be in a semicircle so I can hear the rest of the guys singing," and Andrew had a similar preference for a "horseshoe-shaped" configuration: "That arch we had on Saturday was great [so] you can hear the other sections." Many singers agreed that a semicircular formation was the optimum layout for allowing them to hear each other:

> I like . . . it to be quite a tight semicircle really . . . so you can literally hear the tenors bouncing off you, the basses bouncing off . . . you can hear everybody around you. (Phoebe)

For Joyce, a semicircular formation was linked with improved communication and cohesion when compared to standing in other layouts:

> I prefer semicircle. Well . . . because you can hear the other parts . . . If you're in a straight line, you feel very isolated . . . But you can actually see and communicate almost with the people the other side—you feel more of a whole—when you're singing in [a semicircle] . . . You can hear each other. And that gives you confidence as well. (Joyce)

Sharing visual and auditory cues for words and musical entries improves collaboration and teamwork, which can enhance choral learning, performance quality, and self-confidence (see chapter 4). In a semicircular formation, singers can share positive facial expressions and model positive body language, which adds to their enjoyment:

> I still prefer to sing in a flat horseshoe, so you can see other people . . . I think it does help for you to see people's faces because if they're enjoying it as well, or you can see them with the words, and, you know, you can see them breathing. (Nick)

Barry remembered an occasion when the choir layout did not allow the singers to see or hear each other clearly, with disastrous results:

> We couldn't see each other, and we couldn't feed off each other, and it made it quite awkward. I could hear mistakes going on in the background, and it just didn't go well.

Frank recalled a situation in which the formation of the choir was changed from a less helpful position to the preferred horseshoe shape, and he described the effect that this had on the singers' feelings:

> When we sang in [this church], the arrangement just didn't seem right . . . We were more . . . a flatter semicircle—we were wider, if I remember rightly, and there was something where the basses couldn't hear the sopranos. And then, when we came round like this time [indicates a tighter semicircle], it seemed much better, and everyone was happier.

Singers also preferred choir formations that allowed them to remain within their own vocal sections rather than singing in mixed-voice formats:

> With the majority of stuff . . . then I would sooner stay in the sections, the
> men's section or the tenor section, than I would be mixing. (Andrew)

Only three participants, who described themselves as particularly confident performers, had positive feelings about mixed-voice formations. For these singers, the advantages of mixed-voice layouts were related to perceived improvements in choral blend rather than any impact on confidence levels. In fact, it was generally acknowledged that a higher level of confidence was a prerequisite for using mixed-voice layouts due to the musical familiarity and independence required from each singer. Karen felt that "some people are not confident enough to stand with a soprano one side and a bass the other," and Pamela explained the challenges of this very clearly:

> Sometimes we are mixed up so that you have to know your own part. [The
> conductor] quite regularly will say . . . "I want you all to mix up. I don't want
> you to be alongside people in the same part." And it really is a learning curve
> because you have to know what you're singing, you have to be confident, and
> you've got different voices, different parts all round you, and a completely
> different sound is made as a result.

Other researchers have found that the formation of the choir is less important to singers and listeners than inter-singer spacing.[18] However, the singers that I interviewed felt very strongly that formation affected their ability to hear each other, and that this in turn affected their confidence. They also felt that formations that allowed them to see some of their fellow singers had a positive impact on their confidence because these formations allowed them to receive visual cues and reminders of words and to share positive, nonverbal communication (see chapter 1).

Where preferences about layout have been expressed in other studies, the participants have tended to favor mixed-voice formations because they prefer the perceived choral blend in this configuration.[19] Independent listeners similarly preferred the choral blend achieved in mixed-voice formations.[20] However, the amateur singers that I interviewed felt that mixed-voice layouts had a negative effect on their confidence. They almost unanimously preferred standing next to singers who were singing the same part. Again, the priority for the interviewees was clearly the ease of hearing other singers who could provide musical reinforcement and moral support.

POSITIONING THE PERFORMERS WITHIN THE VENUE

> If you're in a venue that hasn't got brilliant acoustics, you don't hear [the other singers]. It does make a difference where the positioning is. And it also makes a difference where . . . how sort of intimate you are, if you like. (Phoebe)

It is obviously not possible to make sure that there are optimum acoustics or performance spaces in every venue that the choir uses. However, as Phoebe suggests, some of the effects of difficult acoustics or awkwardly shaped venues can be mitigated by using closer spacing and by considering the physical position of the choir. Although the choir's position within the venue and the singer's physical placement within the choir have not prominently featured in previous research, the amateur singers I interviewed felt that both factors affected their ability to hear each other, which had an impact upon their confidence during performance. Nick described an occasion when the choir's position and his own placement negatively affected his experience of the event:

> I was stood right on the front 'cause there was hardly anywhere to stand. I was away from the rest of the guys, right at the front. And I don't think they could hear, so they were singing rubbish in the background, and I was singing complete rubbish out the front and I couldn't hear anybody [laughs]. That was terrible. Actually, that was probably the worst one we've sung.

Celia compared two different rehearsal situations that affected the choir's configuration and the audibility of the other singers. Her story demonstrates that a minor change of position can make a major difference to the singers' perceptions of their performance:

> When we first started rehearsing in the [chapel], we sat in the pews, so it was sopranos on one side of the aisle, altos on the other side of the aisle, and basses and tenors behind us. And then we changed so that we now sit in the choir stalls, again sopranos on one side, altos on the other, tenors behind the sopranos and basses behind the altos. But that makes us closer in, and that's better. That's much, much better.

In this case, moving the singers so that they were closer together helped them to hear each other better, and improved their experience of singing together. Other situational factors can affect whether the singers are in a position where they can see and hear their fellow performers:

> The soloists were immediately in front of us, and then the percussionists, and it was really hard to hear, and indeed to see. So it wasn't the room or the venue

so much as the layout within the venue that made it difficult because it's really hard to pick up your cue because there's too much going on. (Ursula)

Ursula explained that the placement of the soloists and instrumentalists relative to the choir can also block the singers' view of the conductor:

> At other times, the soloists have always been off, you know, not in front of the choir, but to the left or right of it, and I don't know why they were there but . . . and there were three of them and, you know, they were big people. I couldn't see the conductor at all.

The position of the conductor relative to the choir also affects how well the singers can see him or her. In the following case, the conductor's position meant that the singers had to stand at a slightly awkward angle to see him. Frank felt that his own change of position to accommodate this affected his perception of the other singers' voices:

> [The conductor] was a little bit down, at the end of the pews, into the body of the church, and we were looking down . . . For some reason, the voices were going down that way, and we couldn't really hear each other very well.

Placing shorter singers behind taller performers can also limit the sight lines for some singers, like Celia:

> Because I'm not very tall, and if I'm not careful, I can be buried in the middle, and I've got somebody tall in front of me, and I can't see the conductor, and it's just hopeless. Well, not hopeless, but I'm not as comfortable.

These are all important considerations because for many singers, conductor visibility is an important part of performing confidently. Naomi relied on being able to see the conductor as part of managing her nerves:

> If I've got a conductor in front of me, and I'm not very comfortable, or I can see somebody that I know, or it's very bright and I can see them all [the audience], I will concentrate purely on the conductor and that controls me.

For his own confidence, Tim prioritized being able to see the conductor above all other configurational considerations:

Make sure I can see the musical director. That really is my preference. 'Cause sometimes if I get put in a row further back I struggle to see 'cause I'm only short [laughs]. But as long as I can see the [musical director] easily, then I don't mind where I go.

As well as jeopardizing the musical coordination of the choir, being unable to see the conductor during a performance can have a potentially devastating effect on some singers' confidence levels:

Barbara: That's really frightening, if you can't see who's conducting you. That's quite a big problem.

Karen: That's the worst part, if you can't see the conductor . . . and you have to look at the others, to see their mouths moving, to see where you are.

The word "frightening" indicates that seeing the conductor has wider implications than simply keeping track of musical elements of the song such as tempo, dynamics, entries, and endings. The strong feelings expressed here suggest that being able to make eye contact with the group leader provides a degree of moral support as well as musical direction.

INDIVIDUAL PLACEMENT WITHIN THE CHOIR

I like to be with the people I rehearsed with, because you build a rapport. (Angela)

Being in a position to see the conductor is clearly a vital part of confident choral performance for amateur singers, but most singers also have additional concerns about where they are placed within the choir and which singers they regularly sing with. The reasons for this will be explored in this section and expanded on in chapter 4. Most of the singers I interviewed had a strong preference for standing in a certain location relative to other voice parts. They also often favored a particular position in relation to singers in their own section. Although most singers feel more confident when they can hear others who are singing the same part, there were some individual differences in positional preferences. Here, four singers talk about their own favored position within the choir. Phoebe, a soprano, likes "to be really quite opposite the basses," while Frank, a tenor, likes "to be between the basses and the altos in the mixed voice choir." Another tenor, Andrew, said, "If I was the end one of the tenors, and the basses were there, I might be less confident than if I was standing in the middle, with the two tenors each side of me."

Matt, a bass, preferred to hear the melody line rather than the other male harmonies:

> I think hearing the soprano line helps 'cause that's typically the melody and, you know, all the other lines fit into that. That certainly helps. It doesn't matter if we don't hear the tenors, okay? Nothing against the tenors, but it's sometimes a bit easier if you can't hear the tenors 'cause you will clash.

Another experienced bass liked to hear the tenors, while suggesting that his preferences may be due to habituation:

> We always sit in a semicircle and we always stand in a semicircle. [The conductor] likes us like that 'cause then he can hear the whole sound . . . And we do sing a lot better if we're like that. I mean, even though the tenors are singing something slightly different, or a lot different, to what you are, you still like to hear them to make sure you're with them. (Clive)

Consistency of position within the choir can help singers feel confident, partly because they are used to hearing certain neighboring voices. It provides a predictable acoustic ambience in rehearsals, assuming that the same practice room is always used:

> I think it's certainly very helpful that you position yourself in a performance the same as what you do rehearsing. If you're rehearsing, week in, week out, you know, you just get that feel of people 'round about you, and it, to my mind, improves the confidence if you can stand in that same position . . . Certainly I find it more comfortable standing in the same way 'cause it's the environment you're used to—the voices and the sound coming from either side of you. (Doug)

This acoustic predictability makes it easier for singers to feel confident about finding their notes and holding their own vocal line:

> I always like to be in the same relative position to the other singers all the time, because you get used to that environment, and it's just comfort . . . You're used to hearing the juxtaposition of, say, the top tenor and your line, and you're sort of, "Oh, I'm going to be a third below" 'cause sometimes I'm not that brilliant at holding a line. (Frank)

Consistent positions within the choir enable singers to receive musical cues and moral support from trusted, regular neighbors. This relates to the fact that a cohesive environment, choral collaboration, peer learning, reliance on peers, and unofficial choral team leaders all affect confidence levels in amateur choirs (see chapter 4).[21]

FROM REHEARSAL ROOM TO CONCERT VENUE

> It's not the singing that's worrying me, it's where on stage, you know . . . And we all feel comfortable in certain positions, so if you can't get into the position you normally stand in, that can be a bit upsetting. (Barbara)

Singers reported feelings of "comfort," "confidence," or "rapport" when rehearsing and performing in a regular position within the choir. However, this is not always possible; due to the size or shape of the performance space, changes in individual placement are sometimes necessary when the choir moves from the rehearsal setting to the performance venue. In this situation, many choral singers feel "unsettled," "worried," or "upset." The problems seem to arise mainly from changes in auditory feedback when a singer's physical position relative to singers on the same vocal part, or in relation to other voice parts, is altered. Andrew felt that consistency of individual placement within the choir should be maintained, whether the choir is in rehearsal or performing in public, so that the singers feel confident:

> I think, probably if you're in the same position each week, that's the right thing to do . . . I think uniformity, continuity, is important with regards to the rehearsals, but also that the rehearsal then replicates into the concert positions as well 'cause I think you do build confidence by singing with the people around you.

As well as being acoustically disorientating, changes in position can mean that the singers miss out on the emotional and musical benefits of the trust and rapport that they have established with their usual neighbors. In public performances, this mutual support can play a significant role in confidence building, but sometimes the interpersonal benefits are lost in translation from the rehearsal room to the concert venue:

> On the performance night, if you've got that . . . "Ooh! I'm not sitting with the people I've practiced with!" 'Cause we practice sideways, looking at each other, with the men there. And then all of a sudden, for the dress rehearsal, you're looking forwards, and it's completely different . . . with different people. (Angela)

Last-minute changes to choir configuration are particularly problematic for some performers. This is because of the lack of time to acclimatize to alterations in the way in which the room acoustics affect the choral sound and change the singers' ability to hear the rest of the choir. A change of position may mean that a singer cannot hear certain choir members that he or she is used to relying upon. All this is especially difficult to adapt to in unfamiliar venues:

> If it's suddenly lumped on you, "Oh, at this venue, we'll need to do that," then . . . we're going, "No . . . don't do that! It's going to ruin it!" Because you think, "No, we're not going to be able to . . ." (Frank)

Frank's emotive language demonstrates the negative associations with unexpected alterations. His reaction is to catastrophize, imagining that the performance will be disastrous. He tails off with the phrase "we're not going to be able to," showing a severe reduction in self-confidence. Several other singers gave examples of when a configurational change between the rehearsal and performance had caused a deterioration in performance quality, and they described their emotional reactions to this. Don hadn't been able to forget how he felt at one of his first major concerts:

> Last year at the [summer concert] was the most appalling one because of where we stood, and the acoustics. We just couldn't hear each other, and everybody was really disappointed that we hadn't done what we meant to do . . . It was a way we hadn't stood and sung when we had rehearsed . . . We just couldn't hear each other, and we just didn't sing well at all.

Like Don, many singers felt that configurational alterations affected their ability to hear each other, and negative value judgments were attached to this. Emotional reactions included a negative self-evaluation of personal vocal quality and dissatisfaction because the performance was not to the choir's full potential. The perceived drop in performance quality was attributed to a reduced ability to hear the usual cues from other singers when an unfamiliar configuration was introduced. The singers used words such as "worrying," "disappointed," "upsetting," "disconcerting," and "appalling" to highlight the emotional impact of this and its influence upon confidence levels.

Even when the performance is in the same venue as the choir's regular rehearsals, altering choral configuration changes the acoustic effects from the singers' point of view. Ursula's choir always changed their configuration for performances, having rehearsed in a completely different position in the same church:

> Rehearsals are . . . well, they're sideways. So, we're in . . . the choir bit of the church, but we're facing inwards, just standing at an angle to face the conduc-

tor . . . But when we have the concert they turn all the chairs 'round so that we're facing the audience . . . Well, I suppose it's 'cause it's different, and you only get one dress rehearsal with everything in place so when you sing on the night, or at the dress rehearsal, it's disconcerting 'cause you can't hear the same cues, if you like, for how you've coped with . . . throughout the rehearsals . . . Somehow the sound doesn't transmit in the same way, so it is a bit disconcerting.

The obvious question that arises here is "Why don't they rehearse in their concert configuration?" There may be some logistical reasons for this, but it would certainly be helpful to start to acclimatize the singers to their performance position during more than one rehearsal. Another question arising from the above experiences is "Why do last-minute changes occur?" A few answers to these questions will become clear later in the chapter, and some suggestions for remedies will be included in the forthcoming lists of tips and exercises.

Some singers acknowledged that their preferences regarding spacing, layout, and their own physical position within the choir might be largely due to familiarity. Don wondered if having more practice at performing in alternative configurations would increase the choir's confidence when singing in those positions:

It's about comfort and practice . . . Your ears are trained . . . You're listening to people in a different way, so you then get used to the fact that the altos are in front of you instead of opposite you, or however you've arranged it, or the tenors are in front of us instead of to the side of us.

Clive described the mitigating effect that choral experience may have on the need to maintain a regular position in relation to other singers within the choir:

When I first joined them, I tended to keep with a couple of chaps. [This bass] was one because he was accomplished . . . So, yes, I felt a little bit comfortable. But now, quite frankly, I'm not really particularly bothered.

Don noticed the collective progress that his choir made in adapting to different performance situations. They had become more able to adapt to configurational and acoustic changes as they gained experience in performing together:

I think we're stronger now . . . Sometimes all we need is an hour or so in the afternoon to get that right. And we probably wouldn't be full on right, but we can cope with it far more than we could two years ago, when everything had to be really just right, you know. It's familiarity. I guess it would be the same as somebody who's used to playing one piano and then suddenly has something different. That will affect their confidence.

Although performing experience may help to develop confidence in singing in different environmental acoustics and choral configurations, acquiring this experience, by definition, takes a while. The following exercises will help choirs get used to singing in a variety of configurations and will also help them adapt to different choral acoustics. This will encourage a more flexible approach to spacing, layout, choir position, and individual position within the choir.

Configuration Exercises

Choose a familiar piece of music for the choir to sing and then rehearse it with some of the following configurational variations:

- With the singers in their usual voice parts, place them in a semicircular arrangement.
- Try varying the size and shape of the semicircle by increasing or reducing the space between the singers.
- Try varying the order of the voice parts, e.g., B T A S; B A S T, etc.
- Do the same exercise, but with the singers placed in straight lines rather than in a semicircle.
- Place the singers in compact blocks in their voice parts so that there is a block of sopranos, a block of basses, etc.
- Now ask each block of singers to go and stand in a different part of the rehearsal room and repeat the song.
- Place the singers in quartets so that each group has one of each voice type rather than in blocks based on voice parts.
- Ask each quartet to go and stand in a different part of the room and perform the song again.
- Ask the singers to mingle randomly so that they are no longer standing in voice parts.
- In each variation, try changing the amount of space between the singers so that they experience singing in widely spaced and tightly knit formations.
- Try performing different types of music (rounds, call-and-response songs, contrapuntal music, and songs based on block harmonies) in all the above configurations.
- Ask the choir for feedback on how the different variations sounded to them; how easy it was to sing the different types of music in each configu-

ration or position; and how the different performing situations affected their feelings about the music and their own confidence levels.

ACTION STATIONS

The confidence-building effects of rehearsing at the performance venue have already been discussed in relation to polishing the choir's physical presentation and rehearsing practical aspects, such as stage entries and exits (see chapter 2). In this section, the singers again stress the importance of having a chance to acclimatize to the performance venue, this time with an emphasis on helping them to get used to the venue's acoustic properties. Providing only limited opportunities to become accustomed to new acoustic environments can leave singers feeling insecure and unsettled. Celia's choral society sometimes performed in a local chapel, with acoustics that were quite off-putting for the singers:

> In the [chapel we perform in] I find [the acoustics] very difficult. And the noise reverberating. And I'm not confident when I'm in there, particularly about really going for it . . . the sound is different, and we're all anxious. I think everyone's quite anxious in that environment.

Angela felt that having too little time to get to know the idiosyncratic acoustic ambience of some venues can leave the singers doubting themselves:

> Of course, the acoustics change and everything, which is another thing. And sometimes it reverberates, and you think, "Are we behind? Are the men with us?" All that goes on.

Rehearsing in the performance space can reduce potential distractions caused by unfamiliarity with the environment, including the space available as well as differences in the acoustic conditions of the concert venue compared with the rehearsal room. In the first focus group, participants said having the chance to check out the venue was a "security blanket" for the singers:

> Doreen: I find it very useful to go, like, to the church and find out where you are going to stand, how we're going to come on. Having my stage hat on . . . where are we coming on, going off. If you go to a strange place and you're not sure where you're going to stand, how much room you're going to have.
>
> Dawn: And how it sounds as well.

In her interview, Ursula voiced the feelings of many of these singers, who felt that they had insufficient time to adjust to performance locations: "I just wish we could do more rehearsals like that [in the venue]." Frank suggested that practicing in different configurations may help choral singers prepare for any features of performance spaces that may affect inter-singer spacing, choir layout, the position of the choir within the venue, and the placement of the singer within the choir:

> Where it was quite good was when you [the author] said, "Let's bunch up as we're going to do it at the venue." And you had the sopranos in a bunch, and the tenors behind, and then the altos in front on the other side . . . If you're well practiced, and well-rehearsed at singing in different groups, then that is just a variation of what you normally do.

Practicing in different configurations might help singers adapt more quickly when situational factors at the performance venue dictate a change of formation. When it is not possible to arrange rehearsals in the performance venue, practicing in the configuration necessitated by the shape and size of the venue may help to reduce the sense of disorientation and distraction sometimes experienced in an unfamiliar venue. Singers will then acclimatize more quickly to a different acoustic environment and choral configuration. Admittedly, rehearsing in the configuration to be used in the venue may not be as effective as practicing in the actual performance space because the acoustics in the rehearsal room will obviously be different. However, it can familiarize the singers with the way in which their voices interact in this position and give them the opportunity to develop trust and rapport with their new neighbors.

Rehearsing at the performance venue does not prepare the choir for the fact that the acoustic reverberation and absorbency in a venue will usually alter once the audience has arrived. Nevertheless, singers value the increased sense of security derived from opportunities to practice entries and exits; to adapt to the size and shape of the venue; to become comfortable with any changes made to inter-singer spacing, choir position and layout, and individual placement within the choir; and to acclimatize, to some extent, to the conditions created by the interaction of the room acoustics, choral acoustics, and choir configuration. Limited opportunities to rehearse at the concert venue before the performance may be due to room availability or financial concerns (hire fees can be expensive for an amateur choir). However, given the significance of this factor in affecting confidence levels among amateur choral singers, addressing such practicalities may be a priority for some ensembles. The following tips will provide some help with reducing the impact of acoustic and configurational variations.

Tips for Conductors

- Make a site visit to the venue and check whether the size or shape of the performance space will affect the choir's configuration. If so, work out where (and in which formation) the choir will stand, how much inter-singer space there will be, and plan who will stand where. Use this configuration consistently in the rehearsals leading up to the performance.
- During the site visit, check the acoustics of the venue. Try singing a few notes from various places so that you understand how the room acoustics will feel to singers in different parts of the choir.
- If the room acoustics have noticeable idiosyncrasies, check what strategies could be employed to counteract or cope with these. If, for example, there are places where the sound disappears, can the singers stand somewhere else? Even a slight adjustment of position can make a difference in the singers' experience and perception of the performance.
- Prepare the choir for any acoustic challenges by describing these in advance and explaining how they might affect the singers' perception of their own performance. Challenging acoustics often sound worse to the singers than they sound to the audience, so it is worth reassuring the choir about this.
- Explain any strategies that you plan to put in place, such as configurational or positional alterations, to help deal with difficult acoustic environments.
- Take into account any features of the rehearsal space that may affect the choir's acoustic expectations when they are in the performance venue. For example, the rehearsal room may have a lively acoustic ambience with high ceilings, few soft furnishings, and plenty of space, which helps the singers make a bright, resounding, "joyful noise." In contrast, some venues will feel as if they are damping down the choral sound. If the rehearsal room has absorbent acoustics, some venues may seem to overamplify the voices, and an unfamiliar reverberation may leave the singers feeling exposed and insecure.
- Prepare the singers for the above changes in acoustic environment by explaining how they might feel and giving them reassuring but realistic feedback about how the choir sounds in each environment.
- Always have at least one rehearsal in the performance venue.
- Explore ways of increasing the number of rehearsals in the venue.
- Be prepared to give advice about simple adjustments that the singers can make to counteract any acoustic difficulties. For example, to brighten their tone in absorbent acoustics, singers might be reminded to use their smeyes (see chapter 1). However, this guidance should only be given if you are confident in conveying a healthy vocal technique; if not, it is worth seeking advice from an expert voice teacher.

Configuration Checklist for Conductors

At the performance venue, remember to check the following:

- Are all the singers in a position to see you clearly?
- Do all the singers have enough space for their own personal comfort?
- Are the singers positioned closely enough together so that they can hear each other?
- Can each vocal section hear the other parts?
- Can at least some of the singers see each other?
- Are the singers staying within their planned layout? (Sometimes they may drift!)

If your answer to any of these questions is no, try to resolve the issues as quickly as you can.

CHAPTER SUMMARY

My interviews with amateur singers reinforced my informal observation that some acoustic environments can affect their performance quality and confidence levels. The singers raised several significant points regarding the relationship between acoustic conditions, choir configuration within rehearsal and performance spaces, and the placement of individual singers within the choir.[22] These reports diverge from the findings of previous studies, partly due to differences in sample, research focus, and methodology. Other explanations for the preferences discussed in this chapter relate to the musical and social interactions between amateur choral singers, which will be explored in the following chapter. For now, the main points regarding choral acoustics and choir configuration are as follows.

For confident choral performances, amateur singers tend to prefer

- hearing the other singers around them rather than their own voices
- close inter-singer spacing, which enables them to hear each other
- choir formations that allow them to see and hear each other clearly
- singing alongside other singers who are singing the same vocal parts rather than singing in mixed-voice formations
- being in a position where they can see the conductor clearly
- consistency of formation and position

The singers I interviewed suggested the following strategies for taking account of these preferences:

- Arranging more rehearsals in the performance venue when possible in order to acclimatize singers to the interactions between the room acoustics and their voices and help them adjust to any configurational changes necessitated by the size and shape of the performance space.
- Providing more opportunities for developing configurational flexibility during rehearsals to help the singers adjust to any configurational changes determined by the characteristics of performance venues.

Adult amateur singers' preferences regarding their SOR and choral configuration were consistent, regardless of the size or type of choir under discussion. The needs of amateur choral singers, in relation to their SOR and configurational factors, differed markedly from those of their counterparts in earlier studies of university and conservatoire choirs. As very few of the participants in my research had received any musical education beyond secondary school, it seems likely that the interviewees' preference for configurations that allowed them to hear musical cues from fellow singers might be associated with their lower levels of formal musical training relative to the sample groups in the earlier research cited above. One of my earlier studies indicated that higher levels of general musicianship, instrumental tuition, and vocal training all had positive effects, for some adult amateur singers, in terms of reducing music performance anxiety and facilitating confident performance.[23] This suggests that providing extra musical training for amateur singers may be helpful. However, two of the singers who are represented in this chapter had received musical training at an undergraduate level and were very accomplished musicians, but they still expressed the same preferences and insecurities as the other participants.

Finally, there will not be one universal solution when considering the effects of choir formation, position, and spacing. Self-to-other ratio preferences can be affected by room acoustics and reflectors, the size and composition of the choir, individual differences in vocal output, and personal reactions to acoustics and different configurations. However, paying attention to these aspects of choral performance can contribute to creating a musically pleasing choral blend for the audience, establishing a confidence-building acoustic environment for the singers, and helping the singers acclimatize, as far as possible, to the conditions created by the interaction of room acoustics, choral acoustics, and the effects of choir configuration. Considering the specific needs of adult amateur singers when meeting a range of acoustic and situational challenges can also foster trust and rapport between the singers and their conductor. The interactions between choir members and their conductor will be explored in the following chapters.

Chapter Four

Collaboration and Communal Learning

Qualitative researchers always hope to find something new and original about a subject of interest, so our most common modus operandi is to go and directly ask the people who are most likely to know about it. We seek individuals who have "lived experience" of the topic in question because these people are experts on the subject in the context of their own lives.[1] Emergent themes arise spontaneously from open questions and are based entirely on the material that is prioritized by the interviewees. This means that in such a study, there is plenty of room for unexpected, surprising, and exciting results. The element of serendipity is one of the joys of such exploratory research.

It is impossible, however, to enter a research arena in which we have previous experience without a few preconceived ideas about what we will find. This is partly due to our own interests and experience, and partly due to our familiarity with existing research literature. In my case, when I asked the question "Who has influenced your confidence as a choral singer?" I expected to hear a great deal about the input of conductors and singing teachers. This was obviously based on my evaluation of the importance of my own role as a singing teacher and conductor! It was also based on the hitherto limited amount of research literature on performance anxiety among adult choral singers, which has tended to highlight the relationship between the choir and the conductor.[2]

The participants in my research did discuss the notable contribution that a conductor can make to the confidence of choral singers (see chapter 5). However, they also spontaneously discussed the influence of fellow singers, to the extent that this became a major theme. In the spirit of the qualitative aim of representing multiple voices, this theme will now be presented largely in the participants' own words.

COMMUNITY, COMRADESHIP, AND CAMARADERIE

> One of the reasons why we all enjoy it so much is because we have fun together. We're like-minded people so it's a social thing as well as really enjoying the singing, which I think is lovely. (Liz)

The benefits of participation in group singing activities include increased social cohesion, community development, and individual inclusion.[3] Research has shown that choirs for the elderly,[4] the homeless,[5] and other marginalized groups[6] can have a spectacular impact on the social lives and community feeling of their members, reducing isolation and creating group solidarity. In response to this evidence, several musical initiatives have been launched in the United Kingdom, including The Choir with No Name, which is the umbrella title of a set of choirs for people affected by homelessness. Their mission is "to enable marginalized people to make friends, build their confidence and skills, and find their place in society."[7]

The social and individual benefits of group singing in wider society are also well documented,[8] and this was reflected by some of the participants in my study. As a keen sports fan with a successful career, Owen was neither socially disadvantaged nor marginalized. However, when he moved into a new area, he appreciated the way that his singing activities helped him to bond quickly with a whole new circle of friends:

> When I came to [town], I was in the rugby club, and we used to go around the pubs every Christmas and sing carols. But they were a motley crew, and they always wanted me along 'cause I could always start singing the tune, in tune. And that really gave me some confidence.

Singing together has an "ice-breaker effect" because it can accelerate the social bonding process within a group of disparate individuals.[9] This is partly because collective singing imparts a sense of community while bypassing the need to get to know each person individually. Non-human primates spend a great deal of time on social grooming, taking part in activities such as cleaning, stroking, scratching, or massaging each other. Fortunately, the evolution of speech in humans replaced physical grooming with vocal grooming, that is, talking to each other. This saves a lot of time and effort when creating social bonds in human society.[10] Conversing in pairs or small groups is the usual way to introduce ourselves, but bonding through singing together in larger groups is common in many settings beyond the world of formal musical performance. When the crowd sings "Swing Low, Sweet Chariot" at England Rugby Football matches, and when American and Canadian baseball fans sing "Take Me Out to the Ball Game," a palpable feeling of solidarity is created that would be difficult to achieve through any other shared, simultaneous medium of communication. Don discovered this when he went away to college in a remote location. Although he initially found it hard to make friends, shared sporting activities helped him to meet people, and the associated group singing helped him to feel closer to his new companions:

> When I was at [the university], I was in the mountaineering club, and we'd go walking and then meet up in the pub in the evening, and sing old-fashioned Irish rebel songs, folk songs, and whatever. And just being in that camaraderie of men singing together was always good.

The strong impact of group singing upon social cohesion is partly due to the physiological effects of singing together. As singing demands a slower rate of respiration than usual, the heart rate responds by slowing down, creating the calm and unthreatened state that is a precondition for constructive social engagement.[11] Group singing stimulates the production of oxytocin, a neuropeptide involved in strengthening social bonding,[12] and oxytocin is also responsible for collectively synchronized cardiac and respiratory activities.[13] This physiological synchronization between participants can open up channels for sharing emotional expression; in fact, singing together has some advantages over speech. Group singing provides more direct access to stronger feelings, in a similar way to sharing primal vocalizations such as sobbing or laughing.[14] For all of these reasons, singing together predisposes a group to cooperate so that individualistic perspectives are superseded by a group identity with common goals and points of view.[15] The social benefits afforded by singing groups suggest that there is great scope for interpreting amateur choirs as collaborative social units, microcosms of society, hubs of communal learning, and embodiments of community engagement. As we will see, adult amateur singers appreciate the ways in which group dynamics contribute to their experience of group singing activities, with particular reference to collective learning and confidence-building.

The intrinsic enjoyment of singing is a strong motivator for choral participation; as one interviewee put it, "There's nothing like singing with other people in harmony." However, most of the singers I interviewed also attributed much of their enjoyment to having a "great sense of community" and a feeling of solidarity with their fellow singers. This was how Beryl, a soprano with extensive experience singing in church and community choirs, saw it:

> What do I get from it? I think it's the most wonderful thing to be able to blast forth and sing and to be in it with like-minded people.

This was echoed by participants from all types of singing groups, who valued "having fun together," being "on the same wavelength," and feeling as if they were "gelling" as a group. The resultant sense of "community," "comradeship," and "camaraderie" is highly prized and can impart a powerful feeling of musical and social togetherness. Frank shared this uplifting experience:

> All being together—a sort of camaraderie about it. It's good 'cause you feel . . . It's like surfing on the crest of the wave, all four of you [tenors]. And also the whole choir, all together, you know.

THE CHORAL TEAM

The community spirit within a choir can lead to the development of strong social bonds and mutual support systems that can extend beyond the rehearsal sessions into the singers' everyday lives. These chorally based social relationships inspire reciprocal trust and loyalty, which can transfer into a sense of security among the singers. All of this can have a positive effect on the singers' performances, which helps to build their confidence in the quality of their choir. The effects of this social, emotional, and musical bonding are illustrated by Andrew's description of the closeness in a long-established group:

> One of the words we used to use in the male voice choir was comradeship. And if somebody was in trouble, or . . . if they passed away, or a member of the family passed away, the choir was there. It was so, so tight. And I believe that builds good performances. I think that builds a good choir.

Although singing together can accelerate social bonding, deeper friendships obviously do not blossom overnight. The level of support that Andrew experienced is a testament to the commitment of some dedicated amateur choral singers to each other individually and collectively. This mutual commitment can be developed through many hours of singing together in rehearsals and performances. The singers I interviewed often discussed this closeness and its role in building a confident choir, in terms of social cohesion and collaboration. Harry interpreted the choir as an organic entity, which becomes greater than the sum of its parts:

> I have a theory that, for a choir to survive, it's bigger than just the people in it. It's the creation of quality and of grace and of sharing all this stuff, which comes from the order of the choir.

The evolution of the group arises from the combined performance and complex interactions of the group as whole rather than being a simple result of the isolated efforts of individual singers. Of course, the achievements of a choir depend upon the contributions of individuals, but the collective result often resembles a well-oiled machine. Clive, a bass in a male voice choir, used an orchestral analogy to express his awe at being part of this miracle of coordination:

> Suddenly you think to yourself, "My goodness, we are the drums, we are the tubas, we are the bass, and they're this, and they're that, and they're the fiddles, etc." And you can think of a choir as being like an orchestra or a band. And you can see how it all knits together. It's wonderful.

This experience of intense collaboration and precise coordination can add to the enjoyment and satisfaction arising from choral participation. It invites analogies with team projects in other spheres, and interview participants often used vocabulary that reflected this. In the quotation below, Ross links his reflections on choral teamwork with his working life as a project manager. This indicates a quasi-professional attitude to his singing, although his choral activities all take place within the amateur world. Singers commonly make heavy investments of time, effort, emotion, and sometimes finance in their choral participation. In this way, their musical hobbies often become "amateur careers,"[16] which add value to their everyday lives:

> Some of the best projects I've been in have been as part of a team with a common goal . . . And that's what a concert is. It's a project-team coming together to do a one-off thing. And you work on your pieces and you rehearse, and then you deliver on the day.

This feeling of team spirit, along with the singers' commitment and personal investment in their choirs, leads to a sense of pride in their collective achievements. The combination of their awareness of group cohesion and unity, and their intrinsic motivation to contribute to the team effort, helps them to work effectively on their shared goals and has a positive effect on performance quality. Mastery experiences, such as productive rehearsals and successful concert performances, then have a direct effect upon their confidence. This is how Phoebe, a career amateur in a succession of high-quality chamber choirs and choral societies, explained a recent triumph:

> I thought we sang as a choir the best that we sang. So that gave you confidence . . . everybody seemed to be on the right wavelength—we were gelling.

Because choral performances are judged on the group participation of the whole choir, singers are aware of having a shared responsibility to interact constructively with each other. Barbara and her fellow singers in the second focus group agreed that it was "definitely a team thing." For them, one of the major challenges of choral teamwork was the requirement to combine intense musical concentration with a social awareness that allowed "you to be able to listen to the other people and still sing your part." Naomi relished these challenges and felt that collective achievement was key to her enjoyment:

> When . . . we make a good sound—which we do—that makes me feel good. It's definitely a feel-good factor with the choir. And when we do the concerts, we've achieved that goal of so many pieces, and again, it always makes me feel good at the end of a concert.

Sharing responsibility for performance quality, and for helping others learn, creates a sense of group ownership and engagement. This means that singers take pride in the choir's successes and derive confidence from their sense of achievement. Some singers suggested that these effects were magnified when they had shared responsibility for practical aspects of choral performance, such as helping to arrange concerts or raising funds for a charity with personal associations. When Andrew was asked to describe an enjoyable performance in which he had felt particularly confident, he selected a senior citizens concert that he had organized because this had given him a vested interest in the event. This kind of emotional investment in performances has positive effects on the singers' enjoyment, on their sense of belonging and identity as group members, and on their confidence in themselves as valuable contributors to the choir. Clive became quite emotional when describing a concert in which he had a personal stake:

> I've had to have a lot of treatment . . . [My wife] suggested we raise money for the hospital . . . We had the matron of the ward, from the chemotherapy come, and also one of the Sisters . . . And my heart was bursting with pride . . . it was a really, really good experience.

Being involved in the creative process and helping to make artistic decisions, such as choosing repertoire or themes for concert programs, also imparts a sense of ownership, inclusion, and empowerment. Nina liked it when her musical director involved the choir in making improvisational arrangements of songs because it enhanced the choir's identity as a team and increased their "sense of pride" in their achievements: "Oh, we're creating something new!" In the choirs I conduct, I regularly "road test" my own original choral arrangements, and Ross gave me some positive feedback on this:

It's nice to have a conductor . . . who's sharing certain pieces . . . I really enjoy the challenge of helping to develop what the final piece becomes. The creative side of the thing can be extremely wonderful to work with, and to feel part of it.

Providing singers with opportunities for input into decision making and organizational tasks can increase their sense of belonging, group identity, ownership, emotional investment, and engagement in performances, with confidence-boosting effects. Teamwork can also be encouraged through a variety of musical activities, including the following examples.

Team-building Activities

- Work songs and sea shanties have long been used to enhance teamwork, coordination, synchronization, and a sense of participating in "a cause beyond oneself."[17] These traditional songs, among others, are fun to use as choral team-building exercises:

    1. "Haul Away, Joe"
    2. "What Shall We Do With the Drunken Sailor"
    3. "Blow the Man Down"
    4. "Fire Down Below"
    5. "Bound for South Australia"
    6. "The Sloop John B"
    7. "Roll the Old Chariot Along"
    8. "This Old Hammer"
    9. "John Kanaka"
    10. "John Barleycorn"

- Develop coordination and synchronization by setting up a strong rhythmic pattern for these team-building songs. Incorporate some simple movements such as stepping or swaying, or use body percussion, clapping, or stamping.
- Teach a simple round and ask the singers to pick out phrases to use as *ostinati* (repeated motifs). These can then be used to accompany the round or for developing extra harmonies and improvisations. "Rose Red," for example, lends itself beautifully to this exercise.

TRUST, SUPPORT, AND RECIPROCAL PEER LEARNING

Personally, [my confidence] comes from the other chaps who I sing with. That gives me the confidence. (Clive)

Taking group responsibility for performance quality, decision making, creative development, and, in some cases, practical organization are some of the more obvious aspects of working effectively as a choral team. There are also many ways in which singers' personal and musical interactions with each other can affect rehearsal and performance. In Liz's choir, the singers made their own individual contributions to collective achievement and group morale:

> That's the thing with our group: we all encourage each other. We all have different strengths . . . and I think that's really nice. And that helps your confidence if you feel that other people are with you.

All the singers I interviewed gave examples of ways in which choral singers can provide mutual encouragement and moral support. The verbal feedback from other singers was very affirming for Beryl:

> You know what I think's nice? You know [a soprano] stands next to me and I'm ever so nervous . . . saying, "I'll never be able to do this—I can't do this," you know . . . But [she] always encourages me . . . she's encouraging me all the time.

Despite being an accomplished musician and an experienced alto, Naomi still appreciated receiving encouragement and affirmation from her fellow singers. The following vignette illustrates how her choral teammates reacted when she doubted her own ability during a bout of pre-performance nerves and how they provided positive reinforcement once she had successfully overcome her anxieties:

> If it's gone well we'll sit down and go, "Yes!" In fact I said to [a fellow alto] when we'd finished . . . I went, "You won't believe this" . . . 'cause when we went up to do the . . . "Sloop John B" and I was like "I'm dreading this, I'm absolutely dreading this because I know I just don't know this." And she was like "You'll be fine!" And then we came back and I went, "I did it!" . . . And she went, "Ooh, well done! Finally!"

Verbal encouragement or reassurances are sometimes complemented by physical contact to reinforce group cohesion. Harry's chamber choir teammates would sometimes "bolster each other before [going on]" and perhaps "hold an elbow and say, 'Go for it, boy!' or something like that." This kind of physical and verbal support resembles the encouragement that sports team members might exchange during a game. It can help build individual confidence and foster a supportive social learning environment. It can also act as confirmation of the singer's acceptance and integration as a member of the choral team as well as a validation of their individual vocal ability. Praise from Nina's community choir peers helped her "feel positive" about her contribution to the group:

> If someone does a really good job, then we'll say they've done a really good job . . . and the recognition coming from others, and you're sort of like, "Yeah, they think it's okay too! I'm not completely doolally." It's a genuine thing.

Praise and encouragement were particularly highly prized when it came from fellow singers who were perceived as comparatively senior in terms of choral experience, musical knowledge, or vocal skill. Andrew's self-confidence received a welcome boost after this reaction from a semiprofessional soloist in his chamber choir: "All she did was tap me on the shoulder, and that was like a thumbs up—that was good." Similarly, after a long hiatus in his amateur singing career due to pressures of work, Don began to sing occasional solos with his chamber choir and received valuable support from his fellow singers. Peer feedback reinforced his pride in his achievements and helped him to develop confidence in his performance skills:

> A couple of the best comments, or things that have meant most to me, have been when I've done solos . . . and some of the people from the choir have come up and said, "That was really good" because they're people who I sort of appreciate and value their opinions.

Such positive interactions between singers are built upon, and contribute to, the development of a strong rapport and mutual trust. The formation of a group identity based on common interests, experiences, goals, performance values, and achievements helps to develop a sense of trust between fellow singers. This trust can facilitate a supportive, collaborative environment in which effective communal learning and confident performance can take place:

> It's confidence in who you're performing with. Knowing that they know, and that they're going to do what they should. (Barry)

There were occasional concerns about whether singers could trust their fellow performers to remember stage entries and exits, musical cues, and their own vocal lines, all of which can lead to tension during the performance. When a section of the choir had faltered during a dress rehearsal, Frank felt insecure at the concert because he kept wondering, "Oh, are they going to get it this time?" This unsettling feeling affects the confidence of singers both before and during performances, as Barbara explained:

> It's sometimes quite obvious that some people haven't remembered what's been said to them, haven't been listening, or have just completely forgotten what's been said. And you feel nervous because they're not doing what you expect them to.

Fortunately, working together regularly within a choir often leads to empathy and an understanding of each other's strengths and weaknesses. When this rapport develops, it helps create a productive atmosphere of trust and security. Guidance and constructive criticism can then be accepted from respected team members:

> The rapport is good, and that's important as well, isn't it? . . . We're not there to criticize each other, we're there to help each other, and therefore if somebody does get it wrong . . . [If a tenor's] pointed out stuff that I've missed, and I've said, "You're right, I have missed that." . . . So, it's about helping each other, isn't it? . . . To build each other's confidence by working together rather than being self-critical. (Andrew)

This willingness to give and accept feedback from fellow singers can lead to a mutual exchange of knowledge and advice. When Harry reflected on his experience in a long-established chamber choir, he described peer feedback based on affinity and familiarity. His comments embraced the concept of choir rehearsals as learning experiences, with singers contributing to the learning process:

> I know his voice. I trust him. We like each other! [laughs]. This is a tenor. And I nudge him and say, "You made a balls there!" or something like that [laughs]. And he does to me as well, I may hasten to add. It's a two-way traffic. That's what learning's about, isn't it?

This kind of give-and-take is most likely to arise when the choir is functioning as a cohesive, unified team and when choral relationships are founded on trust and mutual support. Tim's workshop experience showed how reciprocal peer learning can spring from a nurturing environment in which singers can develop a sense of individual and collective confidence:

> Certainly, in places like summer schools and workshops, everybody supports everybody else, in a sort of a quiet way. They're watching you and learning

from you, and you're watching them and learning from them. And it's all very comfortable, and confidence-boosting.

Sharing in this type of reciprocal learning process helps singers make the most of their collective skills and aptitudes. In an adult amateur choir, there is generally a diverse membership. The individual singers have various levels of musical and choral experience, technical and vocal training, and baseline self-confidence both in their vocal ability and as a general trait. For this reason, singers often share knowledge, expertise, and moral support to attain their shared goal of competent and enjoyable choral performance. Singers give each other practical help in a variety of ways, including reminding each other of lyrics, pronunciation, starting notes, rhythms, melodies, and harmony lines. Nina, for example, relied on more experienced singers who modeled the pronunciation of words in foreign-language songs:

> When I'm learning a song . . . there'll be members who know it, or at least know the words, so I like to be near them at the start at least just to get a handle on the words 'cause they never sound as they do when they're written, so that's quite helpful.

In one focus group, there was an extended discussion about who relies on whom, which became almost circular as they described these reciprocal processes. In Matt's sketch of team confabulation, the singers are almost performing a discreet version of musical pass the parcel:

> I often find myself turning to [a bass] and saying [whispers], "How does this one go?" And he whispers back, saying, "I don't know. Ask him!" [points to where next singer stands].

Helping each other stay in time with the beat, and understand some of the more complicated rhythms, are important aspects of the choral team effort:

> Sometimes I will count for us both and we'll get the timing. This last one was a lot of counting! . . . And I would start this [tapping beat], and we'd sing together, and the two of us would give it, you know, and feel we did it the best we could do.

Sharing knowledge of musical notation and terminology is also part of collaborative learning. When conductors use technical terms or musical jargon, singers with more musical training or choral experience may enlighten the uninitiated:

I can [also] say to her, "I don't know what that means. What's he [the conduc-
tor] talking about?" And she'll say, "This is . . ." Or save it to the end and tell
me what it is I'm not getting. And then she will equally go, "Don't know what
he's talking about. What's that?" (Angela)

Although musical terminology is a helpful form of shorthand, it should be
used with discretion in mixed-ability singing groups. When inter-singer relationships are based on trust and rapport, singers with different levels of
musical education will spontaneously add to the team effort by translating
some of the more unfamiliar expressions. However, in a less idyllic environment, using terminology and instructions that only some of the participants
fully understand can be divisive. It may undermine the cohesion of the group,
the inclusivity of the collective experience, and the confidence of singers
who feel excluded from the musical conversation. Angela suggested that
conductors sometimes need to remember the needs of less musically in-
formed members:

There are more and more people joining who know a bit more about [music],
and I feel more and more inferior . . . And then they use *words*, and you go,
"Ooh, that's an interesting one" . . . I'm slightly out of my depth with the
choral society, and sometimes I need a little bit of nurturing!

This indicates that the level of musical understanding within a choral group
should be carefully considered so that directions are easily understood by all
present. Time should be taken to ensure that instructions are clear and that
any possibly unfamiliar musical terms are explained or rephrased to clarify
the meaning. Angela ended her discussion of this topic by expressing her
appreciation of a new choral society conductor whose instructions were "a lot
clearer." He provided definitions of terminology so that "the next time he
says that word, you think, 'I know what that means this time. I know what he
wants.'" As a teacher herself, she noted that the conductor was "doing it as a
teacher more." This approach helps the adult learners in the choir increase
their knowledge and capacity for independent learning, based on their musical understanding. Finally, Angela cautioned that false assumptions are
sometimes made by conductors about the knowledge and resources available
to amateur choir members:

It's much better if [a conductor] . . . doesn't assume that everybody in the
masses knows what it's all about. Also, they're not assuming, "When you go
home and do this on the piano" . . . We haven't all got pianos at home.

In a mixed-ability group, some singers will have received more musical training than others. Some of the more challenging aspects of musical performance, or the application of theoretical concepts, can therefore be used as development opportunities for the whole choir. For example, singers with more musical training may be encouraged to share their knowledge. They could be asked to volunteer to explain musical terms or perhaps to outline the "geography" of a song by identifying its structure and pointing out repeats and codas. The strengths and weaknesses of the choral team can thus be accounted for in a way that encourages collaborative learning and contributes to the confidence of everyone in the group. In Nina's choir, the conductor facilitated a collaborative environment in which patience was maintained while everyone learned:

> I think the way we do it is that no one is singled out, so I think that has a definite impact on us feeling like we're a team . . . 'cause we all have to get there. And we all have to sing as a unit. So why single out one person? It's just like "No, we just need to keep going until we all get it right."

Exercises for Building Trust and Rapport

- With the singers standing in pairs, ask them to try to coordinate their breathing using eye contact only. Repeat the exercise in small groups and then in larger groups.
- Now ask them to try to synchronize a single hand clap, first in pairs, then in small groups, and finally in larger groups—or perhaps even with the whole choir.
- With the choir standing in a large circle, set up a rhythm by clapping, stamping or using any part of your body percussively. Make eye contact with one of the singers, who should then copy your rhythm for a couple of bars. The singer should then concoct a rhythmic pattern of her own to pass on to another singer of her choice.
- Still standing in a large circle, set up a simple rhythm using clapping and stamping. I like Queen's "We Will Rock You" pattern. On the strongest beat call out your own name, then the singer on your left should call out his name on the first beat of the next bar, and so on, until everyone has done this. In larger choirs, you could set up several smaller circles to do the exercise simultaneously—chaos will no doubt ensue!
- Repeat the above exercise with creative variations. For example, on the strongest beat of the percussive pattern, singers could be asked to take turns calling out their favorite food, drink, animal, etc.

ROLE MODELS AND TEAM LEADERS

For many singers, "it's nice to feel that you've got some good solid singers around you." They like to be surrounded by "people who know what they're singing" and to have "people who know what they're singing on either side because if I'm not quite sure, I can actually learn from them." This reliance upon more experienced or more competent performers was widely acknowledged by the singers I interviewed, and they usually knew exactly which singers they could rely upon for help with different aspects of rehearsal and performance. The singers' perception of a choral pecking order extended into a friendly rivalry between some of the men, which encouraged striving for higher vocal attainment. Nick's adoption of one of his fellow basses as a role model manifested itself in a kind of choral showboating:

> If I sing next to [him], it's a bit of a competition as well 'cause I don't want to be out-sung by [him], you know [laughs]. I think it lifts my game when I'm stood next to [him], definitely, 'cause I think, you know, he's a really good male singer and I'd like to think that I could sing as well as him. I don't think I can, but I'd like to think I could.

This good-humored competition can enhance performance quality and function as a distraction from performance nerves. Confidence and skills may be developed as the singer improves their own performance by trying to match that of their role model:

> I think it just ups the game a bit . . . 'cause he's very loud . . . He's got a very big tone, very rounded sound too, and I think I sing louder when I'm stood next to him . . . It does help me with my tone and my pitch as well, I think. I just concentrate more. (Nick)

The proximity of a strong singer with reliable intonation can help counteract any distraction caused by less accurate neighbors. More confident singers also have an impact on their peers partly due to emotional contagion (see chapter 1)[18] and partly due to positive modeling, both in musical and emotional terms. In the third focus group, Matt directly addressed his personal role model: "Having you there in the choir really helps me . . . I'd love to be able to sing as well as you!" Singers may also be encouraged to excel by strong soloists:

> He sort of barnstormed when he got the solo bit . . . Having him do that, I noticed that everybody was doing it, even when we did the repeats—we were singing that top note and holding it better, and so again it's been a positive experience. (Nick)

This kind of modeling can be an inspirational factor in the decision to continue singing in choirs or to develop an amateur performance career. George's early years in male voice choirs provided him with a strong motivation to develop his choral chops:

> There was one guy from Wales, and he was absolutely superb. It was one of those things where you sat there listening to him, and you thought, "God, I wish I could sing like that!" . . . And that's what I was doing in the [male voice choir] 'cause I was trying to be as good as that baritone.

Negative role models can also be useful because they provide examples of what not to do or how not to behave. Gordon suggested another benefit of observing less-than-perfect role models: through the "reality check" of watching other amateur singers, he was encouraged to "have a go" at performing, and he gained confidence in his own ability:

> When I first started doing am-dram in 1982, I'd be doing something on stage with people who'd been doing it for years, and we'd sing in pantomimes, and people I was singing on stage with were rubbish! But . . . the audiences loved it. And I thought, "You don't actually have to be brilliant to perform." . . . So that was a positive thing.

All three focus groups and eleven of the sixteen interviewees talked about depending on particular singers for help with various aspects of performance: "Everybody's always jostling to get near the good singers!" (Celia). Certain singers often become informally recognized (usually within their vocal sections but sometimes across the whole choir) as unelected but influential team leaders. These choral team leaders play a major role in facilitating collective learning and encouraging confident performance. They are relied on due to having characteristics such as a strong voice; reliable intonation; an ability to hold the melodic line and retain the harmony; confidence about finding starting notes and making musical entries; fluent sight-reading; a good memory for words or music; or a combination of these advantages. The role of informal team leader usually evolves almost organically, based upon the other singers' perceptions of their relative experience, performance quality, skills, and confidence. Doug admitted that he was helped enormously by "latching on" to his most reliable neighbors:

> I think you do need that someone in a particular piece who knows what they're doing . . . it's good to have that rock. It gives you confidence.

These team leaders were of great importance to many participants, and their mere presence contributed toward the confidence of the singers around them. In the first focus group, Liz painted a vivid picture of singers sharing musical and moral support:

> We've done it quite often . . . sort of lean in, and we know that [this alto] will have the right note. We know when one another has gone a bit wrong and we chivvy [urge] one another along.

During the second focus group, Barbara directly addressed Karen, acknowledging the confidence that her presence gave her:

> You're very confident in what you're singing, and you will always start on the right note. I always feel that maybe I won't, so if you're standing next to me, or [a certain alto] is standing nearby, then I know that if I do falter at any time, I can get back on track.

In the third focus group, Matt and Gordon demonstrated that their team leaders were not necessarily more experienced or longer-standing members of the ensemble, but they supported the singers around them with their own skills in sight-reading, memorization, or pitching:

> Matt: Actually, having you there in the choir really helps me. It really does. It helps me just maintain . . . get the right notes or whatever 'cause I'm subject to straying, and you're consistent.
>
> Gordon: Well, I'm still learning at the moment.
>
> Matt: Yeah, but even from day one, you come in and you're on the notes, and that helps me.

The need to be near an implicitly identified team leader is so important to some singers that it affects where they prefer to sit. Celia likes "being on the front row . . . because the lady next but one to me is good and I can hear . . . she's a good lead." Nick echoed this, saying, "It does make a difference who I stand next to . . . if someone's really confident and can hold the note, then I will hold my notes as well." Andrew agreed that informal choral team leaders affect individual and collective confidence by providing practical help, such as helping singers focus on their starting note:

> I think you do build confidence by singing with the people around you . . . when the others, say the altos and sopranos are singing and we're gonna come

in, I've heard [a tenor] just hum a note, our first note, and . . . that's a confidence builder.

These individuals are often apparently unaware of their informal leadership position or seem reluctant to take credit for their influence within their section or on the whole choir. The unofficial team leader in the bass section of a male voice choir was typical of this:

> I suppose to a great extent we do look to [first bass]. He's been doing it a long time and he's got a damn good bass voice. And so, consequently, you tend to, I suppose, think of him as our leader, if you like. [But] if you said it to him, he'd say, "Oh, don't be so damn soft!" He wouldn't see it that way. (Clive)

Despite these modest inclinations, the informal team leaders are typically more confident about requesting extra help from the choral director. Although these roles are not part of the formal organization of the amateur choir—as section leaders are in a professional orchestra—there is a tendency for more self-assured singers to act as a spokesperson for their vocal section. Comfort may be taken from realizing that even the informal team leader needs extra help at times. Clive perceived this as a mitigating factor in his evaluation of his own competence:

> It's like somebody who's been doing a job for a long, long time. You'd think to yourself, "Well, he knows what he's doing" . . . I mean, there are occasions when we're rehearsing and he'll say, "Can we do so and so again because we're struggling with that bass part," and I think to myself, "Well, if [he] is struggling then I'm bound to be struggling as well."

When singers realize that they have been informally identified as unofficial team leaders, their own confidence is boosted by this awareness of their contribution to the group effort and from the recognition of their skills by their peers. The confidence-building nature of the team leader–team follower dyad is therefore reciprocal. Nina felt validated by the faith that her peers placed in her abilities:

> Among my group of singers—[the] tenor section—there are varying degrees of understanding of musicality, shall we say, so I like to know that at least a few of us have got it . . . 'cause I'm quite bossy and I'll tell them to be quiet or, you know, "Not yet!" [laughs]. "Wait!" . . . The fact that I've only been there for such a short time and they're already looking to me is quite complimentary, I guess.

The influence of informal team leaders on morale as well as on performance quality can be felt as much by their absence as by their presence, as Barry attested: "[This tenor] is very good. And [that baritone]. They're very loud! [laughs]. We miss them when they're not there!" Matt reported the emotional effect of missing his sectional "anchor," which sometimes left him feeling "quite disheartened," while Frank was concerned about the musical impact of the lack of a team leader:

> In the male voice choir . . . If there are key people missing, they tend to get a bit lost, as we do in the second tenors if we've got a few key people missing.

The presence and reliability of these key singers makes a significant difference to the individual singer's sense of security, especially in relation to intonation, finding starting notes, and making timely entries. This is often true even for singers who have a high level of experience and competence. Celia, who attended a school that placed a great emphasis on choral training, now attends a large choral society as well as a small church choir, which she occasionally directs. She explained that the lack of a strong lead can cause her to doubt herself:

> Well, standing next to someone who you know is going to pitch the note right and come in at the right time is good for your confidence 'cause you can sort of go along on their coat tails! But someone who just doesn't come in—I start to think, "Was I wrong? Can they only hear me?"

Clive took this a step further, describing a whole vocal section missing a cue when the unofficial section leader failed to start singing:

> Oddly enough, at our concert . . . we completely missed our entry and [the conductor] looked at us as if to say, "Where the hell are you?" I don't know why, but we all just blanked out! It was odd. And that comes back to having people around you . . . Subconsciously you're looking for your leader to come in, and it didn't happen!

Tips for Conductors

- Allow space in rehearsals for collaborative learning to take place. It can be easy to assume that all conversation between singers is extraneous to the rehearsal, but some of this may be integral to choral teamwork. Try to assess which communications are helpful and which are not. The latter can

then be gently discouraged, while the former can be used to help the singers learn and feel more confident.
- Observe the interactions between the singers and see if you can identify the informal team leaders in your choir. It might then be helpful to situate singers within the choir according to their relative strengths and weaknesses, as well as according to voice type. For example, less accomplished sight readers could be paired with good readers; confident and competent singers could be placed among less confident performers; and those with reliable intonation could be placed near those who pitch less accurately.

Exercises for Developing Team Leaders

- Have a "song share" session occasionally. Ask for volunteers to bring a simple round, call-and-response song, or unison item to teach to the choir. Singers could work in pairs to prepare and present their song for sharing.
- Ask for volunteers to share physical or vocal warm-ups with the choir. Again, this could be done in pairs or small groups rather than individually if singers would rather not work alone.
- In smaller groups, confident and competent singers could be given opportunities to lead sectional rehearsals. Time and resources permitting, mentoring for this could be provided by the conductor.

CLASHES AND CONFLICTS

> You get the singers who, when a mistake is made, they're turning round or pointing it out to you, visibly. What I call "rude performers." They irritate me as well. I know when I've made a mistake. (Pamela)

In this chapter, I may have given the false impression that choral interactions are invariably constructive. Realists will doubtless already have objected that social or task-oriented interactions within choirs are not always as harmonious as I have so far suggested. It is obvious that singers may clash for personal or artistic reasons, and the specter of internal politics can arise in almost any group setting. These scenarios can render the choral learning experience less collaborative than it would be in an ideal world. Problems, in terms of group cohesion and choral sound, can arise when singers do not function well as part of the vocal team. Pamela reported that loud, inaccurate singers seriously "affect my mood," and they sometimes distracted Naomi so much that she would abandon her own vocal line in despair:

> I get really frustrated because when [a certain soprano] . . . thinks she's right, then she sings it really forcefully and, again, sometimes when I know it's not

right, and it affects the altos . . . I give up, because I can't sing against that . . .
so I just don't sing and mime.

Other sources of disturbance and distraction can be "very annoying," particularly singers who talk too much in rehearsals, and even during performances. This made it very difficult for Phoebe to concentrate, and it can create divisions within the choral team if tempers become frayed:

> It [is] quite off-putting and irritating when the conductor is trying to go through parts, or trying to just even talk, and there are groups of people that are talking all the time. And I've even had that in a concert situation, where they've actually been talking behind me, and it really irritates me. I'd have to be like a school teacher: "Will you be quiet?!"

Ursula was similarly outraged by singers who provided a running commentary on proceedings, which could be interpreted as a passive-aggressive reaction to the conductor:

> There's a lady who sits next to me quite often who doesn't stop talking and tutting and muttering, and drives everybody bonkers . . . excruciating irritation. Sometimes to the point where I can't concentrate on the music 'cause I'm waiting for her next rude comment . . . Oh, she comments on the conductor! You know, he sort of says, "Right, all stand," and then "You may sit down" . . . and she'll make comments about him, you know. Just "Can't he make his mind up?" or "Up and down, up and down. It's ridiculous." Just . . . she's really rude! [laughs]. And I want to tell her to shut up.

Even ostensibly positive interactions are not always constructive in the rehearsal environment, as Joyce pointed out:

> I stand next to [a soprano], and sometimes . . . I'm distracted . . . She's such a big laugh . . . But I don't like messing around if it's the real thing, you know. I don't like sort of being distracted.

Balancing choir discipline with providing a favorable environment for collaboration and collective learning is among the most challenging aspects of choral direction, but it makes an important contribution to achieving flow [19] or being in the zone during choral singing. The benefits of entering a state of flow include immersion in the activity, which leads to a loss of self-consciousness and an increase in self-confidence (see chapter 2). The likelihood of achieving flow is reduced by distractions that draw the performer's attention away from the musical activity. Concentration on the task at hand is reduced, self-consciousness intrudes, and performance standards suffer. None of this is conducive to confident musical performance. For these reasons, pulling the singers' attention back to the music, rather than allowing them to focus on extraneous distractions, is likely to have positive effects on performance quality and confidence.

Sadly, a few participants had negative stories to tell about singers who criticized others, sometimes in a way that interfered with the smooth running of rehearsals. This behavior can undermine the conductor as well as adversely affect the concentration and confidence of other singers. Nina was very indignant about negative comments from other singers within the choir: "They might say, 'Oh, you're singing that wrong,' and it's like 'Well, we have a musical director to do that. It's not your place to do it.'" Andrew felt apprehensive about being criticized by a particularly opinionated fellow singer:

> I've heard [this bass] make a couple of comments sometimes to the basses and I think, "Ooh, crikey. If he said that to me" . . . He was criticizing the basses for a note.

Over critical peers can lead to singers doubting their own accuracy or ability. In the face of destructive feedback, excessive fault-finding, or blatant disapproval, singers reported taking offence or blaming themselves. In the most extreme cases, those affected decide to leave their choirs, as Ursula did:

> There was this one lady in [choral society], who is not a very nice lady, and she always kept her finger in her ear [demonstrates]. I'm sitting next to her and . . . [she] really obviously was making the point that I was disturbing her, and she kept saying, "It's a D, it's a D," or whatever it was. So I'd think, "You are so rude" . . . So I left [the choir]. I just assumed I was in the wrong.

Although individuals vary in their reactions to rude, disruptive, or distracting behavior from their choral colleagues, the outcomes are usually negative. Adverse effects on confidence, along with increased self-doubt or discomfort, arise when other singers do not use their skills to enhance the performance of the choral team. Sometimes they use their ability and experience to intimidate other singers rather than to encourage or support them during rehearsals and performances, as Irene found in her church choir:

> One thing that we do have in choir is a lady who's a prima donna; always hits the notes exactly, she thinks! . . . It's very off-putting because you get a snide look and you think, "Is it me? No I don't think so." Then everybody says

afterwards, "She was really flat, wasn't she?" And you think "Phew!" . . . You doubt yourself because she's been singing for years and years and . . . is very confident.

Clive had experienced mass intimidation during a shared concert with other choirs. He felt that his choir had been subjected to collective disdain, which detracted from their collective confidence:

> They [a male voice choir from a specific city] made us feel a little bit inferi-or . . . "You're not quite good enough to be with us" sort of an impression . . . "Why are we singing with *you*?" So I perhaps didn't enjoy it . . . You felt uncomfortable.

Fortunately, encounters like this were reported comparatively rarely. However, when they did occur, they had a significant effect on the enjoyment of choral activities and on the singers' confidence. The responsibilities of the choral conductor include developing an awareness of such interactions and taking appropriate action to mitigate their consequences. This is, of course, easier to say than it is to do, but a selection of strategies for managing choral group dynamics include the following.

Tips for Managing Conflict

- Establish clear ground rules for respectful communication and feedback between the singers.
- Model a team approach to choral learning and performance. This can include presenting yourself as a facilitator in rehearsals and a collaborator in performances.
- Try to use inclusive language that is conducive to cooperation and collaborative learning. Consider mirroring the words and phrases used by my research participants, including "team project," "teamwork," "community," and "collaboration."
- Notice the types of interactions within your choir, both between the singers themselves and between you and the singers. Note whether there are any improvements that could be made in this area (see chapter 5 for advice on conductor feedback).
- Consider discreetly changing the placement of individual singers within the choir if interpersonal harmony is likely to benefit from this.

THE CHOIR AS A COMMUNITY OF PRACTICE

In this section, the interaction between collective learning and choral confidence will be viewed through the lens of some of the most currently relevant psychological concepts. In educational research, an emphasis on the role of the teacher or group leader has been supplemented with an appreciation of the importance of peer interactions, [20] and a collaborative approach to teaching and learning has been advocated. This allows students to be more involved in the learning process rather than reacting passively to a more traditional, teacher-led approach. Although most research on group learning is intended to be applicable to formal educational settings rather than the sphere of adult leisure activities, choral singing shares many features with music learning in the classroom. A choir might not always be seen primarily as having an educational purpose, as classes in a school or college might. However, it is an environment in which the prime target is to learn, whether it is the acquisition of new repertoire, the improvement of performance skills, or the integration of new members as they learn to become fully fledged choral singers. In fact, "everything involved in rehearsing and conducting can be characterized by a teaching paradigm."[21]

Although the conductor usually has the most obviously didactic role, socially supported learning can make a significant contribution to individual and collective confidence in choral ensembles. The importance of peer learning, modeling, and informal mentoring has rarely been acknowledged in traditional "maestro" literature, which has generally emphasized the role of the conductor rather than that of musical group dynamics:

> The key characteristics of group creativity are improvisation, collaboration, and emergence. But we tend to neglect these characteristics. Instead, we often try to attribute the group's creativity to a single person: the group leader, the soloist, the director or conductor.[22]

This approach has been challenged in situated learning theory, in which traditional models of learning based on apprenticeship and mastery have been applied to a wide range of work-related and educational settings.[23] From this perspective, learning is embedded in social life, with a focus on modeling and training by peers, rather than purely concentrated on verbal instruction by teachers or group leaders. As learners add to their skills and experience through peer learning and group practice, they move from peripheral participation to full involvement in group activities.[24] This model shifts the locus of learning from an exclusively teacher-led process to a more collaborative undertaking, sometimes described as a community of practice (CoP).[25] A CoP is a group of people who "share a passion for something that they know how to do and who interact regularly in order to learn how to do it better."[26] They have a shared interest in a common domain, participate in shared activities, and "build relationships that enable them to learn from each other."[27] This is a fitting description of the members of an amateur choir with their shared interest in singing and their joint goals of learning songs together, polishing their musical and vocal delivery of the repertoire, and participating in choral performances.

The amateur choral singers who participated in my research certainly valued a collective approach to achieving their goals, and their social learning had a strong impact on their confidence. If, in the following quotation, we were to substitute "conductor" for "teacher," "singers" for "students," and "choir" for "class," we would have an excellent description of what can happen in a collaborative choral rehearsal in which singers and conductors contribute to the learning process:

> The teacher leads the classroom in group improvisations, rather than acting as a solo "performer" in front of the class "audience." Students become socialized into classroom communities of practice, in which the whole class collaborates in each student's learning.[28]

A brief case study will be threaded through the rest of this section, demonstrating the role of the choral CoP in the induction and development of an individual choir member. This real-life example will provide a useful link between my first-hand observations, the findings from my research data, and the concept of the CoP. In this case study, Katrina was a retired schoolteacher who had recently moved to the area and had joined one of my community choirs several months after it was established. She had no previous choral experience, and her progress during her first few months with the group is presented in installments.

Case Study Part 1: A Newcomer

Katrina had received no musical education, and she had no prior experience of singing with other people until a year ago when she joined one of the female choirs that I conduct. She was not confident in pitching, and she doubted her own accuracy. Her vocal tone was pleasant, but she habitually sang in the male tenor range and found it difficult to pitch alongside the other female singers. Learning and remembering a harmony line was a serious challenge because she tended to drift toward the melody, usually singing the tune an octave lower than written, or sometimes in an entirely different key. Finding the starting note was difficult for her, and she often completely lost her bearings, along with her self-confidence.

Katrina's induction into the choir typifies "legitimate peripheral participation" in a CoP.[29] Newcomers participate within their initial limitations, then add to their experience and learn new skills through continued engagement.[30]

They also interact with "old-timers" who have become relative masters in this context and who provide peer modeling and some verbal instruction. In this way, Katrina undertook a musical and choral apprenticeship in which she learned from her fellow singers as well as the conductor.

Case Study Part 2: A Choral Apprentice

Sometimes Katrina stood very near to me so that I could help her pitch because her tone more closely matched mine than that of the female singers. However, she was not entirely happy with this because she wanted to sing along with her peers. Fortunately, two of the more experienced altos took her under their wing and discreetly helped her to adjust her pitch toward theirs. When learning a new song, these singers gestured to indicate "higher" or "lower," and Katrina responded with a smile as she corrected herself. Her improvements were met with enthusiastic encouragement from the other singers. She became sufficiently self-aware to proactively seek help with her tuning, which she usually requested with subtle eye contact between herself and her fellow singers. During tea breaks, some of the singers habitually retired to a quiet corner with Katrina to help her with extra practice of her part and to record the relevant harmony lines on her mobile phone for later review.

Although the apprenticeship model has traditionally implied a linear relationship between a student and a master, additional learning very often occurs between novices and more experienced apprentices even in the absence of formal apprenticeship systems.[31] Katrina's experience provides a longitudinal example of the benefits of interactions between choral novices and "master singers" and the contribution that this can make to the competence and confidence of newcomers.

Case Study Part 3: A Master Singer

Katrina's transformation into a confident choral singer became obvious during a rehearsal in which her two role models were absent. Katrina was singing the alto part with only one other singer and holding her line extremely well. At one point, Vivienne (an experienced musician) struggled to retain the harmony because she had missed the previous two rehearsals. Katrina turned toward her so that Vivienne could hear her vocal line and gestured to demonstrate the pitch direction. Vivienne and Katrina smiled at each other and sang with gusto. Since then, Katrina has happily managed to participate accurately in rehearsals during which she has been the only singer on her vocal line. She has recently adopted a new choir member, mentoring and encouraging this novice in the same way that she was nurtured when she first arrived.

This case study shows that situated learning is not restricted to novices learning from masters: teaching and learning activities are shared by all members of a CoP. Novices learn from each other as well as from more accomplished old-timers, and different members of the community assume the role of master at different times, depending upon their experience and areas of expertise.[32] Because masters in choirs can be fellow singers with varying degrees of experience, as well as conductors, learning and confidence-building are multidirectional processes, encompassing informal peer mentoring and modeling as well as more formal leadership and directed learning. Reciprocal, collaborative learning among singers is therefore of more importance than might be imagined from the traditional, top-down model of a relatively passive choir being taught by a conductor.

Case Study Part 4: A Full Member of the Choral CoP

When Katrina first arrived, some of the singers from other vocal sections privately expressed concern about her unreliability of intonation. Several singers complained about the distraction that this created and suggested that Katrina should be asked to leave. I resisted this because I wanted the choir to be as inclusive as possible. I asked the other singers to be patient because I knew that Katrina was enjoying the rehearsals and beginning to make progress. I could see that the support she was receiving from her neighbors in the alto section was making a significant contribution to her growing self-confidence. Over the following months, Katrina started to pitch increasingly accurately and to learn her notes more quickly. As her confidence increased, the beauty of her vocal timbre began to shine, and she became an asset to the choir. She also started to risk singing a little higher, and her range began to extend. When learning new harmonies, she sometimes still needed extra help, which often came in the form of peer modeling and informal mentoring from her fellow singers. As time went on, the other singers showed their appreciation of her progress, which further enhanced her confidence. This had a positive impact on her performance as she relaxed into her role as a competent and fully participating member of the choir.

Although Katrina provides an example of a successful choral apprenticeship, her case also demonstrates that newcomers may encounter resistance, opposition, and tensions on the way to full integration as effective, confident, and accepted members of a choral CoP. As well as the socially supported learning and confidence-building support described so far, Katrina's example shows that conflicts and tensions do exist within amateur choral ensembles. Some choral group-learning situations may encompass some of the emotions, experiences, and perceptions in this description of the reality of CoPs:

Mutual relations among participants are complex mixtures of power and dependence, pleasure and pain, expertise and helplessness, success and failure, amassment and deprivation, alliance and competition, ease and struggle, authority and collegiality, resistance and compliance, anger and tenderness, attraction and repugnance, fun and boredom, trust and suspicion, friendship and hatred.[33]

Fortunately, relationships between co-learners do not always need to be positive for effective learning to take place. Mutual engagement is a major component of a CoP, but homogeneity is not always necessary. Co-learners do not always need to get along with each other or even to like each other. In fact, diversity can be a positive factor. The tensions, conflicts, disagreements, and challenges inherent in situations involving sustained group interactions can all be defined as modes of participation and mutual engagement and can contribute to the group-learning process. In Katrina's case, by resisting the pressure to ask her to leave, I was giving her the opportunity to learn from experience; to learn from other choral masters as well as from me; to continue her choral apprenticeship; and to progress from peripheral participation to full membership in the choral community. Working through the teething problems as Katrina was integrated led to constructive developments within the whole choir. The singers acquired a more empathic approach to newcomers; adopted a more tolerant attitude to group learning; obtained an understanding that improvements were possible for all participants; and gained a sense of confidence based on full inclusion for everyone.

Katrina's case illustrates a role change from uncertain novice to confident old-timer as she gained choral experience and skill. Her example encapsulates the life cycle of membership in a social learning environment. Newcomers aspire to emulate the performance of their role models and informal mentors, and they often become masters themselves,[34] passing on their own skills to other learners. They also derive additional confidence from an awareness of their contribution to collective learning and achievement.

BUILDING CONFIDENT CHORAL COPS

My interpretation of amateur choirs as CoPs in which group processes support the development of individual and collective confidence has a strong connection with the main principles of self-efficacy theory.[35] Direct, personal experience is usually the most powerful method of altering self-efficacy beliefs. However, modeling by others is an effective route if the models are similar to the observer, as fellow singers in a choir are likely to be. They are all involved in the activity of group singing for pleasure, and all are following a similar amateur career trajectory, even if they are at different stages of their choral journey. Verbal persuasion may also affect self-efficacy beliefs, but its impact depends upon the individual's perception of the credibility of the person delivering the encouragement in terms of their expertise, prestige, assuredness, and trustworthiness. In an amateur choir, there are opportunities for accessing all three of these approaches to improving perceived self-efficacy. As part of their induction into an effective choral CoP, novice singers gain confidence by acquiring practical experience while observing and learning from their peers and receiving verbal encouragement from trusted and respected fellow singers, as well as from the conductor. All of this has practical, philosophical, and pedagogical implications for choral leadership, and some of these will be outlined below.

As we saw in chapter 3, a change of position within the choir can have a dramatic effect upon the confidence of individual singers. This is partly due to the emotionally disruptive effect of losing the support, rapport, and familiarity of regular neighbors. The adverse effects are especially pronounced when singers are separated from their usual team leaders or role models:

> Week in, week out, everyone sits in the same place, for the rehearsal. Then suddenly—dress rehearsal—"Ooh! Totally different!" . . . So that person that you know always gets that entry—"I know she'll do it"—you can at least see her or hear her. And it gives you a little bit more confidence. And it's not there on the performance 'cause she's gone somewhere else—she's down there. And I can't see her mouth! And that actually, for a nervous singer, is quite something really. (Angela)

Although the relationship between choir position, acoustics, and confidence was also discussed in chapter 3, the physical positioning of individual members of the choral team is worth reviewing here because the musical and social interactions within an amateur choir have such a significant impact upon individual and collective confidence. The contribution of informal choral team leaders may be maximized by careful placement of less confident singers next to more confident performers, non-readers next to more accomplished sight readers, or newcomers next to those who are more familiar with the repertoire, according to the needs of the individuals within the group. Since trust and rapport are such key factors in building supportive musical and social relationships, it is also worth considering social dynamics and internal politics within a choir when placing individuals. Trying to balance all these considerations may seem like a tall order for a conductor, but it is likely to pay dividends in terms of enhancing the learning environment, optimizing teamwork, and building a confident choral CoP.

DEVELOPING THE CHORAL COMMUNITY

When assessing the choir as an effective CoP and planning a strategy for collective confidence-building based on cohesion and collaboration, a useful diagnostic question might be "Does the choir have the main elements of community design in place?" The following checklist is based on Wenger's principal components for the design of healthy CoPs,[36] and it includes suggestions for implementation within the choral context.

Strategies and Suggestions for Choral Community Development

- **Events** can bring the community together and foster a sense of teamwork and group identity. For a choir, these will obviously include performances, but social events also play a useful part in cohesion and identity formation and can be helpful in developing a sense of belonging. This can help singers experience trust and rapport within the choir, which facilitates collective learning and confidence-building. Team-building activities can be used to encourage mutual support and validation, respectful communication, and reciprocal peer learning.
- **Internal leadership** is vital to choral confidence and "enabling the leaders to play their role is a way to help the community to develop."[37] Different forms of leadership might be required in different areas—such as networking, planning, and development—and may be shared between various members. In a choral ensemble, the obvious leader is the conductor, often alongside administrative leaders who may or may not hold formal committee positions, depending upon the organizational structure of the choir. However, singers often take on other unofficial practical and educational roles, including acting as informal team leaders or role models, providing informal mentoring, and taking responsibility for the induction of new members. Part of the conductor's contribution to the choral CoP is to foster the development of these informal leadership roles and to incorporate them into the structure and functioning of the choir. Encouraging these contributions from the singers can enhance their sense of control, ownership, and investment in the group. This can increase self-actualizing factors such as pride in their achievements and confidence in their performances.
- **Connectivity** can include brokering relationships between people who can help each other. This can be part of the role of the conductor and can include identifying potentially mutually beneficial mentoring and peer learning relationships and fostering them as part of collective and individual confidence-building. However, in the spirit of collaboration and cooperation, other members of the choral team should be encouraged to make introductions and connect singers who can provide reciprocal support.

- **Membership** can be healthily maintained by enabling novices to become full members of the choral CoP. Questions related to this include: Does the choir have some form of induction process to accommodate new arrivals? Would some kind of befriending system benefit both old-timers and apprentices? Practical tools might include a choir handbook with information about dress codes, rehearsal arrangements, and performance conventions. And for large choirs, a photo book of all the members can help newcomers get acquainted with their fellow singers. These practical measures are likely to contribute to enhanced confidence as individuals are successfully integrated into the choir.
- **Artifacts** such as documents, equipment, and stories are part of a CoP. For a choir, these can include uniforms, folders, sheet music, concert programs, logos, photographs, recordings, and websites. Choral communities may need to reflect on which artifacts are necessary for their growth and development, and who will be responsible for their creation and maintenance. Useful questions to consider include: Does the choir need a librarian, a uniform subcommittee, a publicity manager, a website designer? Do these roles add to the efficiency of the choir and the collective identity of the group? Does performing these roles add to the members' sense of belonging and personal investment in the community and its activities? All of these are important considerations because a sense of belonging, teamwork, and community can increase choral confidence.
- **Learning projects** can help CoPs "deepen their mutual commitment" by taking "responsibility for a learning agenda."[38] For a choir, this can include taking part in workshops; working with other choirs and conductors; learning new repertoire; trying new styles of music or types of performance; watching choral performances together; participating in exchange visits with other choirs; taking part in music festivals or impromptu performances; and organizing choir tours. Such projects are likely to enhance a collective sense of task mastery and to reinforce the singers' identity as choral performers, and they will therefore increase individual and collective confidence.

CHAPTER SUMMARY

For amateur choral singers, peer relationships play an important part in their experience of group singing. These interactions between fellow singers have a strong impact upon the learning processes, performance quality, and confidence levels within a choir. Group cohesion, teamwork, trust, and rapport help to create a collaborative environment in which effective communal learning can take place. All this helps to establish a firm foundation for enjoyable rehearsals and satisfying performances. These provide confidence-building mastery experiences and reflect Bandura's model (see introduction) for improving perceived self-efficacy. Such positive experiences reinforce the participants' identity as singers, affirm their belief in themselves as accomplished choral performers, motivate them to continue learning and performing, and inspire them to invest time and effort in making further progress. All this can create an upward spiral of successful performances, positive emotional responses, increasing competence, and growing self-confidence.

The singers' emphasis on collaboration and teamwork demonstrates a multidirectional process of choral learning and highlights the influence of fellow choir members upon choral confidence. This reliance on other singers for emotional support and encouragement, as well as musical cues, also has links to the participants' observations on the expression and development of confidence through shared nonverbal communication (see chapter 1), and it directly relates to the situational and configurational aspects discussed in chapter 3. Chapter 5 will focus on the conductor's role, focusing on the effect that his or her verbal feedback can have upon confidence levels in the choir.

Chapter Five

Conductors and Verbal Communication

When imagining a conductor, it is probably quite natural for most people to picture to themselves a long-limbed caricature fulfilling the function of an oversized metronome or, even worse, a human windmill. A quick trawl of the Internet reveals that although this may be a wildly inaccurate and outdated parody of a conductor, these images remain prevalent in popular culture. There is no shortage of pictures of conductors making extravagant gestures with seemingly elastic arms, somewhat reminiscent of Marvel's Mr. Fantastic. The word "conductor" still conjures up the archetypal image of the iconic figure standing on a podium, dominating the performers from a great height, and controlling their every move with his or her gestures. Verbal communication does not usually feature in this widespread stereotype.

In public performances—unless something goes unexpectedly wrong—we rarely hear a conductor speak to the singers. Some choral directors may compère their choir's concerts, but otherwise the audience hardly ever hears the conductor's voice. On the other hand, the singers expect to hear frequently from the conductor during rehearsals because verbal instruction and feedback are usually essential aspects of learning the material and polishing the performance. In the previous chapter, I placed conducting rehearsals within a teaching paradigm. This chapter focuses on the conductor's verbal contribution to enjoyable rehearsals, optimal learning, competent performance, and improvement in choral confidence.

Feedback has been described as "one of the most powerful influences on learning and achievement."[1] The following definition is particularly relevant to learning in choral rehearsals and to achievement in public performances:

Feedback is . . . information provided by an agent (e.g., teacher, peer, book, parent, self, experience) regarding aspects of one's performance or under-standing . . . Feedback thus is a "consequence" of performance.[2]

While feedback and encouragement from fellow choir members was of great significance to the singers I interviewed (see chapter 4), the conductor's verbal communication also plays a very important part in choral learning and achievement. The ways in which a conductor's feedback can influence the confidence of his or her choir will now be presented mainly in the singers' own words.

THE SOURCE OF FEEDBACK

I quite enjoy that feedback . . . not only from peers, but from people like [the conductor]—people that know music. (Colin)

The value of verbal feedback and its role in confidence-building arose during all my focus groups and interviews with choral singers. For singers like Leanne, positive feedback is one of the most significant factors in the devel-opment of confidence:

The feedback you know . . . It's great when we've done a performance and everybody says, "That was great. That was really good."

Although feedback from friends and family is appreciated, people who are emotionally close to the singers are often seen as potentially unreliable sources of feedback due to their desire to play a supportive role. Frank's response to praise from his wife was always "Well, you would say that, wouldn't you?" while Colin felt that audiences are not entirely truthful:

I think people—especially people that you know—won't be honest with you, and say, "That was crap." Because people are too nice, aren't they? And sometimes constructive criticism can help you—actually more so than praise.

Nick thought that audiences tend to be mindful of the feelings of amateur singers and give encouragement, regardless of performance quality:

People are there supporting their families, and they know that people are nervous . . . And they'll give you a clap even if you're crap, right? [laughs]. Because that's polite, isn't it?

Many singers believed that opinions from their conductors were more likely to be honest and impartial than feedback from family and friends, which was likely to be biased or flattering. Nina felt validated as a singer by praise from her conductor:

> My mum's always said I could sing, but she's my mum! [laughs]. So you take that with a little pinch of salt. But feedback from the musical director saying, "We need to get you singing some solos and stuff" is worth its weight in gold to me 'cause I respect her, and she's giving that feedback, so I think, "Okay, I'll give it a go!"

When I asked the interviewees an open question about the sources of their confidence, they often talked about positive feedback from conductors. Liz's experience epitomizes self-efficacy theory in action, illustrating the practical associations between positive feedback, task mastery, and increased self-confidence:

> I felt very unsure when I joined the choir because I hadn't sung really for years and years and years. It's just the more you do . . . feedback from yourself [the conductor] when you say, "Hey, that sounded really, really good." . . . Once you know you're successful when you do things, even just you [the conductor] saying, "That's good." . . . If you succeed at something then it gives you confidence, and then you go from strength to strength.

Verbal encouragement is most effective in developing self-efficacy if the person giving the encouragement is seen as trustworthy and credible.[3] Although feedback from respected choral peers is greatly valued by many amateur singers[4] and is an important factor in choral learning,[5] the influence of the conductor cannot be overestimated. The majority of interviewees described "people in the know" as particularly influential sources of verbal feedback:

> I suppose, really, if people like [the conductor], people that know music, that perform, say it's good, that's fine. It's nice for an audience member to do it as well, but if you get it from a professional, that's even more, that's even better. (Andrew)

Some interviewees felt that respecting the opinion of the person providing feedback could be more important than personal rapport. Phoebe saw her conductor as a credible musical expert, and therefore she trusted and valued his opinion despite her personal dislike of his manner:

Even somebody that has been quite harsh and actually quite critical, and very difficult to get on with, like the musical director at [my choir], who's now retired—he was incredibly nasty and sometimes really undermined your confidence. But equally, when he did praise you, or whatever, I actually really liked his praise, because I respected him. So, as harsh as he was, and sometimes as much as I hated him, I actually did respect his ear for music and what he was doing.

The power inherent in feedback from conductors means that their praise can be a strong motivational factor for singers:

The conductor at the time said, "You're one of my best sopranos," which was a real boost, you know. And I thought, "Wow! That's wonderful!" And then I thought, "Well, I must keep this up." (Pam)

The impact of conductor feedback can be magnified in the case of some older adult singers who might be quite alone in their everyday lives, perhaps after a divorce or bereavement, and who may have no significant other to provide support and encouragement for their choral activities. When I asked Celia if she had anybody who is supportive to her singing, or who might give her some feedback after a performance, she said, "No, not really. Apart from what we get from the conductor afterwards." This reinforced for me the importance of trying to provide meaningful and constructive feedback to adult choral singers. The influential nature of feedback from "musical experts" who "know what they're talking about" places a great responsibility on choral conductors. Since their negative and positive feedback are both taken very seriously by amateur singers, conductors can contribute to undermining confidence as well as boosting it.

THE POWER OF PRAISE

The praise . . . Somebody actually saying, "You can do it—don't be frightened of it. You actually can do it and you're doing it quite well" . . . that gives you so much confidence. (Una)

Praise consists of "positive evaluations made by a person of another's products, performances, or attributes," and it is an influential form of social reinforcement.[6] Receiving praise can have beneficial effects on behavior and it can stimulate positive emotions, which can help to raise the recipient's self-esteem.[7] Positive feedback from the conductor is particularly valued by most singers. When asked if there were any things that a conductor might do or say that might affect her confidence, Naomi talked about the benefits of receiving praise from the conductor:

> In a good way—if [it's] positive . . . which is what you [the author] do when we sound good, you tell us.

For Ursula, positive feedback is a counterweight to criticism and a spur to improving performance:

> I think a lot of praise, you know, a lot of "Yeah, that's brilliant! You got that right" 'cause then when [the conductor] says that we didn't get that right, it doesn't feel all negative. So I think it's helpful to give you a lot of praise for the good bits. And also 'cause it helps you to aspire to the good bits if you think, "Yeah, actually, that went well."

Angela had noticed that some conductors, especially those who are used to working with children, do not always recognize the need of adult learners for praise:

> I think sometimes, with adults, peoples' transition into "I'm okay with children but now I'm dealing with adults" is tricky, and they forget that we want to be praised as well.

This is especially important when dealing with amateur singers, who are participating as part of their leisure. Again, Angela explained how she felt about this:

> I do like it when [conductors] say something positive. It may be rubbish, but there must be something positive about it . . . given that it's a pleasure, it's a hobby, it's in your free time . . . Yes, be constructive with your criticism. That's absolutely fine. But please find something nice to say. We want to come out of it on a high.

Although praise from conductors is highly prized by choral singers, it is taken more seriously if it is specific to aspects of their performance rather than simply generalized verbal encouragement. Specific praise provides more detailed information about which aspects of performance have resulted in a positive evaluation. It also shows which aspects the feedback-giver particularly values.[8] The recipient of the feedback is then in a better position to repeat successful performances or continue to make the desired improvements. For example, it is very helpful to the singers if a conductor says,

"Your diction was excellent throughout the last song. I could hear every word this time. And your tuning was much better in the last four bars. Let's do it again and see if we can do it just as well." They know exactly why the conductor is pleased with their performance, and they will be more able to replicate their success than if he or she simply says, "That was great, guys. Well done." Praising specific aspects of a singer's performance, rather than dispensing general praise, is therefore far more constructive and confidence-building.

Routine, nonspecific praise that is repeated frequently and dispensed almost automatically can become meaningless.[9] This can be an occupational hazard for conductors because of the repetitive nature of musical rehearsals,[10] especially in choirs where there are few fluent sight singers and constant repetition is the principal mechanism for learning notes. Adult choral singers interpret generalized, anodyne praise as insincere, and it can cast doubt upon the honesty and credibility of their conductor. Mistrusting their conductor's judgment can lead singers to question the quality of their performance, which then has a negative effect on their perception of their own ability and upon their self-confidence. Singers can harbor serious doubts about a musical director's discernment and integrity when automatic praise seems to have developed into a nervous tic:

> If you're working with somebody that continually says, "That's good. That's good. That's good," you find yourself thinking, "Is it?" (Tim)

Overeffusive praise, coupled with a lack of specific critique, is another source of doubt about the intentions, judgment, or honesty of the conductor. Adult amateur singers are usually perceptive enough to know whether the feedback is sincere:

Barbara: [The conductor] could be very fulsome in her praise after a concert.

Karen: Oh, it was always the best concert ever, so . . . you never knew . . .

Barbara: If there was any truth in it. There was a sort of element that, unless there is some relation to the truth, you know . . . There has to be some criticism along with the praise.

Karen: Some reality.

Barbara: So you know that it's real, that you're not living in cloud cuckoo land about whether you can do it or not. And we don't want to go out and make a racket. We want people to enjoy what we're doing. And we want to do it right.

Karen: Yeah . . . Sometimes you can hear for yourself if something is wrong, can't you? And you don't want to get away with it . . . You need some honesty.

The importance of finding an effective balance of criticism and praise will be discussed further in the next section. For now, here is a summary of the main points about praise-giving in adult amateur choirs.

A Quick Guide to Giving Meaningful Praise

Effective praise is

- specific rather than general
- detailed, so that high-quality choral performances can be replicated
- based on performance-related evaluation rather than on personal attributes
- generous but not overeffusive
- realistic and sincere
- expressive
- varied and creatively articulated rather than repetitive
- delivered thoughtfully rather than as a routine response

BALANCING THE AMOUNT OF POSITIVE AND NEGATIVE FEEDBACK

> The feedback—the confidence comes from somebody actually saying, "Actually, that was good!" And usually people don't do that . . . You don't hear either way. (Frank)

Many choral singers felt that more generous quantities of feedback from their conductor would increase their confidence, and some of them reported a lack of feedback, either positive or negative. Colin felt that more information about his choir's performance would be useful, but he also wondered if the feedback was always genuine, which sometimes made him doubt himself:

> I think it's good to get people to tell you . . . And that doesn't happen very often, believe it or not. People won't be honest with you, when you are singing.

Angela was frustrated by receiving minimal, nonspecific feedback, and she was worried about the implications of this:

Choral society feedback? They'll just say, "There were some good things in it." This is what we get from [our conductor]: "There were some very good things in there." So you know it wasn't very good.

While generosity of praise plays an important part in developing confidence, a shortage of criticism is also problematic for choral singers:

Barbara: You need criticism as well as praise because if you work in a void, where nothing is said, you don't know where you are.

Karen: You feel insecure.

Leanne: Yeah.

Barbara: And I've had that in my working life, where nothing was ever said, one way or the other, about what you were doing, and so you don't know if it's good, bad, or indifferent. And you actually end up as a wreck, because you don't understand it.

Karen: You start doubting yourself.

A healthy balance between praise and criticism can help to establish that the conductor's feedback is genuine and trustworthy. A lack of criticism can lead singers to question their conductor's honesty, judgment, and credibility. These doubts can affect collective and individual confidence:

Karen: [In my community choir] it was a bit anything goes, more or less, you know. There wasn't . . . I didn't feel that [the conductor] was being strict enough with us.

Barbara: Not enough criticism.

Karen: Not enough criticism. And that made me feel uncertain of whether or not I did things right, because . . . I couldn't rely on [the conductor] to say if I did things wrong . . . I had my confidence almost eroded.

Barbara: At one point, she really knocked it out of us.

In educational settings, knowing that a teacher's "silence is never meaningless or innocent to students (they think it either implies tacit approval or signifies condemnation)" reminds us of "the need constantly to say out loud what we're thinking."[11] Likewise, a dearth of any kind of feedback leaves choral singers feeling uncomfortable, uncertain, and apprehensive because they are left trying to guess the conductor's thoughts on their performance quality and progress within rehearsals. Without feedback, the singers also have no idea about the choral director's standards and expectations of them, and they end up relying upon their intuition and imagination to extrapolate what they need to do:

> Thinking about a show recently that I did, the [musical director] was very quiet and didn't say much . . . That didn't feel right. (Tim)

Guesswork is obviously not a reliable source of information about the conductor's opinions. After a rehearsal in which the basses in one of my choirs had been prone to wander from their allotted harmony line, the only bass who had been consistently accurate asked me, "Why did you keep smiling at me tonight?" "Because you were singing so well and managing to stick to your notes regardless of what everyone else was doing," I replied. "Oh!" he exclaimed, "I thought you were trying to tell me that I was in the wrong." From that, I learned that giving clear verbal feedback during rehearsals can be much more effective than relying purely on body language.

Remembering to give generous amounts of straightforward, honest, verbal feedback helps to delineate the performance standards required by the conductor. It also helps to establish trust between the conductor and the singers. Andrew wanted the truth, however painful, from his choral director so that faults could be corrected:

> I think it's to be honest—to be honest with the section . . . So if something isn't right, then say it . . . "Basses, that didn't sound right. Tenors, that timing is wrong, completely wrong." And you go through it.

A lack of specific, realistic criticism, combined with vague verbal encouragement, can seriously undermine the credibility of the conductor and reduce the value of his or her feedback. Frank made it clear that singers are very aware of occasions when a conductor is either avoiding facing reality or not telling the whole truth:

> You don't get the constructive criticism. No. There comes a point where I think he feels he's flogging a dead horse. Very occasionally he'll drop a piece 'cause it really is a nonstarter. But other times we'll just go with it. And you know [a fellow singer] and I are always chatting, and [he'll] say, "That was crap!" And I'll say, "It *was* crap!" [laughs]. And [our conductor] will say, "That's all right. That's nice."

According to the singers I interviewed, the amateur choir's needs for more feedback that is honest and specific are not always met. A lack of specificity in both praise and criticism can cause singers to doubt the conductor's sincerity and credibility and reduce the acceptance and meaningfulness of the feedback. Pamela had very strong feelings about being praised inappropriately while faults were left uncorrected:

> I find constant praise irritating. When things are not good, and the conductor says, "Oh, that was very good." Rubbish! No, be honest. Be honest, and say, "Well, look, I'm not happy with such and such. We have to get this right."

Although singers value realistic, constructive feedback, overcritical approaches usually have a discouraging outcome. Like overeffusive praise, an excessive amount of criticism can reduce the perceived validity of the feedback. Clive felt that the conductor of his male voice choir indulged in needless fault-finding. He wondered if this indicated the limitations of the conductor rather than those of the singers:

> We've had overcriticism, maybe. Or a little bit of nit-picking. [Our conductor] can be a little bit nit-picky. And I think, in a way, I get the impression that when he'll say something probably about the dynamic in a particular piece, or he didn't like them notes there, I think to myself, "Mmmm. Is that all you've got to say? Can't you think of anything else?" Maybe it's just for the sake of having something to say!

Adult amateur singers appreciate a conductor's ability to provide a balanced combination of honest feedback, constructive criticism, praise, and encouragement. This helps to give them confidence in their conductor's judgment and trustworthiness. It also helps them to make progress in response to the feedback and to have confidence that their performance is genuinely improving. Angela offered her own recipe for mixing meaningful feedback with a dash of clarity and mutual respect:

> Well, I think one word of encouragement, and two words of explanation that we can understand, and six criticisms is a formula! [laughs]. I think just one bit of praise will cover quite a lot of other stuff, but don't just keep [impersonates a conductor growling and cracking a whip]. And not be patronizing, but be clear with your explanation . . . Yeah. Just be a bit more human. But praise of any sort is what everybody thrives on, you know—even the dog!

Like Angela, most singers expressed a desire for larger amounts of praise and more detailed verbal feedback from their conductors. Generous amounts of specific positive feedback help to establish trust and rapport, create a collaborative learning environment,[12] improve performance quality, build self-confidence among the singers, and encourage the singers to have confidence in their conductor. This contrasts with some music education research in which high levels of "teacher talk" had a negative effect on the students' attentiveness, achievement, and emotions.[13] This may partly be due to the focus of my research, as most of the previous research on conductor feedback has been related to attainment and attention in classroom settings rather than to confidence levels among adult amateur singers.

Some of the research into school and college classroom situations is not transferrable to adult amateur choral rehearsals because of differences in age and motivation. Some music education studies have found that schoolchildren and students usually obtain adequate positive reinforcement simply from participating in musical activities.[14] They generally prefer this intrinsic reward to verbal interaction;[15] their priority tends to be to keep playing or singing rather than listening to their teachers talking. Performing successfully can provide useful intrinsic feedback, and for university-level musicians, this is often sufficient to reduce performance anxiety and to allow them to achieve a state of flow.[16] This usually helps to reduce self-consciousness and increase self-confidence (see chapter 2). However, for amateur choral singers, the feedback derived from the performance itself is not always sufficient to build their confidence. They are more reliant upon external sources of feedback, particularly from trusted peers[17] and their conductors.

CONSTRUCTIVE CRITICISM

Criticism is often divided into two contrasting categories, usually described as "constructive" and "destructive." In my focus groups and interviews, there was widespread agreement among the singers that more constructive criticism would be useful, and that destructive criticism is never helpful. The following definitions explain why this is the case.

Constructive criticism is "specific in content" and "considerate in tone," makes "no attributions concerning the causes behind the subjects' poor performance," and "contains no threats."[18] Conversely, destructive criticism is more general in content, inconsiderate in tone, attributes poor performance to personal factors, and sometimes includes threats. Unsurprisingly, confidence is more negatively affected by receiving destructive criticism than by constructive criticism, and emotional reactions to destructive criticism often impair performance. This becomes part of a cycle of declining performance quality and diminishing confidence. Constructive criticism does not have the same negative impact, however, which suggests that "it is not the delivery of negative feedback, per se, that produces such effects; rather, the manner in which such information is conveyed seems to play a crucial role."[19]

Constructive criticism is expected, and even welcomed, by most singers. Clive explained his philosophical attitude to this:

> I'm not offended by negatives. If they say, "That's not right, we'll have to do it again," that doesn't bother me . . . At least if it's constructive criticism, then that's fine.

Singers view criticism as constructive when it is detailed, performance-specific, delivered in a positive manner, and counterbalanced with praise. Barry gave an example of this from his experience with a community choir:

> If [conductors] just stood there and listened and criticized, and you didn't get any positive feedback, then that would knock your confidence a bit. When criticism's constructive, you don't mind. And the sort of things that [my conductor] said were constructive criticism . . . It was a very slow song and it needed to be smooth, and we were hopping along. And she said, "Oh, it needs to be smoother than that. Let it flow." That sort of thing you don't mind. Because when you do it again, you do it like that and she goes, "Great!"

Justified constructive criticism from the conductor is generally accepted quite cheerfully, while undeserved negative feedback has an unsettling effect and can cause resentment among the singers:

> If it's right, then it doesn't really worry me 'cause I like to get it right . . . If you feel it's unjust, then it rattles you a bit, but you move on. As long as it's justified, I think. (Frank)

Several singers gave examples of the content and delivery of constructive criticism that they found helpful. Matt felt that it should be done "in such a way that it's a pleasant conversation" and that "a positive manner" is essential when giving negative feedback. Because the style of delivering negative feedback can be more influential than the content, it has a strong effect upon the reception and impact of the feedback. Harry felt that his conductor's "gentlemanly" style of communication was helpful in maintaining a cooperative and upbeat atmosphere:

> Our conductor is a very gentle, good rehearser. He doesn't coerce anybody. He's a noncoercer. "Very good, but . . ." is the line, you know, rather than "You were singing flat!"

Pamela described her ideal experience of both criticism and praise from a conductor:

> If a section's doing really well, to say, "I like it. I want it just like that." Or if somebody's too loud, to quieten them down. To make contact in a nice way, so that people's feelings aren't hurt.

Like praise, constructive criticism helps to foster confidence among amateur singers if it is related to specific aspects of their performance because it then helps them to understand the conductor's expectations and provides detailed information about how to make improvements.

A Quick Guide to Giving Constructive Criticism

To be effective, criticism needs to be

- specific rather than general
- based on performance-related evaluation rather than personal attributes
- detailed
- considerate in tone
- honest without being painfully blunt
- delivered with good humor
- nonthreatening and noncoercive
- varied and creative rather than repetitive
- accompanied by suggestions about how to improve the singers' performance

DESTRUCTIVE CRITICISM

As well as building confidence and encouraging choral singers, the authoritative nature of conductor feedback can have a marked demotivating or dispiriting effect on singers, especially when destructive criticism is used. This can include personal rather than performance-related critique, feedback that is lacking in respect and consideration for the singers, and criticism that feels threatening to the recipient. The impact of destructive feedback is compounded if individuals are singled out for public criticism. Frank remembered a conductor's tactless way of correcting individual errors and the devastating results of this:

> [Our musical director] once picked out a guy . . . We were doing some [Gilbert and Sullivan], and he said, "I can hear somebody not quite right," and he homed in on it . . . and he didn't quite go, "And it's you!" But it was like that.

And this guy was destroyed by it. He never came back. He left after that rehearsal because he felt he'd been singled out.

Similar incidents, in which choral singers had been deterred from continuing to participate, featured in several interviews. This kind of public criticism was sometimes out of proportion to the perceived error and did not necessarily reflect the skill of the singer concerned:

> We did some particularly technically difficult work, and [my friend] repeatedly made some mistake in the diction, in a particular place, and the conductor got off the stage, walked straight across to my friend, stood in front of her and said [bangs table violently], "No! That's such and such!" And my friend said, "Oh, I felt so awful. In front of everybody." And [she] lost her confidence. And she's since left. And I'm really sad about it. She had a nice voice, with quite a bit of depth to it, you know. (Pamela)

Several singers told me about instances in which they had left choirs for this reason:

> I was with [a choir] for about four years, an absolutely fantastic choir, but the pressure was so enormous. [The conductor had] to win everything; everything had got to be perfect and she would point out, she would stick her finger— fortunately I was never on the front—she would pick people out and criticize and the pressure got so great I thought I'd burst. She had a go at one of my friends and [my friend] said, "I don't like this." And I said, "No, I don't like this." So we both made a joint decision that we wouldn't go anymore and it was such a relief. (Doreen)

Although these interviewees later found other opportunities to sing, being singled out for public criticism had far-reaching effects upon their confidence. Participants in one of the focus groups shared their experiences of this:

> Una: A musical director dressed me down in front of [everyone] and . . . I was never going to sing again. It really knocked my confidence and I thought, "If that's what they think of me I don't want to come anymore."

> Beryl: "I must be rubbish" . . . You get that feeling, "I must be rubbish."

In some instances, individually targeted destructive criticism permeated the singers' faith in their own general vocal and musical ability as well as having an adverse effect on their confidence in themselves as choral performers. The following focus group extract describes bullying, harassment, and personal victimization:

> Barbara: I think your name was the first one I learned in [choir] because [the conductor] was always saying, "Karen, you've got it wrong!"
>
> Karen: She always would. If anything went wrong, it was always my fault. And then I really began thinking I was a really awful singer, and that I couldn't hear if I was wrong, because I went home and listened to my recordings and it sounded right to me, and yet I was always told I was wrong! And then one day, someone next to me said, when she was saying it again, "But you were not even singing that part!" And suddenly the penny dropped, that I was just, you know . . . It was a personal thing.
>
> Barbara: It was a personal thing. And if you feel you're being victimized, like that . . .
>
> Karen: And I really got so insecure that I really thought . . . I recorded everything I was doing, and I listened to it, and I thought, "To me, it sounds right." And then I thought, "Oh, maybe I haven't got any sense of music. Maybe I can't hear if it's wrong!" And I began to doubt my own ability.

Constantly singling out a particular section of the ensemble also has destructive effects on performance quality and choral confidence. Phoebe described it like this:

> I think sometimes conductors can really undermine the confidence not just of individuals but of certain groups—so the soprano group or, you know, whoever is the weakest link. They can really undermine their confidence, and that just makes the group underperform even more. So I think it's got to be done in the right way.

Andrew gave several examples of different male voice choir conductors who repeatedly knocked the confidence of sections, individuals, and the whole ensemble:

> [This conductor] used to do it all the time. If not individuals, it was certainly sections. [He] would show up sections. And I think that's not helpful . . . This guy used to really be quite nasty. And he used to lose his rag when, say, the basses or the baritones didn't get it right . . . He would do it line by line. In fact, sometimes he would do it even half a line . . . "These three do it. You three do it" . . . His predecessor—he used to do the same . . . It hurt, you know. If you didn't get it right . . . If you didn't get it right, he would belittle you . . .

People used to think, "Oh shit," and they used to be afraid then, to actually sing out, because they were afraid to get it wrong.

Singers unanimously characterized destructive criticism as demotivating and likely to affect their confidence levels adversely, not only regarding specific performances but in relation to their general self-efficacy for singing. Ursula's choral society always rehearsed with a chorus master who was replaced by another conductor for all their public performances:

The [conductor] who takes it on the night [of the concert]—he comes in on the penultimate rehearsal, and I think every time we've gone away and said, "Actually, I'm not going to come on Sunday. There's no point. We're just rubbish. I don't know what I'm supposed to be doing. I don't know my words. I don't know my notes." And it seems to be, yeah, that your confidence . . . my confidence drops, and I think, "I'm not going to do it!"

This conductor's negative effect on the choir's morale is explained by his tempestuous style of communication:

[The conductor] does throw himself around and stamp a lot. I mean, in time with the music, but really . . . there's a lot of histrionics. And I think it makes us all feel . . . On the basis that we all get it wrong, I assume that we all feel that we're just useless.

These scenarios were surprisingly common, and many singers used strongly emotive language to describe them. Their feelings of being "victimized," "belittled," "hurt," "undermined," "afraid," and "destroyed" indicate the damage to confidence that results from feedback that is inconsiderate or threatening in tone and that attributes poor performance to personal factors. Destructive criticism like this creates a downward spiral of inhibited responses, impaired performance, reduced task mastery, and low self-confidence.

Although earlier research proposed that adult musical participation is largely predicted by early life experiences,[20] more-recent studies of adult amateur musicians demonstrate the significance of later events. Musical identity development is now seen as an ongoing process that continues throughout our lifetime.[21] The effect of verbal feedback on adult amateur singers can therefore be substantial. It can add to their self-confidence as vocal performers and reinforce their identity as accomplished choral singers. Sadly, it can also have the opposite effect.

COMMUNICATION STYLE

Criticism is, predictably, more acceptable to amateur choral singers when delivered in a thoughtful, considerate, and nonthreatening manner. Common sense tells us that no singer will perform well or enjoy the experience while feeling humiliated or under threat. Equally self-evident is the fact that everyone responds better to respectful communication. Ideally this is based on rapport, reinforces mutual trust, and is designed to have constructive outcomes. To paraphrase Bananarama's advice on getting results, It ain't what you say it's the way that you say it!

Ursula was one of many singers who articulated the fact that mutual respect is key to a good working relationship between conductors and choirs:

> I think it's got to be mutual respect. And I think sometimes you get conductors who just have a hint of being a bit too much of "the maestro" [indicating quotation marks]. You know, come on, it's just a small choir in [name of town]! And you need to feel as though you're an important part of the set-up, really. So I would look for someone who does respect you, and can still command respect himself.

Respect between the singers and the conductor can be eroded, along with their self-confidence, if the conductor's approach toward the choir is not appropriate to the age and ability of the members. Andrew pointed out that this works both ways because singers are bound to lose respect for a conductor who does not behave respectfully:

> [The conductor] was a teacher, and he had seventy men which he treated like boys . . . He was well respected for his musical ability, but he wasn't respected for the way he treated people. And, quite honestly, that upset a lot of people.

Many participants highlighted situations in which they had been treated like children by their conductors, especially by those who were teachers in their day jobs. In Celia's choral society, this did not go down well at all:

> [The conductor] used to get a bit petulant with us and treat us sometimes like he would the children, I think. And because we're adults, and most of us ladies were older than him [laughs], we took umbrage really.

Angela's choral society conductor was also a school teacher who displayed a condescending attitude toward the adults in his choir:

And, not be patronizing, but be clear with your explanation. And getting radgy [irritable], you know [impersonates conductor muttering under his breath], and then standing there with that supercilious "I'm waiting for you to stop chattering" . . . and deliver that in a patronizing way as well, you know [mimics pompous conductor]: "I've got some notices here and you just have a bit of a chat—okay, that'll do!" [claps hands authoritatively].

Conductors who treat adult choir members like children were contrasted with those who adopt a more facilitative, egalitarian, and respectful attitude. Harry, who had over fifty years of wide-ranging choral experience, compared these different attitudes to delivering verbal feedback. He also suggested a couple of alternative approaches that were more likely to yield positive results:

[Conductors] sometimes [assuming schoolmasterly tone] "Now we're going to have to bash through this to get this one right!" [groans]. So it needs to be the positive, musical approach. And not the blamey approach. It's the approach that says, "I'm all right and you're all right." Not "I'm all right but you lot are not. I've got to work on you!"

The schoolmasterly approach can sometimes become dictatorial, with very negative results as far as mutual respect and collective confidence are concerned. Singers reported that these confrontational approaches often had a negative effect on the rehearsal environment. Phoebe's conductor's personal criticism and aggressive manner caused Phoebe to question her motivation for singing:

I have worked with conductors that just . . . well, it's totally unreasonable. They rant. They absolutely rant. And it gets really quite personal. And it's sort of a case of, you know, "I may as well pack my bags and go home. I don't come and do this for this, that and the other"—total ranting. And obviously that undermines your confidence. And you stand there and think, "What am I doing here? Why am I putting myself through this?" So, I think that's not great.

Celia felt that "petulance" and "having a hissy fit . . . doesn't work with older people," although I would argue that it is not effective or professional in any situation. Respectful verbal feedback, phrased considerately and delivered appropriately for adult participants, helps to establish a positive rehearsal environment and to develop confident performance. Sadly, this was often most clearly illustrated when singers gave examples of less positive styles of conductor communication. When comparing various past conductors, Andrew concluded that aggressive and dictatorial behavior were not preconditions for choral success:

> He used to bang the table and say, "This is not . . ." you know—especially if we were leading up to a competition, then he used to go ape-shit. [His successor] was entirely different. He was a school teacher, but he was a different persona completely. And everybody had great respect for [him]. And, to be honest, technically, he wasn't far off [his more aggressive predecessor]. He was as good as [him] and he took the choir to some good concerts and competitions, and we won, so there's nothing to be said for it, that aggression.

Ursula said, "It's important they make you feel comfortable. I mean, [the singers] don't have to be there. So they can't conduct a choir if there isn't a choir to conduct." Andrew agreed that as amateur singers participate in choirs as part of their leisure, they do not expect musical goals to be attained at the expense of enjoyment or respect:

> Even though [the conductor] was good at what he did, and the choir was probably the best it had ever been, there was this animosity against him because he was such a condescending, patronizing bloke, you know what I mean? And so therefore there's a balance between certainly knowing your music but treating people with the respect that they deserve. 'Cause we're all volunteers, at the end of the day.

The voluntary nature of amateur choral singing may account for the amounts of praise and constructive criticism that are most useful for confidence-building among adult amateur singers. While negative feedback can sometimes be effective in obligatory activities, largely due to avoidance considerations, positive feedback is usually more effective in voluntary pursuits.[22] An overdose of negative feedback often results in withdrawal from voluntary pastimes, as demonstrated by the singers who left their choirs because of destructive criticism, particularly when delivered publicly and with personal connotations.

Tips for Avoiding Giving Destructive Criticism

- Avoid singling out individual singers or small sections of the choir for criticism.
- Deliver any critical comments respectfully and thoughtfully.
- Use age-appropriate content, language, and style when delivering a critique.

- Try to adopt an egalitarian and facilitative approach to delivering feedback.
- Adopt the "I'm all right and you're all right" perspective rather than the "I'm all right but you're not" perspective.
- Deliver all feedback calmly, objectively, and considerately.
- If you are tempted to give a searing critique, take a deep breath and count to ten!

INDIVIDUAL NEEDS WITHIN THE CHOIR

Since their choral singing is part of their leisure, amateur singers often prioritize the creation of a relaxed atmosphere, with some opportunities for social interaction, and a conductor's use of humor can be helpful with this. Sonia had been rather wary of joining my open-access women's choir until she realized that I generally adopt a light-hearted approach to rehearsing:

> When I first started I thought, "If they get cross or if everything's a bit serious, I'm not gonna like this. But the first time you went into your fits of giggles I thought, "No, we'll be all right" [laughs]. Because okay, it's all gone wrong, so what. Let's have a giggle and then we'll try again. Then I thought, "Okay, it's going to be fine" 'cause I can't take too much seriousness. It's not good for me.

On the other hand, it was important to Andrew that while rehearsals in my mixed chamber choir were fun, there was also enough discipline to allow the choir to make progress:

> We have a bit of a laugh, and you close it down if it gets too bad. And you have a laugh as well with us . . . When something goes wrong . . . there's normally a bit of banter goes across the sections, that we enjoy. 'Cause you have to. But then, when the learning needs to be done, we get down to the nitty gritty of it.

Andrew and Sonia had subtly different expectations of the amount of "seriousness" and "banter" that they preferred during rehearsal. It is important for conductors to be aware of these variations in preferences, to assess their own choir's needs for social as well as musical interaction, and to try to accommodate these when communicating with the singers. Other participants discussed the importance of matching the conductor's approach to the ability of the singers and of having realistic expectations of adult amateur choirs. Frank told me about a conductor who had sped through rehearsals with a choir who had been drawn together specifically for a one-off fund-raising concert:

I mean, you can always do with a bit more rehearsal but . . . I just thought, "Cor, blimey! What standard does he think we are?!" I mean, we were just a scratch choir!

When taking over a new choir, it is always worth taking time to get to know the singers' strengths and weaknesses before committing to a concert program. Barry felt that his conductor was expecting too much of the singers. This can make them feel inadequate, knock their confidence, and impair their enjoyment:

I think the new leader wanted to move along too quickly. I think what she'd done was she'd committed herself to a performance and had been a bit ambitious in the time scale. And she was trying to do all these new songs, with harmonies . . . and we just couldn't keep up . . . and she kept saying, "Come on. Sing the song with me. I'm dragging you along!" 'cause we were having to wait for the note on there [indicates keyboard] so that we knew what to sing. So she was playing it and then we were catching up, so she was dragging us along. So I thought, "Ooh, no. No, no. We can't keep up with this." It was just hard work.

These problems can arise even with well-established conductors who have been working with their choir for some time. Frank remembered some demoralizing rehearsals with his regular conductor at a large choral society:

[The conductor] comes in, goes through the line, goes "La la la," sopranos "La la la"—'cause they're all fine 'cause they're singing the tune—basses "La la la." "Right, now we'll do it!" And that's it, you know! . . . You just got the impression "I'm not going to spend any more time on this! This is enough! You've done it!" As though he was with a professional chorus . . . We all felt pretty ropey!

These examples illustrate some of the dangers of providing minimal feedback and limited instruction. This can be due to time pressures or over-ambitious targets, but it gives the impression that the conductor has not taken account of the needs of the singers. It also implies that he or she cannot be bothered to provide more detailed information to help them to improve their performance. This can be very frustrating and dispiriting for the singers, and it can reduce their confidence in themselves and in the conductor.

Although some amateur singers are highly skilled and experienced and may have received musical training, others may have no previous choral experience or musical education at all. Feedback and verbal instruction are only effective if they are pitched at an appropriate level and delivered in a way that facilitates positive feelings among the singers. Angela felt that some conductors made too many assumptions about the skills and knowledge of the singers in their choirs:

> They forget that there's a lot of us that are kind of [whispers] very amateur . . .
> It's much better if somebody [explains musical terms and symbols] and
> doesn't assume that [we know] what it's all about.

She appreciated that her new choral society conductor had started to familiarize the singers with some of the technical aspects of choral singing rather than making assumptions about their pre-existing knowledge:

> Those kind of things I'm now beginning to understand because [our conduc-
> tor] is using the words—instead of just saying whatever and expecting that we
> all know, he's actually explaining it.

The pros and cons of using musical jargon were discussed in detail in chapter 4. However, it is worth repeating here that for some singers, musical terminology is a mystery and its overuse can obscure the meaning of verbal feedback. Conductors can help to demystify musical terms by providing brief explanations, when time permits. Alternatively, by using the terms in a clear context, they can enable singers to extrapolate the meaning for themselves.

Even when the conductor has considered the musical and social needs of an adult amateur choir and tried to pitch his or her teaching and communication style appropriately, it is still a challenge to account for the different learning styles, skill levels, experience, and learning abilities that coexist within a mixed group of amateur singers. Doug was aware of these variations within his choir:

> Some people can maybe pick it up fairly quickly and are on the ball maybe
> after a run through, but not everybody might be the same. Really, it takes me a
> bit longer to get to the heart of the matter.

Andrew recognized that trying to cater to the diverse requirements of adult amateur singers can sometimes be difficult for a conductor:

> When you've got a choir of seventy, and you've got lots of readers, and lots of
> non-readers, and people that take longer to learn it, then your tolerance . . .
> you're gonna lose your rag aren't you?

He recommended a patient approach, from the singers as well as the conductor, that allows for the different learning needs of individual choir members:

> Some of us take longer to learn something than others. Therefore, you're as good as your slowest learner, I suppose, aren't you? To a certain extent. To carry that slowest learner for a bit longer, until he gets it.

Singers also vary regarding their personal reaction to criticism and praise. In response to destructive criticism, some individuals increase their efforts, while others suffer reductions in performance quality, motivation, and self-efficacy.[23] Likewise, the way in which singers interpret praise can vary individually, creating a range of emotional and cognitive responses that can affect their performance and self-confidence.[24] Some singers simply may not apply feedback constructively, and others may react defensively to criticism, especially if they prioritize reinforcing their self-belief above fulfilling musical learning goals.[25]

A singer's general self-efficacy or confidence may also affect their response to feedback. Highly self-efficacious learners respond well to positive feedback that is delivered at an early stage of the learning process. This helps them cope with subsequent negative feedback and react constructively. Less self-efficacious learners are demotivated by early positive feedback because they fear that their future performances of the task may be less successful.[26] Learners with low self-efficacy are also more likely to experience negative emotions when negative feedback is received and to attribute their perceived failure to ability rather than effort.[27] This means that they tend to interpret negative feedback as a personal slur rather than as a spur to work on improving their performance. This will be the case if a singer believes that their ability is finite rather than seeing their own potential for development.[28] To counteract this, it is important to emphasize that singing is a skill that can be developed rather than a fixed, unchanging "talent."[29] Most people can make improvements to their vocal performance with regular practice and a little guidance. Due to time pressures and the constraints of working with larger groups, choral conductors are not usually in a position to train individuals to improve their vocal technique. However, providing regular, gentle vocal warm-ups can help singers to feel prepared for the demands of choral rehearsal and performance and may help them to feel more secure in their vocal ability (see chapter 2).

Ross pointed out that a singer's personal ability to cope with criticism can vary according to his or her physical and psychological state. He appreciated the occasions when his conductor recognized this and responded appropriately:

Some nights I'm absolutely [exhausted] . . . But in general you [the author] seem to sense that, and therefore you don't criticize me when I'm clearly not in a fit state to be singing, and probably shouldn't have bothered coming [laughs]. And I just want to get down to the pub and have a couple of pints, you know!

He remembered being very sensitive to verbal feedback when he first started singing in a choir after a long break from performing. He attributed his increased capacity to deal with this feedback to the trust and rapport that he and I had now developed. When I asked Ross what kind of comments might affect his confidence during a rehearsal, this was his reply:

In the early days, anything! [laughs]. Just the fact that you decided you had to have a word with me, suggests I'm not doing it right. And therefore, "Oh shit! I knew I couldn't cope with this." Whereas now I think I'd be reasonably balanced. I don't think it would knock my confidence. And I think that's just 'cause of the relationship that you and I have . . . Because you're my teacher and my mentor, or whatever, in a musical sense, then I've got a relationship where I don't worry . . . You wouldn't say something unless it needed saying.

Ross felt that getting used to their musical director's personality and modus operandi can help singers to accept and interpret feedback. Likewise, getting to know the singers and being able to interpret their moods and receptivity to feedback can help conductors phrase their criticism and praise appropriately. Regarding getting to know the singers, Angela mentioned basic social skills that we take for granted in everyday life, that is, recognizing and acknowledging the people we meet:

I mean, a conductor in a big group, doesn't necessarily know you individually—I find that slightly unnerving, in that they are a bit remote. And sometimes you think, "Week after week, for I don't know how many years, you have been conducting me, and then I see you in the street, or I see you at school, or I see you wherever it is, and you don't acknowledge me." And I'm thinking, "Hello!" And they just look at you, and you think, "Am I really anonymous? Have you really never noticed me?"

Angela found this sense of anonymity very disconcerting; it made her feel insignificant, as if she did not matter to her choral society conductor. She compared this distant attitude to that of other conductors who validate their singers by the simple process of getting to know their names:

Compare and contrast that with the person who conducts us in [my other choir]—the choir mistress at church, who I know incredibly well—she's taught my daughter this and that, and it's all very matey—nobody could sneak in there and not be known by name . . . [a] busy lady, but knew us all by name.

This is not rocket science, but it does help the singers feel as if they belong and have value within their choirs, which can contribute to their self-confidence as choral singers. Other aspects of the conductor's role, though, are less straightforward, and these will be considered later in this chapter. For now, here are some strategies for getting to know your singers.

Tips for Getting to Know the Singers and Establishing Rapport

- When a new choir member arrives, ask them about their singing experience and their perception of their voice—and their name!
- If you are new to a choir, try to get to know the singers by showing an interest in their musical background—and establish trust by being reassuring if their musical experience and training happens to be minimal.
- Get to know the names of the singers as quickly as you can. If your memory for names is not reliable, provide name badges for the singers until you have learned most of them.
- In large choirs, a photobook of all the participants with their names and voice types attached can help everyone to get to know each other.

Exercises for Learning Names

- Ask the singers to stand in a circle. Set up a steady clapping or stamping rhythm. On the strongest beat of the pattern call out your own name. The singers should then take it in turns to do the same, progressing clockwise around the circle.
- Set up the same circle and rhythmic pattern. Make eye contact with one of the singers and call out his or her name. He or she should then do the same with one of their fellow singers so that you end up playing a figurative game of "pass the parcel" with the singers' names. If you are working with a new choir or singers who do not yet know each other well, it would be useful to distribute name badges before doing this exercise.

ACCOUNTING FOR CHORAL DIVERSITY

Providing a helpful amount of honest and detailed feedback with an optimal balance of constructive criticism and praise that is delivered in an appropriate style and at a suitable level for the singers (while accounting for individual needs) is a formidable but stimulating task. Several singers acknowledged the demands, for their conductors, of working with mixed-ability amateur choirs composed of individuals from a wide range of musical, educational, cultural, and social backgrounds. Pamela had this advice for conductors:

> You've got to remember that people who sing come from all walks of life. Some are very academic, some are very practical . . . They're different people. Different characters coming together. But they're coming together to sing.

All adult learners, whether they are learning to make pottery at a summer school, completing a master's degree in accounting, or singing in a choir, have different needs and priorities,[30] and these can become increasingly divergent with increased life experience.[31] Not all amateur choral groups are comparable because the membership of such groups varies and adult singers have an infinite range of different personal traits. Responses to feedback, and preferences regarding praise and criticism, are also subject to individual variations. These include how confident the singers are in the first place, their general mood when they receive the feedback, and their age and experience.

Some of the principles of teaching adults in other contexts apply to amateur choral rehearsals. These include taking into account the experience, knowledge, and insight of adult learners and adopting a collaborative, facilitative approach to suit the composition of the group (see chapter 4).[32] This requires flexibility on the part of group leaders[33] and a willingness to adapt their teaching or leadership style to suit the needs of adult singers.[34] In other areas of adult learning, the interpersonal qualities and teaching style of group leaders are often more significant than the lesson content,[35] and this also seems to be true for adult amateur choral singers.

Providing confidence-building verbal feedback in amateur choirs necessitates considering the needs of the individual singer as well as the whole group. This requires empathic attempts to view feedback from the perspective of the members and trying to target it to an appropriate level for the recipients. A helpful approach is to consider your style of communication and the balance between positive and negative feedback within the context of the amateur singers' needs for developing self-confidence, meeting their performance goals, and acquiring new musical skills and repertoire in a social learning environment. Choral leaders may also need to develop a range of teaching strategies and organizational approaches so that they can accommodate the spectrum of needs, skills, experience, confidence levels, modes of learning, and responses to verbal feedback that usually exist within a mixed group of adult amateur singers.

As if all this were not challenging enough, a complicating factor is that group feedback of the kind that a choral ensemble generally receives can be "confounded by perceptions of relevance to oneself or to other group members,"[36] which can reduce the effectiveness of the feedback.[37] Choral singers may interpret praise or criticism as relevant to themselves as individuals, to the whole choir, or to other members of the ensemble exclusively. Bearing in mind the universal dislike, among choral singers, of singling out individuals or small sections of the choir for criticism, it is wise to avoid this where possible. One of the most useful tools is specific, task-oriented criticism that helps singers to understand what needs to be improved and how they can achieve this rather than making them feel that they are personally under fire.

Tips for Working with Adult Choirs of Mixed Ability

- Remember that adult amateurs attend choirs as part of their leisure; consider their social expectations as well as their achievement needs.
- Consider the age, experience, and skill levels of the singers. Set suitable goals and give appropriate feedback.
- Observe the choir carefully when teaching them a new song. Learn about their individual and collective strengths and weaknesses.
- Try to set goals appropriately so that the singers are challenged enough to maintain their interest but are also comfortable enough to enjoy their singing.
- Remember to give explanations of musical terminology, and demonstrations of technical points, if the singers seem to be in any doubt.
- Observe the behavior and emotional reactions of singers during rehearsals and performances. Try to identify how the singers learn most effectively and what helps them to sing most confidently.
- Try to develop a rapport with the singers so that you get to know how their moods affect their performance and so that you can react sympathetically and constructively.
- Never prioritize musical achievement over the emotional, psychological, or physical well-being of the singers.

PAUSE FOR REFLECTION

With great power comes great responsibility.
—Voltaire

Some of the interview and focus group extracts in this chapter will no doubt have been uncomfortable to read. Some of the singers' reports on the impact of feedback (or lack of it) from conductors is, at the very least, worrying and, in some cases, quite disturbing. Even if our own style of communication is impeccable, it is sobering to consider the powerful effect that our words and behavior potentially have upon the emotions and confidence levels of the singers we conduct.

Carrying out these interviews has impressed upon me that choral conductors, sometimes unwittingly, wield a great deal of authority. This can create unforeseen as well as intended consequences every time we communicate with our choirs. The power inherent in all verbal communication from conductors therefore places a great responsibility upon all conductors. This power is partly derived from our status, among the choirs we conduct, as musical experts and leaders. Because the singers see us as experts in the choral domain, they trust and respect our opinions and take our feedback seriously. Empirical research in other fields has shown that the credibility and status of assessors as perceived experts significantly affect the acceptance and value of their criticism and praise. In fact, the perceived status of the feedback provider can be as influential as the content of the feedback.[38]

The quotations in this chapter will no doubt have provided food for thought for all conductors, whether or not we have ever indulged in any of the more extreme behaviors described in some of the interviews. For me, simply learning that some choral directors habitually use various forms of destructive feedback has given me serious cause for contemplation. There is certainly plenty of ground for reflection on the way in which some conductors reportedly interact with amateur singers and on why this might happen.

It is possible that some of the reported problems may be associated with training, or lack of it. Until comparatively recently, very few British musicians were "first study" conductors, and there was relatively little systematic training for this demanding field of expertise. Despite the introduction of specific conductor training in some higher education institutions, not all conductors of amateur choirs have had the benefit of this. In the United Kingdom, there are alternative routes to conductor training via commercial organizations, but access to courses may be limited by time commitments, geographic location, and financial considerations. Even those who have received formal conductor training during their academic studies may not have been trained with the expectation that they would conduct anything other than a professional ensemble of some kind. Getting ready for life after an intensive musical education does not always include preparation for the reality that most conductors will work with amateur groups at some point.

Personally, I would strongly recommend that all budding choral conductors work with at least one adult amateur choir as part of their training since amateur choral singing is the most accessible and widespread form of musical participation.[39] Conducting adult amateur group singing activities can provide experience in a wide range of performances, teaching and learning situations, and choral repertoire. It can also provide priceless training in a variety of musical and interpersonal skills and can aid in the consolidating of existing skills. I also recommend shopping around for an affordable but reputable training course. If this is not available, it can be invaluable to recruit an experienced choral director to act as a mentor and role model and to watch (and participate in) as many choral rehearsals and performances as possible. However, training is not the only solution to the problems described in this chapter because some of the featured conductors had received training of some kind. Also, there are many untrained conductors who are very proficient and who maintain an exemplary rapport with their choirs. Other factors in ineffective conductor communication may simply include lack of experience with adult amateur choirs or the conductor's own confidence issues. Conversely, overconfidence may also affect how some conductors relate to their choirs. Some of the teaching frameworks discussed in the next chapter may be helpful for developing facilitative relationships with amateur singers and might be recommended to inexperienced or trainee conductors.

In case you were wondering, I did not ask the interviewees loaded or leading questions about choral directors. When I presented my work at a conductors' conference at the University of Oxford, I was asked if I had "invited singers to bitch about their conductors"! The answer to this is no, I did not ask anyone to tell me about all the awful things that their choir leaders might do or say. All the quotations in this chapter arose from nondirective, open questions. In the focus groups, I asked singers to tell me about "any individuals who have had a positive or negative effect" on their confidence. Because the focus group participants had a lot to say about conductors, I included two related questions in the subsequent one-to-one interviews: "What characteristics or behavior might be helpful in a conductor? and What might not be so helpful?"

The final quotation in this section comes from Andrew as he summarizes some of the main prerequisites for confidence-building communication between conductors and adult amateur choral singers. These include a conductor's demonstrable credibility based on technical know-how; mutual trust, rapport, and respect; honest and constructive feedback; a balance between good humor and a disciplined approach to learning; space for enjoyment and socializing; and a willingness to relax and celebrate the choir's achievements. As it happens, Andrew is talking about one of my own choirs, but the following extract has been selected for its aptness rather than as a self-aggrandizing ploy! I realize that I don't always get it right, but it's good to know that I've managed to please some of the people some of the time.

> In regards to the choir now, I'm going to be straight. Your technical abilities are second to none—and I mean that—as well as your rapport . . . The thing is, if you don't like something, you'll say it . . . There has to be a certain amount of enjoyment but, I'm sorry, but I am there to learn that music as best as we can learn it, and sing it the best we can. Then, when we've done it properly, then we'll pat ourselves on the back and socialize. And I think we do that with yourself 'cause you've got a nice balance between the two.

CHAPTER SUMMARY

Positive feedback from conductors is highly prized by adult amateur choral singers. Credible praise and justifiable, constructive criticism are especially valuable to choirs. However, some singers reported that the feedback in amateur choral rehearsal and performance situations was not always beneficial for improving performance and building confidence. Shortcomings were reported in the amount of feedback, the content and style of delivery, the balance between praise and criticism, and the credibility and trustworthiness of the feedback received. In sum,

- A high rate of verbal feedback helps build confidence.
- A lack of verbal feedback has an adverse effect on confidence.
- Verbal feedback is only meaningful if perceived as credible and trust-worthy.
- Specific details in both praise and criticism add credibility and improve performance.
- Singers place a premium on verbal feedback from choral conductors.
- Destructive criticism has negative effects on performance and confidence.
- Criticizing individual singers has a negative impact on performance and confidence.
- Mutual rapport and respect are essential in all verbal feedback.
- Constructive criticism balanced with realistic, credible praise is the ideal combination.

Specific, trustworthy praise and constructive criticism are essential tools for the choral conductor because they are motivational and confidence-building. Destructive criticism and confrontational styles of communication have equally dramatic effects, including reducing performance quality, decreasing motivation, and undermining the confidence of the singers. The interviewees felt that in some cases, their conductors had not fully considered the maturity of the singers, their skill levels, and their requirements for learning support. Some participants also felt that their conductors had not fully accounted for the implications of the amateur status of choir members, whose motivation for participating in choral activities is often based on enjoyment and social cohesion as much as (or perhaps, for some individuals, more than) musical achievement.

The singers I interviewed sometimes felt that some of the more destructive feedback arose from prioritization of musical attainment over their needs for enjoyment, supported learning, and confident performance.[40] This reflects Charles Leonhard's criticism of choral directors in educational settings who are sometimes guilty of adopting a "quasi-professional" approach and using singers to further their own musical ambitions rather than prioritizing the singers' learning and enjoyment of their choral experience.[41] Chapter 6 will briefly summarize some of the ways in which the singers' learning, achievement, and enjoyment can be firmly placed at the center of their choral activities.

Chapter Six

Singer-Centered Choral Conducting

A leader is best when people barely know he exists. When his work is done, his aim fulfilled, they will say, We did it ourselves.
—Lao Tzu

The research on which this book is largely based was inspired by many years of practical experience. When I was a teenager, my early forays into the world of amateur performance in choirs and operatic societies gave me a firm foundation for my musical career. They gave me my first insights into the world of amateur choral performance and kindled my interest in teaching and conducting singers. My subsequent professional work as a performer, teacher, and conductor has given me countless opportunities to observe and interact with a wide range of other singers and conductors. In some cases, my research has confirmed my informal observations and subjective experiences of choral participation and conducting; in other cases, the research has yielded some unexpected results.

Throughout I have tried to give center stage to the adult amateur singers who generously gave their time in interviews and shared their feelings, perceptions, thoughts, and opinions about their group singing activities. I have examined their contributions through the lens of several psychological concepts, including self-efficacy, emotional contagion, flow, situated learning, and communities of practice. In this concluding section, I will introduce a few final ideas to illustrate my philosophy as a choral conductor, and I hope that these will be helpful to others.

Having established that choral rehearsal is a multidirectional learning environment in which interpersonal relationships and verbal and nonverbal communication are paramount, I would like to introduce the concept of human compatible learning (HCL).[1] This was originally proposed by Leon Thurman and Graham Welch as a constructive approach to teaching singing in educational environments, and I believe that it can also provide a useful framework for establishing trust and rapport between choral singers and conductors. It has great potential for facilitating learning and goal attainment in choirs and for helping to develop confident choral performance. I delightedly recognized the concept of HCL as soon as I discovered it because I realized that it perfectly chimed with my own approach to teaching and conducting. HCL also neatly reflects many of the needs and preferences of the singers I interviewed.

When I first mentioned the concept of HCL to one of my students, she asked me, "What's the opposite of that, then? Robot compatible learning?" In fact, the opposite would be "human antagonistic learning," and describing this will help to delineate HCL. In the previous chapter, singers reported instances of "human antagonistic" behavior—including destructive criticism, making an example of individuals, and using disrespectful styles of communication—that adversely affected their performance quality and confidence. In contrast to this, HCL fosters an egalitarian, facilitative, and cooperative approach that is based on mutual trust and respect. This approach can build a strong rapport between the choir and conductor, provide firm foundations for the choral team, and help the singers to perform more confidently.

I suggest that applying HCL principles to choral conducting and teaching means providing encouragement and optimal support for learning; giving space for singers to learn collaboratively from each other as well as from the conductor; using nonjudgmental and nonthreatening language to make improvements to performance; and providing rehearsal environments in which mutual respect, empathy, and pleasant emotional states can be generated in all concerned—including the conductor. All of this can have a positive influence on aspects of learning such as attention and memory, which can improve performance and satisfaction all around.[2]

In HCL, the teacher takes on the role of a "senior learner"[3] who is learning alongside the student rather than perceiving him- or herself as a leader who is expected to have all the answers. For less experienced conductors, adopting the role of a senior learner can remove some of the pressure of feeling obliged to deliver flawless leadership. For more experienced conductors, identifying oneself as a senior learner can encourage openness, rapport, and trust between the conductor and the singers. Choral conductors can apply HCL by positioning themselves in a facilitative role and by stressing that skills and knowledge are shared between all the participants. This collaborative approach helps to build an effective community of practice (CoP; see chapter 4) in which learning takes place through interactive processes between learners and senior learners. A dynamic, multidirectional network of reciprocal learning relationships can then develop within the choir rather than a comparatively stagnant, one-way process in which the conductor teaches and the singer learns.

In the choral context, adopting the role of a senior learner can enable the conductor to learn from the singers as well as teach them. It entails listening to the singers not just when they are singing, but also when they are expressing opinions or feelings. Singers usually welcome opportunities to give as well as receive feedback. They may wish to discuss the repertoire, the pace of learning, their strengths and weaknesses, their perception of musical or acoustic challenges, and the kind of help that they would like from the conductor and their peers. An openness to suggestions obviously needs to be balanced by making careful distinctions between genuine, valid concerns and more trivial or contentious communications from singers. It is worth keeping in mind that we can't please all the people all the time, no matter how hard we try. And sometimes people are impossible to please! Having said that, it is still worth listening.

In some choirs I have observed, the singers seem to have been trained not to ask questions or show that they are struggling with any aspect of rehearsal. I find that singers communicate more openly and develop more rapport with me when I consistently reassure them (and demonstrate) that it is okay to ask questions, to ask for help, or to admit that they haven't "got" something. I have also found that being a senior learner means listening to their feedback about my own performance and learning to make any necessary improvements. It also means never being afraid to admit that I have made a mistake, which happens on a regular basis! One of the joys of conducting is the fact that there is always something new to learn, for me as well as for the singers. Learning to be a conductor never ends, as every group of singers is different and I need to adapt accordingly.

Making the most of the whole choir's potential as a community of senior learners also entails allowing the singers opportunities to listen to and learn from each other. During rehearsals, conductors may instinctively limit interactions between singers to avoid unnecessary disruptions. However, peer interactions often include sharing useful information, informal mentoring, and providing mutual support and encouragement. These interactions are an integral part of reciprocal peer learning and can help to build individual and collective confidence. An awareness of this can enable conductors to help singers to make the most of the social learning situation by encouraging teamwork and team leadership.

As a young conductor, I often felt disheartened when singers were talking among themselves instead of giving me their undivided attention. Recognizing that they are often working collaboratively (see Katrina's case study in chapter 4) rather than gossiping or talking about the weather has helped me to relax and give them time to do this when appropriate. Although choir discipline is obviously vital, I have found that it can be balanced with opportunities for constructive peer interaction. Finding this balance is not always easy; it takes careful judgment, patience, and a willingness to experiment with communal modes of learning. It also requires self-confidence on the part of the conductor because sharing power as well as knowledge can sometimes be daunting.[4] However, it is likely to pay dividends in terms of enhanced choral relationships, more effective learning, improved goal attainment, increased self-confidence, and greater enjoyment for everyone involved.

Applying the concept of HCL to choral rehearsal and performance helps to place the singer at the center of group singing activities. This philosophy has much in common with the "person-centered" approach to counseling that was originally developed by Carl Rogers and has subsequently been applied to teaching, with positive effects on attendance and self-confidence.[5] In person-centered teaching, teachers are viewed as learning facilitators rather than leaders, and the core values are congruence (genuineness), empathy, and unconditional positive regard for others, that is, working in a nonjudgmental way. Person-centered teaching also tends to be more process- than content-oriented: learning how to learn is often the outcome. This empowers students to take more control of their learning and to adapt to different learning situations. Rogers believed that teaching based on person-centered values can give people the confidence to grow in ways that are beyond all expectations.[6] I have found that adopting similar values can facilitate singer-centered choral conducting, with similar benefits for the choir.

When trying to develop a singer-centered approach to choral direction, finding out about the singers' understanding of the core values, goals, and functions of the choir is a prerequisite. In communities of practice, achieving cohesion and competence depends upon the participants' shared understanding of the purpose of their joint efforts.[7] Different interpretations of a choir's priorities can lead to clashes, fragmentation, and a lack of unity. This in turn can lead to impaired performance quality and reduced individual and collective confidence. I learned this lesson the hard way when working with a new choir in which the members could not agree among themselves on their aims and objectives. Half of the singers wanted the choir to be a non-auditioned, open-access community group singing purely for fun; the other half wanted to be a high-quality choral society singing complex sacred music for discerning audiences. This led to friction between the singers and made it very difficult to plan rehearsals and choose repertoire or program concerts. In the end, it seemed easier to propose forming two separate choirs!

Some choirs may see themselves as having pedagogical aims because they are mainly concerned with teaching people to sing, while others may be more performance-oriented or may highly value both performance- and process-based goals.[8] Some groups may prefer not to sing in front of an audience at all and would class themselves as "non-performing choirs."[9] Yet others may prioritize the social opportunities provided by group singing activities, and the music may be of secondary importance to their members.

Although the singers in a choir all contribute to communal learning and collective confidence levels, it may fall to the conductor to establish whether the singers agree with each other about their goals and to assess whether any adjustments need to be made to their expectations so that group cohesion and performance satisfaction can be maximized. This requires attentive listening, discussion, negotiation, and possibly facilitating some compromises. It also means that conductors may sometimes end up re-evaluating and adjusting their own expectations and goals to ensure that their modus operandi and the needs of the choir are mutually compatible.

The complex individual and collective needs of a mixed group of adult amateur singers can affect every decision that a conductor makes. Selecting suitable repertoire, facilitating deep learning, arranging satisfying performances, encouraging collaboration, communicating effectively, considering choir acoustics, and choosing the optimum configuration for a particular choir in a particular venue all depend upon the experience, skills, and preferences of the singers within the group. These factors all make a significant difference to performance quality and confidence levels within the choir. All of this highlights the complexity of the role of the choral conductor. However, the objective of this book is not to simplify or minimize the conductor's role but to give extra insight into the perspective of those who are central to choral activities—the singers.

It is demanding to juggle the various musical, social, and learning needs of the individuals within different choirs, but the rewards can be immense. From my own experience, I realize that we cannot be all things to all people, and as conductors, we all have our own strengths and weaknesses. In some cases, we can capitalize upon the former and improve upon the latter. In other cases, I have found that it is worth recognizing that we cannot be expected to do everything and sometimes we must delegate some aspects of our role to other choir members. In larger choirs, for example, we may make the most of choral "team leaders" by asking them to take some responsibility for doing an informal skills audit of their section and conveying the singers' learning needs to us. Fortunately, despite the unique challenges of choral direction, there is a very simple take-home message that can help us to build confident choirs: get to know the singers!

FINAL CHECKLIST FOR CONDUCTORS

Getting to know your choir—a few important questions about the singers:

- What are their strengths and weaknesses?
- What is their previous choral experience?
- What is their musical background?

- What are their aims and aspirations?
- Which performance targets will challenge them sufficiently to maintain their interest, while being attainable enough to be satisfying?
- How much practice and preparation do they need for different songs and events?
- How can they be empowered to build their choral skills and knowledge?
- Who are their team leaders?
- What skills and knowledge do the team leaders have?
- How do different singers react to criticism and praise?
- How does their mood affect their performance and confidence levels?
- How do environmental factors affect their singing and confidence?
- Do I know their names?!

I realize that simply asking these questions will not suddenly transform a choir into a wellspring of self-efficacy. However, I hope that carefully considering the answers, and making use of some of the tips and exercises scattered throughout this book, will help choral conductors develop a range of strategies for encouraging choral cohesion, collaboration, competence, and confidence.

It occurs to me that listening has been one of the main themes of this book, and it has played a starring role in this concluding section. In my research projects, my own role has been as a supporting actor: my function has been to listen to the adult amateur singers I interviewed and to honor their contributions by representing their voices as faithfully as I could. In group singing activities, singers expect to listen to their fellow performers, and they derive musical security and interpersonal support from being in a position to hear each other clearly. Likewise, conductors specialize in listening to their choirs to evaluate choral blend, vocal tone, rhythmic coordination, and expressive aspects of performance. In addition to musical listening, other forms of interpersonal listening contribute to performance quality, choral teamwork, and confidence levels in choirs. Listening judiciously to questions and feedback from singers, as well as listening to their vocal performance, can help conductors to accommodate their needs, develop effective teaching strategies, plan enjoyable rehearsals, and create satisfying performances. Giving singers opportunities to communicate with each other by sharing their knowledge and skills in rehearsals can help choirs to become socially and musically cohesive, to work cooperatively and collaboratively, and to focus on performing as a team.

The nonverbal communication essential to choral confidence-building, which includes modeling and sharing positive body language, also requires singers and conductors to pay close attention to each other. And maybe that is the true essence of the confident choir—it is a choir in which genuine attention is paid to the singers as well as to the conductor and the music. In a confident choir, we all keep our eyes and ears wide open, communicate openly with each other, learn collaboratively, and sing expressively. Most important of all, singers and conductors alike can then enjoy rehearsing and performing together and can have fun making music.

Over the years, many of the singers that I have met have highlighted the considerable contribution that conductors can make to their choral performance, their enjoyment of the process of singing together, and their confidence in themselves as singers. They have also acknowledged the wide-ranging demands placed on conductors of adult amateur choirs and the influence of these conductors on their musical, social, and cultural life. In the spirit of my singer-centered philosophy, I will leave the final words in this section to one of the singers I interviewed. Tim summarized the benefits of a facilitative approach, which places the conductor alongside the singers as a full member of the choral team and in a supportive, empathic, and empowering role:

> I've worked with musical directors who've done everything for you, including singing if necessary. They breathe for you, they look at you, and they're with you all the way. It doesn't matter if it's you as an individual, or you as a group, if the musical director is with you, then it really boosts the confidence.

Conclusion

Throughout this book, the perceptions and experiences of adult amateur choral singers have helped me shed light on the ways in which choirs can learn together, improve their performance quality, and enhance their confidence. All the social and musical interactions discussed by the singers I interviewed can be viewed through the lens of Csikszentmihalyi's flow theory,[1] which can be applied to group performances as well as solo work. Group flow is "a property of the entire group as a collective unit" that can help individual members attain their own state of flow.[2] Being in a flow state, otherwise known as being "in the zone," helps singers lose their self-consciousness and perform with increased individual and collective confidence. During group flow, musicians feel that everything is coming together naturally, that co-performers can anticipate each other's actions, and that they can achieve more during collaborative efforts than they might achieve individually.[3]

For the adult amateur choral singers that I have met during my work as a conductor, teacher, and researcher, group dynamics, communal learning, and collective achievement all make significant contributions to their self-confidence. Many singers view the choir as a team and derive confidence from trusting and relying upon their team members. As the "team manager," the conductor can maximize this sense of teamwork by adopting a facilitative role, by encouraging constructive interactions, and by allowing space for collaboration within rehearsals. The sense of belonging that can develop in an effective choral team can help the singers become immersed in their musical experiences and enter a confidence-enhancing state of flow.

FACILITATING FLOW

The conductor plays a pivotal role in confidence-building in the choir because he or she can contribute to an environment in which flow states are attainable. Auspicious conditions for achieving flow can be created by encouraging collaborative and cohesive relationships; providing carefully balanced constructive criticism and positive feedback; setting clear and realistic shared goals; preparing meticulously for all the musical and practical elements of presenting a confident performance; and modeling confident body language, posture, and deportment.

It has been suggested that emotional contagion can play a role in the transfer of flow between music teachers and their students,[4] and this may also be true for conductors and singers. Conductors might also profitably explain the concept of flow to singers so that they are able to "explore for themselves times of optimal experience and become more mindful of when flow occurs and in which kind of situations."[5] Singers may then become aware of which conditions are most likely to engender a state of flow, and they may be able to share the responsibility for trying to create these conditions. Unfortunately, however, it is not possible to induce flow states at will or to guarantee that certain scenarios will result in group flow; we can only aim to provide favorable conditions in which flow may occur.[6]

The conductor's contribution to facilitating group flow partly involves reducing extraneous distractions so that the singers' concentration on the performance can be as complete as possible. This includes dealing with acoustic issues; considering the impact of choir configuration; preparing the choir for performing in different venues; providing opportunities for singers to become accustomed to different choir configurations; and making sure singers can hear each other well enough to receive musical feedback and vocal cues.

Any insecurities about a choral performance limits the singers' ability to access a flow-inducing state of immersion in the music and reduces their enjoyment. The skills of the singers therefore need to match the challenges of the performance, and thorough preparation of every aspect of the performance is essential. For the conductor, getting to know the singers' strengths and weaknesses can help with suitable repertoire selection and the application of appropriate rehearsal strategies.

THERE ARE LIMITS!

Unfortunately, "some individuals might be constitutionally incapable of experiencing flow."[7] This may be due to excessive self-absorption or self-consciousness, attentional disorders, or stimulus overinclusion. This means that some people find it exceptionally difficult to filter out distractions and concentrate on the task in hand. Creating a personal flow state or facilitating group flow will therefore not always be achievable goals for the choral director. Furthermore, the attainment of these goals cannot be viewed as the conductor's sole responsibility, bearing in mind the functioning of the choir as a community of practice with opportunities for peer learning, modeling, mentoring, and collaboration. The potential effects of negative, as well as positive, emotional contagion between singers can also affect the likelihood of entering a flow state. However, the conductor's adoption of a personal and professional approach that is likely to stimulate flow conditions (including the provision of a rehearsal environment that is conducive to collaborative learning, cooperative interaction, and optimal experience) will contribute to the development of individual and collective confidence within the choral community of practice.

PERSONAL REFLECTIONS UPON PROFESSIONAL PRACTICE

For me, it has been very helpful to recognize the ways in which I can contribute to facilitating confidence-building flow states in group singing activities. The main elements include selecting appropriate repertoire, setting challenging but achievable goals, preparing thoroughly, encouraging teamwork, reducing extraneous sources of distraction, reminding singers to adopt positive body language, and providing constructive feedback. These are very simple strategies, but I quickly know it if I happen to forget them in any of the choirs I conduct! It has also been useful to realize that it's not all about me. As a younger conductor, I was sometimes daunted to feel the weight of the responsibility for the learning, achievement, and enjoyment of a large group of diverse adult amateur singers.

The insights acquired from the singers I interviewed, as well as my own practical experience as a teacher and conductor, have helped me adopt a more relaxed and collegial attitude in some ways. It is important to acknowledge the powerful impact that a conductor's verbal and nonverbal communication can have upon a choir. However, positioning myself as a senior learner,[8] facilitator, and member of the choral team has helped me to be more forgiving of my own faults and mistakes; to accept negative feedback from the singers without feeling that I have failed in some way; to fully appreciate positive feedback and to share this with the choir as my co-performers; and to take into account the effect of group dynamics upon learning and performance rather than feeling that I am responsible for absolutely everything that happens in this context. Sharing the challenges and achievements, the tasks of communal learning and problem-solving, and the joys (and occasional stresses!) of rehearsing and performing with the rest of the choral team adds to the pleasure of the work.

A CONDUCTOR'S MISSION STATEMENT

I hope that sharing these perspectives will encourage other conductors to explore ways of building confident choirs. Seeing our choirs blossom is one way of building our own confidence as leaders of group singing activities. And of course, it works both ways since a confident conductor is likely to inspire confidence in others. A few years ago, a friend introduced me to Marianne Williamson's poem "Our Deepest Fear," which exhorts us to re-lease ourselves from the fear of revealing our own innate power and to allow ourselves the freedom to shine. Her wisdom had a liberating effect on me, and I have spent many years pointing my students in the direction of her inspirational words. For me as a conductor and teacher, the following extract has become my mantra:

> *As we let our own light shine, we unconsciously*
> *Give other people permission to do the same.* [9]

Notes

INTRODUCTION

1. "Singing Europe," a pilot study edited by the European Choral Association—Europa Cantat, realized in the frame of the VOICE European Cooperation project with the support of the European Union (2015), www.singingeurope.org.

2. Gunter Kreutz et al., "Effects of Choir Singing or Listening on Secretory Immunoglobulin A, Cortisol, and Emotional State," *Journal of Behavioral Medicine* 27, no. 6 (2004).

3. Liz Mellor, "An Investigation of Singing, Health and Well-Being as a Group Process," *British Journal of Music Education* 30, no. 2 (2013).

4. Stephen Clift and Grenville Hancox, "The Significance of Choral Singing for Sustaining Psychological Wellbeing: Findings from a Survey of Choristers in England, Australia and Germany," *Music Performance Research* 3 (2010).

5. Elizabeth Cassidy Parker, "Exploring Student Experiences of Belonging within an Urban High School Choral Ensemble: An Action Research Study," *Music Education Research* 12, no. 4 (2010).

6. Michael Murray and Alexandra Lamont, "Community Music and Social/Health Psychology: Linking Theoretical and Practical Concerns." *Music, Health and Wellbeing* 76 (2012).

7. Caroline Bithell, *A Different Voice, a Different Song: Reclaiming Community through the Natural Voice and World Song* (New York: Oxford University Press, 2014).

8. Ian Bostridge, *A Singer's Notebook* (London: Faber & Faber, 2011); Renée Fleming, *The Inner Voice: The Making of a Singer* (New York: Penguin, 2005); and Robert Tear, *Singer Beware: Cautionary Story of the Singing Class* (London: Hodder & Stoughton, 1995).

9. Daniel Barenboim and Phillip Huscher, *A Life in Music* (New York: Arcade Publishing, 2002); and Leonard Slatkin, *Conducting Business: Unveiling the Mystery behind the Maestro* (Milwaukee, WI: Amadeus Press, 2012).

10. Robert A. Stebbins, *The Barbershop Singer: Inside the Social World of a Musical Hobby* (Toronto: University of Toronto Press, 1996); and Robert A. Stebbins, *Between Work and Leisure* (New Brunswick, NJ: Transaction Publishers, 2004).

11. Ibid.

12. Johannes F. L. M. Van Kemenade, Maarten J. M. Van Son, and Nicolette C. A. Van Heesch, "Performance Anxiety among Professional Musicians in Symphonic Orchestras: A Self-Report Study," *Psychological Reports* 77, no. 2 (1995); and Andrew Steptoe, "Negative Emotions in Music Making: The Problem of Performance Anxiety," in *Music and Emotion:*

Theory and Research, ed. Patrik N. Juslin and John A. Sloboda (Oxford: Oxford University Press, 2001).

13. Jennifer L. Abel and Kevin T. Larkin, "Anticipation of Performance among Musicians: Physiological Arousal, Confidence, and State-Anxiety," *Psychology of Music* 18, no. 2 (1990); Paul G. Salmon, "A Psychological Perspective on Musical Performance Anxiety: A Review of the Literature," *Medical Problems of Performing Artists* 5, no. 1 (1990); and Dianna Kenny, *The Psychology of Music Performance Anxiety* (New York: Oxford University Press, 2011).

14. Jennifer L. Abel and Kevin T. Larkin, "Anticipation of Performance among Musicians: Physiological Arousal, Confidence, and State-Anxiety," *Psychology of Music* 18, no. 2 (1990); and Dianna Kenny, Tim Driscoll, and Bronwen Ackermann, "Psychological Well-Being in Professional Orchestral Musicians in Australia: A Descriptive Population Study," *Psychology of Music* 42, no. 2 (2014).

15. Dianna T. Kenny, James M. Fortune, and Bronwen Ackermann, "Predictors of Music Performance Anxiety during Skilled Performance in Tertiary Flute Players," *Psychology of Music* 41, no. 3 (2013); and Donald L. Hamann and Martha Sobaje, "Anxiety and the College Musician: A Study of Performance Conditions and Subject Variables," *Psychology of Music* 11, no. 1 (1983).

16. Claudia Spahn, Matthias Echternach, Mark F. Zander, Edgar Voltmer, and Bernhard Richter, "Music Performance Anxiety in Opera Singers," *Logopedics Phoniatrics Vocology* 35, no. 4 (2010); and Glenn D. Wilson, *Psychology for Performing Artists: Butterflies and Bouquets* (London: Jessica Kingsley Publishers, 1994).

17. Dianna T. Kenny, Pamela Davis, and Jenni Oates, "Music Performance Anxiety and Occupational Stress among Opera Chorus Artists and Their Relationship with State and Trait Anxiety and Perfectionism," *Journal of Anxiety Disorders* 18, no. 6 (2004); and Charlene Ryan and Nicholle Andrews, "An Investigation into the Choral Singer's Experience of Music Performance Anxiety," *Journal of Research in Music Education* 57, no. 2 (2009).

18. Michael J. Bonshor, "Musical Performance Anxiety amongst Adult Amateur Singers: The Effects of Age, Experience and Training," MA dissertation (University of Sheffield, 2002).

19. Jennifer L. Abel and Kevin T. Larkin, "Anticipation of Performance among Musicians: Physiological Arousal, Confidence, and State-Anxiety," *Psychology of Music* 18, no. 2 (1990); Paul G. Salmon, "A Psychological Perspective on Musical Performance Anxiety: A Review of the Literature," *Medical Problems of Performing Artists* 5, no. 1 (1990); and Dianna Kenny, *The Psychology of Music Performance Anxiety* (New York: Oxford University Press, 2011).

20. Michael J. Bonshor, "Confidence and the Choral Singer: The Effects of Choir Configuration, Collaboration and Communication," PhD dissertation (University of Sheffield, 2014).

21. Jonathan A. Smith, "Semi-structured Interviewing and Qualitative Analysis," in *Rethinking Methods in Psychology*, ed. Jonathan A. Smith, Rom Harre, and Luk Van Langenhove (London: Sage Publications, 1995); and Jonathan A. Smith, Paul Flowers, and Michael Larkin, *Interpretative Phenomenological Analysis* (London: Sage Publications, 2009).

1. CONVEYING AND CULTIVATING CONFIDENCE

1. *Collins Dictionary and Thesaurus*, 2nd ed. (Glasgow: HarperCollins, 2000).

2. *Oxford Dictionary of English* (Oxford: Oxford University Press, 2003).

3. Albert Bandura, "Self-Efficacy: Toward a Unifying Theory of Behavioral Change," *Psychological Review* 84, no. 2 (1977).

4. Albert Bandura, "Self-Efficacy Mechanism in Human Agency," *American Psychologist* 37, no. 2 (1982): 122.

5. Aleksandra Luszczynska, Benicio Gutiérrez-Doña, and Ralf Schwarzer, "General Self-Efficacy in Various Domains of Human Functioning: Evidence from Five Countries," *International Journal of Psychology* 40, no. 2 (2005): 81.

6. Robin S Vealey, Megan Garner-Holman, Susan Walter Hayashi, and Peter Giacobbi, "Sources of Sport-Confidence: Conceptualization and Instrument Development," *Journal of Sport and Exercise Psychology* 20, no. 1 (1998).

7. Albert Bandura and Nancy E. Adams, "Analysis of Self-Efficacy Theory of Behavioral Change," *Cognitive Therapy and Research* 1, no. 4 (1977).

8. Donald L. Hamann and Martha Sobaje, "Anxiety and the College Musician: A Study of Performance Conditions and Subject Variables," *Psychology of Music* 11, no. 1 (1983).

9. Paul G. Salmon, "A Psychological Perspective on Musical Performance Anxiety: A Review of the Literature," *Medical Problems of Performing Artists* 5, no. 1 (1990); and Andrew Palmer, *Divas in Their Own Words* (Nottingham, UK: Vernon Press, 2000).

10. Sara Solovitch, *Playing Scared: My Journey through Stage Fright* (London: Bloomsbury Publishing, 2015).

11. Laurence Olivier, *On Acting* (London: Weidenfeld and Nicolson, 1986).

12. Paul M. Lehrer, "A Review of the Approaches to the Management of Tension and Stage Fright in Music Performance," *Journal of Research in Music Education* 35, no. 3 (1987); and C. L. Barney Dews and Martha S. Williams, "Student Musicians' Personality Styles, Stresses, and Coping Patterns," *Psychology of Music* 17, no. 1 (1989).

13. Michael J. Bonshor, "Musical Performance Anxiety amongst Adult Amateur Singers: The Effects of Age, Experience and Training" (MA diss., University of Sheffield, 2002).

14. Mimi Bong and Einar M. Skaalvik, "Academic Self-Concept and Self-Efficacy: How Different Are They Really?" *Educational Psychology Review* 15, no. 1 (2003).

15. Albert Bandura, "Self-Efficacy: Toward a Unifying Theory of Behavioral Change," *Psychological Review* 84, no. 2 (1977).

16. Ibid.

17. Leon Thurman and Graham Welch, *Bodymind and Voice: Foundations of Voice Education*, 2nd ed. (Iowa City, IA: National Center for Voice and Speech, 2000).

18. Sabine Stepper and Fritz Strack, "Proprioceptive Determinants of Emotional and Nonemotional Feelings," *Journal of Personality and Social Psychology* 64, no. 2 (1993): 211.

19. John H. Riskind and Carolyn C. Gotay, "Physical Posture: Could It Have Regulatory or Feedback Effects on Motivation and Emotion?" *Motivation and Emotion* 6, no. 3 (1982).

20. Pablo Briñol, Richard E. Petty, and Benjamin Wagner, "Body Posture Effects on Self-Evaluation: A Self-Validation Approach," *European Journal of Social Psychology* 39, no. 6 (2009).

21. Ibid.

22. Albert Bandura, "Self-Efficacy Mechanism in Human Agency," *American Psychologist* 37, no. 2 (1982).

23. Albert Bandura, "Self-Efficacy: Toward a Unifying Theory of Behavioral Change," *Psychological Review* 84, no. 2 (1977).

24. Charles Darwin, *The Expression of the Emotions in Man and Animals* (New York: Philosophical Library, 1872), 361.

25. Paul Ekman, "Facial Expressions of Emotion: New Findings, New Questions," *Psychological Science* 3 (1992).

26. Dana R. Carney, Amy J. C. Cuddy, and Andy J. Yap, "Power Posing: Brief Nonverbal Displays Affect Neuroendocrine Levels and Risk Tolerance," *Psychological Science* 21, no. 10 (2010).

27. Fritz Strack, Leonard L. Martin, and Sabine Stepper, "Inhibiting and Facilitating Conditions of the Human Smile: A Nonobtrusive Test of the Facial Feedback Hypothesis," *Journal of Personality and Social Psychology* 54, no. 5 (1988): 768.

28. James D. Laird, "Self-Attribution of Emotion: The Effects of Expressive Behavior on the Quality of Emotional Experience," *Journal of Personality and Social Psychology* 29, no. 4 (1974): 475.

29. Paul Ekman, "Facial Expressions of Emotion: New Findings, New Questions," *Psychological Science* 3 (1992).

30. Ibid., 35.

31. Ralph Adolphs, "Neural Systems for Recognizing Emotion," *Current Opinion in Neurobiology* 12, no. 2 (2002); and Barbara Wild, Michael Erb, Michael Eyb, Mathias Bartels, and Wolfgang Grodd, "Why Are Smiles Contagious? An fMRI Study of the Interaction between Perception of Facial Affect and Facial Movements," *Psychiatry Research: Neuroimaging* 123, no. 1 (2003).

32. Daniel S. Messinger, Alan Fogel, and K. Laurie Dickson, "What's in a Smile?" *Developmental Psychology* 35, no. 3 (1999).

33. James C. McKinney, *The Diagnosis and Correction of Vocal Faults: A Manual for Teachers of Singing and for Choir Directors*, revised ed. (Nashville, TN: Genevox, 1994).

34. Richard Miller, *On the Art of Singing* (New York: Oxford University Press, 1996).

35. Paul Ekman, Richard J. Davidson, and Wallace V. Friesen, "The Duchenne Smile: Emotional Expression and Brain Physiology: II," *Journal of Personality and Social Psychology* 58, no. 2 (1990): 342.

36. *The Concise Oxford Dictionary* (Oxford: Oxford University Press, 1996).

37. Richard Rodgers and Oscar Hammerstein II, *The King and I* (New York: Williamson Music, 1951).

38. Patsy Rodenburg, *Presence: How to Use Positive Energy for Success in Every Situation* (London: Penguin, 2007).

39. Tanya L. Chartrand and John A. Bargh, "The Chameleon Effect: The Perception-Behavior Link and Social Interaction," *Journal of Personality and Social Psychology* 76, no. 6 (1999).

40. Paul Ekman, "Facial Expressions of Emotion: New Findings, New Questions," *Psychological Science* 3 (1992).

41. Irina Falkenberg, Mathias Bartels, and Barbara Wild, "Keep Smiling!" *European Archives of Psychiatry and Clinical Neuroscience* 258, no. 4 (2008).

42. Vittorio Gallese and Alvin Goldman, "Mirror Neurons and the Simulation Theory of Mind-Reading," *Trends in Cognitive Sciences* 2, no. 12 (1998): 495.

43. Simon Wessely, "Mass Hysteria: Two Syndromes?" *Psychological Medicine* 17, no. 1 (1987): 109.

44. Richard J. Levine, "Epidemic Faintness and Syncope in a School Marching Band," *JAMA* 238, no. 22 (1977).

45. M. E. K. Moffatt, "Epidemic Hysteria in a Montreal Train Station," *Pediatrics* 70, no. 2 (1982).

46. Robert E. Bartholomew and Simon Wessely, "Protean Nature of Mass Sociogenic Illness," *British Journal of Psychiatry* 180, no. 4 (2002).

47. Robert E. Bartholomew and Francois Sirois, "Epidemic Hysteria in Schools: An International and Historical Overview," *Educational Studies* 22, no. 3 (1996).

48. Richard Rodgers and Oscar Hammerstein II, *The King and I* (New York: Williamson Music, 1951).

49. Ibid.

50. Paul Ekman, "Facial Expressions of Emotion: New Findings, New Questions," *Psychological Science* 3 (1992); Sabine Stepper and Fritz Strack, "Proprioceptive Determinants of Emotional and Nonemotional Feelings," *Journal of Personality and Social Psychology* 64, no. 2 (1993); and Fritz Strack, Leonard L. Martin, and Sabine Stepper, "Inhibiting and Facilitating Conditions of the Human Smile: A Nonobtrusive Test of the Facial Feedback Hypothesis," *Journal of Personality and Social Psychology* 54, no. 5 (1988).

51. Dana R. Carney, Amy J. C. Cuddy, and Andy J. Yap, "Power Posing: Brief Nonverbal Displays Affect Neuroendocrine Levels and Risk Tolerance," *Psychological Science* 21, no. 10 (2010).

52. Amy J. C. Cuddy, Caroline Ashley Wilmuth, and Dana R. Carney, "The Benefit of Power Posing before a High-Stakes Social Evaluation," *Harvard Business School Working Paper* 13-027 (2012).

53. Dana R. Carney, Judith A. Hall, and Lavonia Smith LeBeau, "Beliefs about the Nonverbal Expression of Social Power," *Journal of Nonverbal Behavior* 29, no. 2 (2005).

54. Amy J. C. Cuddy, Caroline Ashley Wilmuth, and Dana R. Carney, "The Benefit of Power Posing before a High-Stakes Social Evaluation," *Harvard Business School Working Paper* 13-027 (2012).

55. Dana R. Carney, Amy J. C. Cuddy, and Andy J. Yap, "Power Posing: Brief Nonverbal Displays Affect Neuroendocrine Levels and Risk Tolerance," *Psychological Science* 21, no. 10 (2010).

56. Amy J. C. Cuddy, Caroline Ashley Wilmuth, and Dana R. Carney, "The Benefit of Power Posing before a High-Stakes Social Evaluation," *Harvard Business School Working Paper* 13-027 (2012).

57. Ibid.

58. Amy Cuddy, *Presence: Bringing Your Boldest Self to Your Biggest Challenges* (London: Hachette, 2016).

59. Dana R. Carney, Amy J. C. Cuddy, and Andy J. Yap, "Power Posing: Brief Nonverbal Displays Affect Neuroendocrine Levels and Risk Tolerance," *Psychological Science* 21, no. 10 (2010).

60. Liz Garnett, *Choral Conducting and the Construction of Meaning: Gesture, Voice, Identity* (Farnham, UK: Ashgate, 2009), 170; my italics.

61. James M. Jordan, *Evoking Sound: Fundamentals of Choral Conducting and Rehearsing* (Chicago: GIA Publications, 1996), 9.

62. Abraham Kaplan, *Choral Conducting* (New York: Norton, 1985).

63. Paul F. Roe, *Choral Music Education*, 2nd ed. (Englewood Cliffs, NJ: Prentice Hall, 1983).

64. James F. Daugherty and Melissa C. Brunkan, "Monkey See, Monkey Do? The Effect of Nonverbal Conductor Lip Rounding on Visual and Acoustic Measures of Singers' Lip Postures," *Journal of Research in Music Education* 60, no. 4 (2013).

65. John Baker Hylton, *Comprehensive Choral Music Education* (Englewood Cliffs, NJ: Prentice Hall, 1995), 95.

66. Gordon Reynolds, *The Choirmaster in Action* (London: Novello, 1972), 6.

67. Elizabeth Valentine, "Alexander Technique," in *Musical Excellence: Strategies and Techniques to Enhance Performance*, ed. Aaron Williamon (Oxford: Oxford University Press, 2004).

68. Leon Thurman and Graham Welch, *Bodymind and Voice: Foundations of Voice Education*, 2nd ed. (Iowa City, IA: National Center for Voice and Speech, 2000).

69. Daniela Coimbra, Jane Davidson, and Dimitra Kokotsaki, "Investigating the Assessment of Singers in a Music College Setting: The Students' Perspective," *Research Studies in Music Education* 16, no. 1 (2001): 15.

2. PRACTICE, PREPARATION, AND PRESENTATION

1. Don Black, Christopher Hampton, and Andrew Lloyd Weber, *Sunset Boulevard* (London: Really Useful Group, 1993).

2. A. Edwards, *Streisand: A Biography* (New York: Rowman & Littlefield, 2016).

3. Michael J. Bonshor, "Musical Performance Anxiety amongst Adult Amateur Singers: The Effects of Age, Experience and Training" (MA diss., University of Sheffield, 2002).

4. Misse Wester, "Fight, Flight or Freeze: Assumed Reactions of the Public during a Crisis," *Journal of Contingencies and Crisis Management* 19, no. 4 (2011).

5. Trevor J. Powell and Simon J. Enright, *Anxiety and Stress Management* (London: Routledge, 1990).

6. Glenn D. Wilson, "Performance Anxiety," in *The Social Psychology of Music*, ed. David J. Hargreaves and Adrian C. North (Oxford: Oxford University Press, 1997), 230.

7. Paul M. Lehrer, "A Review of the Approaches to the Management of Tension and Stage Fright in Music Performance," *Journal of Research in Music Education* 35, no. 3 (1987): 145.

8. Dianna Kenny, *The Psychology of Music Performance Anxiety* (New York: Oxford University Press, 2011).

9. Aaron Williamon, *Musical Excellence: Strategies and Techniques to Enhance Performance* (New York: Oxford University Press, 2004).

10. Andrew Steptoe, "Performance Anxiety: Recent Developments in Its Analysis and Management," *Musical Times* 123, no. 1674 (1982).

11. Jennifer L. Abel and Kevin T. Larkin, "Anticipation of Performance among Musicians: Physiological Arousal, Confidence, and State-Anxiety," *Psychology of Music* 18, no. 2 (1990).

12. Paul M. Lehrer, "A Review of the Approaches to the Management of Tension and Stage Fright in Music Performance," *Journal of Research in Music Education* 35, no. 3 (1987).

13. Michael J. Bonshor, "Musical Performance Anxiety amongst Adult Amateur Singers: The Effects of Age, Experience and Training" (MA diss., University of Sheffield, 2002).

14. Paul Salmon, R. Schrodt, and Jesse Wright, "A Temporal Gradient of Anxiety in a Stressful Performance Context," *Medical Problems of Performing Artists* 4, no. 2 (1989).

15. Dianna Kenny, *The Psychology of Music Performance Anxiety* (New York: Oxford University Press, 2011).

16. Stanley J. Rachman, *Anxiety* (Hove, UK: Psychology Press, 1998).

17. Dianna Kenny, *The Psychology of Music Performance Anxiety* (New York: Oxford University Press, 2011), 75.

18. Mihalyi Csikszentmihalyi, *Flow: The Psychology of Happiness* (London: Random House, 2002), 71.

19. Kazuhisa Shibata et al., "Overlearning Hyperstabilizes a Skill by Rapidly Making Neurochemical Processing Inhibitory-Dominant." *Nature Neuroscience* 20, no. 3 (2017).

20. Hermann Ebbinghaus, *Über das Gedächtnis: Untersuchungen zur Experimentellen Psychologie* (Leipzig: Duncker & Humblot, 1885).

21. Kazuhisa Shibata et al., "Overlearning Hyperstabilizes a Skill by Rapidly Making Neurochemical Processing Inhibitory-Dominant." *Nature Neuroscience* 20, no. 3 (2017).

22. Mihalyi Csikszentmihalyi, *Flow: The Psychology of Happiness* (London: Random House, 2002).

23. Bernard S. Cayne, *The New Lexicon Webster's Dictionary of the English Language* (New York: Lexicon, 1990).

24. Mihalyi Csikszentmihalyi, *Flow: The Psychology of Happiness* (London: Random House, 2002).

25. Leon Thurman and Graham Welch, *Bodymind and Voice: Foundations of Voice Education*, 2nd ed. (Iowa City, IA: National Center for Voice and Speech, 2000).

26. Hajo Adam and Adam D. Galinsky, "Enclothed Cognition," *Journal of Experimental Social Psychology* 48, no. 4 (2012).

27. Andrew H. Gregory, "The Role of Music in Society: The Ethnomusicological Perspective," in *The Social Psychology of Music*, ed. David J. Hargreaves and Adrian C. North (Oxford: Oxford University Press, 1997).

28. Glenn D. Wilson, *Psychology for Performing Artists: Butterflies and Bouquets* (London: Jessica Kingsley Publishers, 1994).

29. Jane W. Davidson, "The Social in Musical Performance," in *The Social Psychology of Music*, ed. David J. Hargreaves and Adrian C. North (Oxford: Oxford University Press, 1997).

30. Graham Welch, "The Genesis of Singing Behavior," in *Proceedings of the Sixth International Conference on Musical Perception and Cognition*. CD-ROM, Department of Psychology, University of Keele, UK. 2000.

31. Solomon E. Asch, "Opinions and Social Pressures," *Scientific American* 193 (1955).

32. Joel Wapnick, Alice Ann Darrow, Jolan Kovacs, and Lucinda Dalrymple, "Effects of Physical Attractiveness on Evaluation of Vocal Performance," *Journal of Research in Music Education* 45, no. 3 (1997).

33. Noola K. Griffiths, "'Posh Music Should Equal Posh Dress': An Investigation into the Concert Dress and Physical Appearance of Female Soloists," *Psychology of Music* 38, no. 2 (2010).

34. Sandra A. Howard, "The Effect of Selected Nonmusical Factors on Adjudicators' Ratings of High School Solo Vocal Performances," *Journal of Research in Music Education* 60, no. 2 (2012).

35. Daniela Coimbra, Jane Davidson, and Dimitra Kokotsaki, "Investigating the Assessment of Singers in a Music College Setting: The Students' Perspective," *Research Studies in Music Education* 16, no. 1 (2001).

36. Mihalyi Csikszentmihalyi, *Flow: The Psychology of Happiness* (London: Random House, 2002).

37. David J. Foster, Daniel A. Weigand, and Dean Baines, "The Effect of Removing Superstitious Behavior and Introducing a Pre-performance Routine in Basketball Free-Throw Performance," *Journal of Applied Sport Psychology* 18, no. 2 (2006).

38. Jared L. Bleak and Christina M. Frederick, "Superstitious Behavior in Sport: Levels of Effectiveness and Determinants of Use in Three Collegiate Sports," *Journal of Sport Behavior* 21, no. 1 (1998).

39. Mari Womack, "Why Athletes Need Ritual: A Study of Magic among Professional Athletes," in *Sport and Religion*, ed. Shirl J. Hoffman (Champaign, IL: Human Kinetics, 1992).

3. CHORAL ACOUSTICS AND CHOIR CONFIGURATION

1. Leon Thurman and Graham Welch, *Bodymind and Voice: Foundations of Voice Education*, 2nd ed. (Iowa City, IA: National Center for Voice and Speech, 2000).

2. Johan Sundberg, *The Science of the Singing Voice* (DeKalb: Northern Illinois University Press, 1987).

3. Sten Ternström and Duane Richard Karna, "Choir," in *The Science and Psychology of Music Performance: Creative Strategies for Teaching and Learning*, ed. Richard Parncutt and Gary McPherson (New York: Oxford University Press, 2002), 269.

4. Sten Ternström, "Hearing Myself with Others: Sound Levels in Choral Performance Measured with Separation of One's Own Voice from the Rest of the Choir," *Journal of Voice* 8, no. 4 (1994): 300.

5. Ibid., 293.

6. Ibid., 294.

7. Richard Alderson, *Complete Handbook of Voice Training* (New York: Parker Publishing Company, 1979).

8. Sten Ternström, "Preferred Self-to-Other Ratios in Choir Singing," *Journal of the Acoustical Society of America* 105, no. 6 (1999): 3563–74.

9. Sten Ternström, "Hearing Myself with Others: Sound Levels in Choral Performance Measured with Separation of One's Own Voice from the Rest of the Choir," *Journal of Voice* 8, no. 4 (1994).

10. Michael J. Bonshor, "Confidence and Choral Configuration: The Affective Impact of Situational and Acoustic Factors in Amateur Choirs," *Psychology of Music* (2016), doi:10.1177/0305735616669996.

11. James F. Daugherty, "Spacing, Formation, and Choral Sound: Preferences and Perceptions of Auditors and Choristers," *Journal of Research in Music Education* 47, no. 3 (1999); James F. Daugherty, "Choir Spacing and Formation: Choral Sound Preferences in Random, Synergistic, and Gender-Specific Chamber Choir Placements," *International Journal of Research in Choral Singing* 1, no. 1 (2003); and Elizabeth Ekholm, "The Effect of Singing Mode and Seating Arrangement on Choral Blend and Overall Choral Sound," *Journal of Research in Music Education* 48, no. 2 (2000).

12. Ibid; and Christopher Aspaas, Christopher R. McCrea, Richard J. Morris, and Linda Fowler, "Select Acoustic and Perceptual Measures of Choral Formation," *International Journal of Research in Choral Singing* 2, no. 1 (2004).

13. Michael John Bonshor, "Collaboration in the Choral Context: The Contribution of Conductor and Choir to Collective Confidence," in *Proceedings of the International Symposium on Performance Science Held at the University of Music and Performing Arts, Vienna*, 2013; and Michael John Bonshor, "Confidence and the Choral Singer: The Choir as a Community of Practice," in *Choral Singing: Histories and Practices*, ed. Ursula Geisler and Karin Johansson (Newcastle upon Tyne, UK: Cambridge Scholars Publishing, 2014).

14. Elizabeth Ekholm, "The Effect of Singing Mode and Seating Arrangement on Choral Blend and Overall Choral Sound," *Journal of Research in Music Education* 48, no. 2 (2000).

15. Christopher Aspaas, Christopher R. McCrea, Richard J. Morris, and Linda Fowler, "Select Acoustic and Perceptual Measures of Choral Formation," *International Journal of Research in Choral Singing* 2, no. 1 (2004).

16. Sten Ternström and Duane Richard Karna, "Choir," in *The Science and Psychology of Music Performance: Creative Strategies for Teaching and Learning*, ed. Richard Parncutt and Gary McPherson (New York: Oxford University Press, 2002), 269.

17. Ibid., 273.

18. James F. Daugherty, "Spacing, Formation, and Choral Sound: Preferences and Perceptions of Auditors and Choristers," *Journal of Research in Music Education* 47, no. 3 (1999); and James F. Daugherty, "Choir Spacing and Formation: Choral Sound Preferences in Random, Synergistic, and Gender-Specific Chamber Choir Placements," *International Journal of Research in Choral Singing* 1, no. 1 (2003).

19. Christopher Aspaas, Christopher R. McCrea, Richard J. Morris, and Linda Fowler, "Select Acoustic and Perceptual Measures of Choral Formation," *International Journal of Research in Choral Singing* 2, no. 1 (2004).

20. James F. Daugherty, "Spacing, Formation, and Choral Sound: Preferences and Perceptions of Auditors and Choristers," *Journal of Research in Music Education* 47, no. 3 (1999).

21. Michael John Bonshor, "Confidence and the Choral Singer: The Effects of Choir Configuration, Collaboration and Communication" (PhD diss., University of Sheffield, 2014); Michael John Bonshor, "Confidence and the Choral Singer: The Choir as a Community of Practice," in *Choral Singing: Histories and Practices*, ed. Ursula Geisler and Karin Johansson (Newcastle upon Tyne, UK: Cambridge Scholars Publishing, 2014); Michael John Bonshor, "Collaboration in the Choral Context: The Contribution of Conductor and Choir to Collective Confidence," in *Proceedings of the International Symposium on Performance Science Held at the University of Music and Performing Arts, Vienna*, 2013; and Michael Bonshor, "Sharing Knowledge and Power in Adult Amateur Choral Communities: The Impact of Communal Learning on the Experience of Musical Participation," *International Journal of Community Music* 9, no. 3 (2016).

22. Michael J. Bonshor, "Confidence and Choral Configuration: The Affective Impact of Situational and Acoustic Factors in Amateur Choirs," *Psychology of Music* (2016), doi:10.1177/0305735616669996.

23. Michael J. Bonshor, "Musical Performance Anxiety amongst Adult Amateur Singers: The Effects of Age, Experience and Training" (MA diss., University of Sheffield, 2002).

4. COLLABORATION AND COMMUNAL LEARNING

1. Jonathan A. Smith, Paul Flowers, and Michael Larkin, *Interpretative Phenomenological Analysis* (London: Sage Publications, 2009).

2. Charlene Ryan and Nicholle Andrews, "An Investigation into the Choral Singer's Experience of Music Performance Anxiety," *Journal of Research in Music Education* 57, no. 2 (2009).

3. Michael Murray and Alexandra Lamont, "Community Music and Social/Health Psychology: Linking Theoretical and Practical Concerns," *Music, Health and Wellbeing* 76 (2012).

4. Jane E. Southcott, "And as I Go, I Love to Sing: The Happy Wanderers, Music and Positive Aging," *International Journal of Community Music* 2, nos. 2–3 (2009).

5. Betty A. Bailey and Jane W. Davidson, "Adaptive Characteristics of Group Singing: Perceptions from Members of a Choir for Homeless Men," *Musicae Scientiae* 6, no. 2 (2002).

6. Genevieve A. Dingle, Christopher Brander, Julie Ballantyne, and Felicity A. Baker, "'To Be Heard': The Social and Mental Health Benefits of Choir Singing for Disadvantaged Adults," *Psychology of Music* 41, no. 4 (2013): 405–21; and Betty A. Bailey and Jane W. Davidson, "Effects of Group Singing and Performance for Marginalized and Middle-Class Singers," *Psychology of Music* 33, no. 3 (2005).

7. The Choir with No Name, "Our Mission," http://choirwithnoname.org/about/mission.

8. Colin Durrant and Evangelos Himonides, "What Makes People Sing Together? Socio-Psychological and Cross-Cultural Perspectives on the Choral Phenomenon," *International Journal of Music Education* 1 (1998); and Liz Mellor, "An Investigation of Singing, Health and Well-Being as a Group Process," *British Journal of Music Education* 30, no. 2 (2013).

9. Eiluned Pearce, Jacques Launay, and Robin I. M. Dunbar, "The Ice-Breaker Effect: Singing Mediates Fast Social Bonding," *Open Science* 2, no. 10 (2015).

10. Leslie C. Aiello and Robin I. M. Dunbar, "Neocortex Size, Group Size, and the Evolution of Language," *Current Anthropology* 34, no. 2 (1993).

11. Stephen W. Porges, "Orienting in a Defensive World: Mammalian Modifications of Our Evolutionary Heritage. A Polyvagal Theory," *Psychophysiology* 32, no. 4 (1995).

12. David Huron, "Is Music an Evolutionary Adaptation?" *Annals of the New York Academy of Sciences* 930, no. 1 (2001).

13. Viktor Müller and Ulman Lindenberger, "Cardiac and Respiratory Patterns Synchronize between Persons during Choir Singing," *PloS one* 6, no. 9 (2011): e24893.

14. Bruce Richman, "On the Evolution of Speech: Singing as the Middle Term," *Current Anthropology*, 34, no. 5 (1993).

15. Björn Vickhoff, *A Perspective Theory of Music Perception and Emotion* (Gothenburg, Germany: University of Gothenburg, 2008); Elisabeth Pacherie, "Framing Joint Action," *Review of Philosophy and Psychology* 2, no. 2 (2011); Scott S. Wiltermuth and Chip Heath, "Synchrony and Cooperation," *Psychological Science* 20, no. 1 (2009); and Tamás Dávid-Barrett and R. I. M. Dunbar, "Cooperation, Behavioral Synchrony and Status in Social Networks," *Journal of Theoretical Biology* 308 (2012).

16. Robert A. Stebbins, *The Barbershop Singer: Inside the Social World of a Musical Hobby* (Toronto: University of Toronto Press, 1996); and Robert A. Stebbins, *Between Work and Leisure* (New Brunswick, NJ: Transaction Publishers, 2004).

17. D. J. Levitin, *The World in Six Songs: How the Musical Brain Created Human Nature* (London: Penguin, 2008)

18. Irina Falkenberg, Mathias Bartels, and Barbara Wild, "Keep Smiling!" *European Archives of Psychiatry and Clinical Neuroscience* 258, no. 4 (2008).

19. Mihalyi Csikszentmihalyi, *Flow: The Psychology of Happiness* (London: Random House, 2002).

20. A. Goodrich, "Peer Mentoring in a High School Jazz Ensemble," *Journal of Research in Music Education* 55, no. 2 (2007): 94–114; and Lucy Green, *Music, Informal Learning and the School: A New Classroom Pedagogy* (Aldershot, UK: Ashgate Publishing, 2009).

21. Harry E. Price and James L. Byo, "Rehearsing and Conducting," in *The Science and Psychology of Music Performance: Creative Strategies for Teaching and Learning*, ed. Richard Parncutt and Gary McPherson (New York: Oxford University Press, 2002), 336.

22. Keith R. Sawyer, "Group Creativity: Musical Performance and Collaboration," *Psychology of Music* 34, no. 2 (2006): 153.

23. Jean Lave and Etienne Wenger, *Situated Learning: Legitimate Peripheral Participation* (New York: Cambridge University Press, 1991).

24. Ibid.

25. Etienne Wenger, *Communities of Practice: Learning, Meaning and Identity* (Cambridge: Cambridge University Press, 1998).

26. Etienne Wenger, "Knowledge Management as a Doughnut: Shaping Your Knowledge Strategy through Communities of Practice," *Ivey Business Journal* 68, no. 3 (2004): 2.

27. Etienne Wenger, "Communities of Practice: A Brief Introduction," https://scholars-bank.uoregon.edu, 2011.

28. Keith R. Sawyer, "Group Creativity: Musical Performance and Collaboration," *Psychology of Music* 34, no. 2 (2006): 163.

29. Jean Lave and Etienne Wenger, *Situated Learning: Legitimate Peripheral Participation* (New York: Cambridge University Press, 1991).

30. Ibid.

31. Etienne Wenger, "Communities of Practice: A Brief Introduction," https://scholars-bank.uoregon.edu, 2011.

32. Jean Lave and Etienne Wenger, *Situated Learning: Legitimate Peripheral Participation* (New York: Cambridge University Press, 1991), 92.

33. Etienne Wenger, *Communities of Practice: Learning, Meaning and Identity* (Cambridge: Cambridge University Press, 1998), 77.

34. Jean Lave and Etienne Wenger, *Situated Learning: Legitimate Peripheral Participation* (New York: Cambridge University Press, 1991).

35. Albert Bandura, "Self-Efficacy: Toward a Unifying Theory of Behavioral Change," *Psychological Review* 84, no. 2 (1977).

36. Etienne Wenger, "Communities of Practice and Social Learning Systems," *Organization* 7 (2000): 225–46.

37. Ibid., 231.

38. Ibid.

5. CONDUCTORS AND VERBAL COMMUNICATION

1. John Hattie and Helen Timperley, "The Power of Feedback," *Review of Educational Research* 77, no. 1 (2007): 81.

2. Ibid.

3. Albert Bandura, "Self-Efficacy: Toward a Unifying Theory of Behavioral Change," *Psychological Review* 84, no. 2 (1977).

4. Michael Bonshor, "Choral Confidence: Some Effects of Choir Configuration, Cohesion and Collaboration," *The Phenomenon of Singing* 9 (2014); and Michael John Bonshor, "Collaboration in the Choral Context: The Contribution of Conductor and Choir to Collective Confidence," in *Proceedings of the International Symposium on Performance Science Held at the University of Music and Performing Arts, Vienna,* 2013.

5. Michael John Bonshor, "Confidence and the Choral Singer: The Effects of Choir Configuration, Collaboration and Communication" (PhD diss., University of Sheffield, 2014); and Michael John Bonshor, "Confidence and the Choral Singer: The Choir as a Community of Practice," in *Choral Singing: Histories and Practices,* ed. Ursula Geisler and Karin Johansson (Newcastle upon Tyne, UK: Cambridge Scholars Publishing, 2014).

6. David E. Kanouse, Peter Gumpert, and Donnah Canavan-Gumpert, "The Semantics of Praise," *New Directions in Attribution Research* 3 (1981): 98.

7. Wulf-Uwe Meyer, "Paradoxical Effects of Praise and Criticism on Perceived Ability," *European Review of Social Psychology* 3, no. 1 (1992).

8. David E. Kanouse, Peter Gumpert, and Donnah Canavan-Gumpert, "The Semantics of Praise," *New Directions in Attribution Research* 3 (1981).

9. Ibid.

10. Tucker Biddlecombe, "Assessing and Enhancing Feedback of Choral Conductors through Analysis and Training," *International Journal of Research in Choral Singing* 4 (2012).

11. Stephen D. Brookfield, *The Skillful Teacher: On Technique, Trust, and Responsiveness in the Classroom* (San Francisco: John Wiley & Sons, 2015), 36.

12. Michael John Bonshor, "Confidence and the Choral Singer: The Effects of Choir Configuration, Collaboration and Communication" (PhD diss., University of Sheffield, 2014); and Michael John Bonshor, "Confidence and the Choral Singer: The Choir as a Community of Practice," in *Choral Singing: Histories and Practices,* ed. Ursula Geisler and Karin Johansson (Newcastle upon Tyne, UK: Cambridge Scholars Publishing, 2014).

13. Jessica Nápoles, "The Relationship between Type of Teacher Talk and Student Attentiveness," *Journal of Music Teacher Education* 16, no. 1 (2006); Jessica Nápoles and Angel M. Vázquez-Ramos, "Perceptions of Time Spent in Teacher Talk: A Comparison among Self-Estimates, Peer Estimates, and Actual Time," *Journal of Research in Music Education* 60, no. 4 (2013); Robert L. Spradling, "The Effect of Timeout from Performance on Attentiveness and Attitude of University Band Students," *Journal of Research in Music Education* 33, no. 2 (1985); Anne C. Witt, "Use of Class Time and Student Attentiveness in Secondary Instrumental Music Rehearsals," *Journal of Research in Music Education* 34, no. 1 (1986); and Cornelia

Yarbrough and Harry E. Price, "Prediction of Performer Attentiveness Based on Rehearsal Activity and Teacher Behavior," *Journal of Research in Music Education* 29, no. 3 (1981).

14. Robert L. Spradling, "The Effect of Timeout from Performance on Attentiveness and Attitude of University Band Students," *Journal of Research in Music Education* 33, no. 2 (1985); and Anne C. Witt, "Use of Class Time and Student Attentiveness in Secondary Instrumental Music Rehearsals," *Journal of Research in Music Education* 34, no. 1 (1986).

15. Jessica Nápoles, "The Relationship between Type of Teacher Talk and Student Attentiveness," *Journal of Music Teacher Education* 16, no. 1 (2006); Jessica Nápoles and Angel M. Vázquez-Ramos, "Perceptions of Time Spent in Teacher Talk: A Comparison among Self-Estimates, Peer Estimates, and Actual Time," *Journal of Research in Music Education* 60, no. 4 (2013); and Cornelia Yarbrough and Harry E. Price, "Prediction of Performer Attentiveness Based on Rehearsal Activity and Teacher Behavior," *Journal of Research in Music Education* 29, no. 3 (1981).

16. Joann Marie Kirchner, "The Relationship between Performance Anxiety and Flow," *Medical Problems of Performing Artists* 23, no. 2 (2008).

17. Michael Bonshor, "Choral Confidence: Some Effects of Choir Configuration, Cohesion and Collaboration," *The Phenomenon of Singing* 9 (2014); Michael John Bonshor, "Collaboration in the Choral Context: The Contribution of Conductor and Choir to Collective Confidence," in *Proceedings of the International Symposium on Performance Science Held at the University of Music and Performing Arts, Vienna*, 2013; Michael John Bonshor, "Confidence and the Choral Singer: The Effects of Choir Configuration, Collaboration and Communication" (PhD diss., University of Sheffield, 2014); and Michael John Bonshor, "Confidence and the Choral Singer: The Choir as a Community of Practice," in *Choral Singing: Histories and Practices*, ed. Ursula Geisler and Karin Johansson (Newcastle upon Tyne, UK: Cambridge Scholars Publishing, 2014).

18. Robert A. Baron, "Negative Effects of Destructive Criticism: Impact on Conflict, Self-Efficacy, and Task Performance," *Journal of Applied Psychology* 73, no. 2 (1988): 200.

19. Ibid., 204.

20. Jane W. Davidson, Michael J. A. Howe, Derek G. Moore, and John A. Sloboda, "The Role of Parental Influences in the Development of Musical Performance," *British Journal of Developmental Psychology* 14, no. 4 (1996); and Michael J. A. Howe, Jane W. Davidson, and John A. Sloboda, "Natural Born Talents Undiscovered," *Behavioral and Brain Sciences* 21, no. 3 (1998).

21. Alexandra Lamont, "The Beat Goes On: Music Education, Identity and Lifelong Learning," *Music Education Research* 13, no. 4 (2011).

22. Dina Van Dijk and Avraham N. Kluger, "Positive (Negative) Feedback: Encouragement or Discouragement," in *The Annual Convention of the Society for Industrial and Organizational Psychology, New Orleans, Louisiana*, 2000.

23. Albert Bandura and Daniel Cervone, "Differential Engagement of Self-Reactive Influences in Cognitive Motivation," *Organizational Behavior and Human Decision Processes* 38, no. 1 (1986).

24. Robert A. Baron, "Negative Effects of Destructive Criticism: Impact on Conflict, Self-Efficacy, and Task Performance," *Journal of Applied Psychology* 73, no. 2 (1988); Jere Brophy, "Teacher Praise: A Functional Analysis," *Review of Educational Research* 51, no. 1 (1981); and David E. Kanouse, Peter Gumpert, and Donnah Canavan-Gumpert, "The Semantics of Praise," *New Directions in Attribution Research* 3 (1981).

25. John Hattie and Helen Timperley, "The Power of Feedback," *Review of Educational Research* 77, no. 1 (2007).

26. William B. Swann, Brett W. Pelham, and Thomas R. Chidester, "Change through Paradox: Using Self-Verification to Alter Beliefs," *Journal of Personality and Social Psychology* 54, no. 2 (1988).

27. John Hattie and Helen Timperley, "The Power of Feedback," *Review of Educational Research* 77, no. 1 (2007).

28. Carol S. Dweck, *Mindset: The New Psychology of Success* (London: Random House, 2006).

29. Graham F. Welch, "We Are Musical," *International Journal of Music Education* 23, no. 2 (2005).

30. Brian Findsen, *Learning Later* (Malabar, FL: Krieger Publishing, 2005).

31. Alexandra Withnall, *Improving Learning in Later Life* (Abingdon, UK: Routledge, 2009).

32. Andrea Creech, Susan Hallam, Hilary McQueen, and Maria Varvarigou, "The Power of Music in the Lives of Older Adults," *Research Studies in Music Education* 35, no. 1 (2013); and Andrea Creech, Maria Varvarigou, Susan Hallam, Hilary McQueen, and Helena Gaunt, "Scaffolding, Organizational Structure and Interpersonal Interaction in Musical Activities with Older People," *Psychology of Music* 42, no. 3 (2014).

33. Alexandra Withnall, *Improving Learning in Later Life* (Abingdon, UK: Routledge, 2009).

34. James Cox, "Rehearsal Organizational Structures Used by Successful High School Choral Directors," *Journal of Research in Music Education* 37, no. 3 (1989).

35. Deborah L. Duay and Valerie C. Bryan, "Learning in Later Life: What Seniors Want in a Learning Experience," *Educational Gerontology* 34, no. 12 (2008); and Feliciano Villar, Montserrat Celdran, Sacramento Pinazo, and Carme Triado, "The Teacher's Perspective in Older Education: The Experience of Teaching in a University for Older People in Spain," *Educational Gerontology* 36, nos. 10–11 (2010).

36. John Hattie and Helen Timperley, "The Power of Feedback," *Review of Educational Research* 77, no. 1 (2007): 93.

37. David A. Nadler, "The Effects of Feedback on Task Group Behavior: A Review of the Experimental Research," *Organizational Behavior and Human Performance* 23, no. 3 (1979).

38. Victor M. Catano, "Relation of Improved Performance through Verbal Praise to Source of Praise," *Perceptual and Motor Skills* 41, no. 1 (1975); Victor M. Catano, "Effectiveness of Verbal Praise as a Function of Expertise of its Source," *Perceptual and Motor Skills* 42, no. 3 (1976); and C. G. Stock, "Effects of Praise and Its Source on Performance," *Perceptual and Motor Skills* 47 (1978): 43–46.

39. Stephanie E. Pitts, *Valuing Musical Participation* (Aldershot, UK: Ashgate Publishing, 2005).

40. Michael Bonshor, "Conductor Feedback and the Amateur Singer: The Role of Criticism and Praise in Building Choral Confidence," *Research Studies in Music Education* (2017), doi:10.1177/1321103X17709630.

41. Brian Gorelick and Charles Leonhard, "The Choral Rehearsal: A Laboratory for Musical Learning and Aesthetic Responsiveness," *Choral Journal* 51, no. 4 (2010).

6. SINGER-CENTERED CHORAL CONDUCTING

1. Leon Thurman and Graham Welch, *Bodymind and Voice: Foundations of Voice Education*, 2nd ed. (Iowa City, IA: National Center for Voice and Speech, 2000).

2. Ibid.

3. Ibid.

4. Michael Bonshor, "Sharing Knowledge and Power in Adult Amateur Choral Communities: The Impact of Communal Learning on the Experience of Musical Participation," *International Journal of Community Music* 9, no. 3 (2016).

5. Carl R. Rogers, Harold C. Lyon, and Reinhard Tausch, *On Becoming an Effective Teacher: Person-Centred Teaching, Psychology, Philosophy, and Dialogues with Carl R. Rogers and Harold Lyon* (Abingdon, UK: Routledge, 2013).

6. Ibid.

7. Etienne Wenger, "Communities of Practice and Social Learning Systems," *Organization* 7, no. 2 (2000).

8. Martin Ashley, *Contemporary Choral Work with Boys* (Oxford: Compton Publishing, 2014).

9. Caroline Bithell, *A Different Voice, a Different Song: Reclaiming Community through the Natural Voice and World Song* (New York: Oxford University Press, 2014).

CONCLUSION

1. Mihalyi Csikszentmihalyi, *Flow: The Psychology of Happiness* (London: Random House, 2002).

2. R. Keith Sawyer, "Group Creativity: Musical Performance and Collaboration," *Psychology of Music* 34, no. 2 (2006): 158.

3. Ibid.

4. Arnold B. Bakker, "Flow among Music Teachers and Their Students: The Crossover of Peak Experiences," *Journal of Vocational Behavior* 66 (2005).

5. Karen Wesson and Ilona Boniwell, "Flow Theory: Its Application to Coaching Psychology," *International Coaching Psychology Review* 2, no. 1 (2007): 39.

6. Mihalyi Csikszentmihalyi, *Flow: The Psychology of Happiness* (London: Random House, 2002).

7. Ibid., 84.

8. Leon Thurman and Graham Welch, *Bodymind and Voice: Foundations of Voice Education*, 2nd ed. (Iowa City, IA: National Center for Voice and Speech, 2000).

9. Marianne Williamson, *A Return to Love* (New York: HarperCollins, 1992).

Bibliography

Abel, Jennifer L., and Kevin T. Larkin. "Anticipation of Performance among Musicians: Physiological Arousal, Confidence, and State-Anxiety." *Psychology of Music* 18, no. 2 (1990): 171–82.

Adam, Hajo, and Adam D. Galinsky. "Enclothed Cognition." *Journal of Experimental Social Psychology* 48, no. 4 (2012): 918–25.

Adolphs, Ralph. "Neural Systems for Recognizing Emotion." *Current Opinion in Neurobiology* 12, no. 2 (2002): 169–77.

Aiello, Leslie C., and Robin I. Dunbar. "Neocortex Size, Group Size, and the Evolution of Language." *Current Anthropology* 34, no. 2 (1993): 184–93.

Alderson, Richard. *Complete Handbook of Voice Training.* New York: Parker Publishing Company, 1979.

Asch, Solomon E. "Opinions and Social Pressures." *Scientific American* 193 (1955): 31–35.

Ashley, Martin. *Contemporary Choral Work with Boys.* Oxford: Compton Publishing, 2014.

Aspaas, Christopher, Christopher R. McCrea, Richard J. Morris, and Linda Fowler. "Select Acoustic and Perceptual Measures of Choral Formation." *International Journal of Research in Choral Singing* 2, no. 1 (2004): 11–26.

Bailey, Betty A., and Jane W. Davidson. "Adaptive Characteristics of Group Singing: Perceptions from Members of a Choir for Homeless Men." *Musicae Scientiae* 6, no. 2 (2002): 221–56.

———. "Effects of Group Singing and Performance for Marginalized and Middle-Class Singers." *Psychology of Music* 30, no. 3 (2005): 269–303.

Bakker, Arnold B. "Flow among Music Teachers and Their Students: The Crossover of Peak Experiences." *Journal of Vocational Behavior* 66, no. 1 (2005): 26–44.

Bandura, Albert. "Self-Efficacy Mechanism in Human Agency." *American Psychologist* 37, no. 2 (1982): 122–47.

———. "Self-Efficacy: Toward a Unifying Theory of Behavioral Change." *Psychological Review* 84, no. 2 (1977): 191–215.

Bandura, Albert, and Nancy E. Adams. "Analysis of Self-Efficacy Theory of Behavioral Change." *Cognitive Therapy and Research* 1, no. 4 (1977): 287–310.

Bandura, Albert, and Daniel Cervone. "Differential Engagement of Self-Reactive Influences in Cognitive Motivation." *Organizational Behavior and Human Decision Processes* 38, no. 1 (1986): 92–113.

Barenboim, Daniel, and Phillip Huscher. *A Life in Music.* New York: Arcade Publishing, 2002.

Baron, Robert A. "Negative Effects of Destructive Criticism: Impact on Conflict, Self-Efficacy, and Task Performance." *Journal of Applied Psychology* 73, no. 2 (1988): 199–207.

Bartholomew, Robert E., and Francois Sirois. "Epidemic Hysteria in Schools: An International and Historical Overview." *Educational Studies* 22, no. 3 (1996): 285–311.

Bartholomew, Robert E., and Simon Wessely. "Protean Nature of Mass Sociogenic Illness." *British Journal of Psychiatry* 180, no. 4 (2002): 300–306.

Biddlecombe, Tucker. "Assessing and Enhancing Feedback of Choral Conductors through Analysis and Training." *International Journal of Research in Choral Singing* 4 (2012): 2–18.

Bithell, Caroline. *A Different Voice, a Different Song: Reclaiming Community through the Natural Voice and World Song.* New York: Oxford University Press, 2014.

Black, Don, Christopher Hampton, and Andrew Lloyd Weber. *Sunset Boulevard.* London: Really Useful Group, 1993.

Bleak, Jared L., and Christina M. Frederick. "Superstitious Behavior in Sport: Levels of Effectiveness and Determinants of Use in Three Collegiate Sports." *Journal of Sport Behavior* 21 (1998): 1–15.

Bong, Mimi, and Einar Skaalvik. "Academic Self-Concept and Self-Efficacy: How Different Are They Really?" *Educational Psychology Review* 15, no. 1 (2003): 1–40.

Bonshor, Michael J. "Choral Confidence: Some Effects of Choir Configuration, Cohesion and Collaboration." *The Phenomenon of Singing International Symposium IX.* St. Johns, Newfoundland: Memorial University, 2014.

———. "Collaboration in the Choral Context: The Contribution of Conductor and Choir to Collective Confidence." *Proceedings of the International Symposium on Performance Science.* Vienna: University of Music and Performing Arts, 2013. 749–54.

———. "Conductor Feedback and the Amateur Singer: The Role of Criticism and Praise in Building Choral Confidence." *Research Studies in Music Education,* 2017. doi:10.1177/1321103X17709630.

———. "Confidence and Choral Configuration: The Affective Impact of Situational and Acoustic Factors in Amateur Choirs." *Psychology of Music,* 2016. doi:10.1177/0305735616669996.

———. "Confidence and the Choral Singer: The Choir as a Community of Practice." In *Choral Singing: Histories and Practices.* Edited by Ursula Geisler and Karin Johansson, 185–207. Newcastle upon Tyne, UK: Cambridge Scholars Publishing, 2014.

———. "Confidence and the Choral Singer: The Effects of Choir Configuration, Collaboration and Communication." PhD dissertation, University of Sheffield, 2014.

———. "Musical Performance Anxiety amongst Adult Amateur Singers: The Effects of Age, Experience and Training." MA dissertation, University of Sheffield, 2002.

———. "Sharing Knowledge and Power in Adult Amateur Choral Communities: The Impact of Communal Learning on the Experience of Musical Participation." *International Journal of Community Music* 9, no. 13 (2016): 291–305.

Bostridge, Ian. *A Singer's Notebook.* London: Faber & Faber, 2011.

Briñol, Pablo, Richard E. Petty, and Benjamin Wagner. "Body Posture Effects on Self-Evaluation: A Self-Validation Approach." *European Journal of Social Psychology* 39, no. 1 (2009): 1053–64.

Brookfield, Stephen D. *The Skillful Teacher: On Technique, Trust, and Responsiveness in the Classroom.* San Francisco: John Wiley & Sons, 2015.

Brophy, Jere. "Teacher Praise: A Functional Analysis." *Review of Educational Research* 51, no. 1 (1981): 5–32.

Carney, Dana R., Amy J. C. Cuddy, and Andy J. Yap. "Power Posing: Brief Nonverbal Displays Affect Neuroendocrine Levels and Risk Tolerance." *Psychological Science* 21, no. 10 (2010): 1363–69.

Carney, Dana R., Judith A. Hall, and Lavonia Smith LeBeau. "Beliefs about the Nonverbal Expression of Social Power." *Journal of Nonverbal Behavior* 29, no. 2 (2005): 106–23.

Catano, Victor M. "Effectiveness of Verbal Praise as a Function of Expertise of Its Source." *Perceptual and Motor Skills* 42, no. 3 (1976): 1283–86.

———. "Relation of Improved Performance through Verbal Praise to Source of Praise." *Perceptual and Motor Skills* 41, no. 1 (1975): 71–74.

Cayne, Bernard S., ed. *The New Lexicon Webster's Dictionary of the English Language.* New York: Lexicon, 1990.

Chartrand, Tanya L., and John A. Bargh. "The Chameleon Effect: The Perception-Behavior Link and Social Interaction." *Journal of Personality and Social Psychology* 76, no. 6 (1999): 893–910.

The Choir with No Name. "Our Mission." http://choirwithnoname.org/about/mission.

Clift, Steven, and Grenville Hancox. "The Significance of Choral Singing for Sustaining Psychological Well-Being: Findings from a Survey of Choristers in England, Australia and Germany." *Music Performance Research* 3, no. 1 (2010): 79–96.

Coimbra, Daniela, Jane Davidson, and Dimitra Kokotsaki. "Investigating the Assessment of Singers in a Music College Setting: The Students' Perspective." *Research Studies in Music Education* 16, no. 1 (2001): 15–32.

Collins Dictionary and Thesaurus. Second edition. Glasgow: HarperCollins, 2000.

The Concise Oxford Dictionary. Oxford: Oxford University Press, 1996.

Cox, James. "Rehearsal Organizational Structures Used by Successful High School Choral Directors." *Journal of Research in Music Education* 37, no. 3 (1989): 201–18.

Creech, Andrea, Maria Varvarigou, Susan Hallam, Hilary McQueen, and Helena Gaunt. "Scaffolding, Organizational Structure and Interpersonal Interaction in Musical Activities with Older People." *Psychology of Music* 42, no. 3 (2014): 430–47.

Creech, Andrea, Susan Hallam, Hilary McQueen, and Maria Varvarigou. "The Power of Music in the Lives of Older Adults." *Research Studies in Music Education* 35, no. 1 (2013): 87–102.

Csikszentmihalyi, Mihalyi. *Flow: The Psychology of Happiness.* London: Random House, 2002.

Cuddy, Amy. *Presence: Bringing Your Boldest Self to Your Biggest Challenges.* London: Hachette, 2016.

Cuddy, Amy J. C., Caroline Ashley Wilmuth, and Dana R. Carney. "The Benefit of Power Posing before a High-Stakes Social Evaluation." *Harvard Business School Working Paper* 13-07 (2012): 1–18.

Darwin, Charles. *The Expression of the Emotions in Man and Animals.* New York: Philosophical Library, 1872.

Daugherty, James F. "Choir Spacing and Formation: Choral Sound Preferences in Random, Synergistic, and Gender-Specific Chamber Choir Placements." *International Journal of Research in Choral Singing* 1, no. 1 (2003): 48–59.

———. "Spacing, Formation, and Choral Sound: Preferences and Perceptions of Auditors and Choristers." *Journal of Research in Music Education* 47, no. 3 (1999): 224–38.

Daugherty, James F., and Melissa C. Brunkan. "Monkey See, Monkey Do? The Effect of Nonverbal Conductor Lip Rounding on Visual and Acoustic Measures of Singers' Lip Postures." *Journal of Research in Music Education* 60, no. 4 (2013): 345–62.

Dávid-Barrett, Tamás, and R. I. M. Dunbar. "Cooperation, Behavioural Synchrony and Status in Social Networks." *Journal of Theoretical Biology* 308 (2012): 88–95.

Davidson, Jane W. "The Social in Musical Performance." In *The Social Psychology of Music.* Edited by David J. Hargreaves and Adrian C. North, 209–28. Oxford: Oxford University Press, 1997.

Davidson, Jane W., Michael J. A. Howe, Derek G. Moore, and John A. Sloboda. "The Role of Parental Influences in the Development of Musical Performance." *British Journal of Developmental Psychology* 14, no. 4 (1996): 399–412.

Dews, Barney C. L., and Martha S. Williams. "Student Musicians' Personality Styles, Stresses, and Coping Patterns." *Psychology of Music* 17 (1989): 37–47.

Dingle, Genevieve A., Christopher Brander, Julie Ballantyne, and Felicity A. Baker. "'To Be Heard': The Social and Mental Health Benefits of Choir Singing for Disadvantaged Adults." *Psychology of Music* 41, no. 4 (2013): 405–21.

Duay, Deborah L., and Valerie C. Bryan. "Learning in Later Life: What Seniors Want in a Learning Experience." *Educational Gerontology* 34, no. 12 (2008): 1070–86.

Durrant, Colin, and Evangelos Himonides. "What Makes People Sing Together? Socio-Psychological and Cross-Cultural Perspectives on the Choral Phenomenon." *International Journal of Music Education* 1 (1998): 61–71.

Dweck, Carol S. *Mindset: The New Psychology of Success*. London: Random House, 2006.

Ebbinghaus, Hermann. *Über das Gedächtnis: Untersuchungen zur Experimentellen Psychologie*. Leipzig: K. Buehler, 1885.

Edwards, A. *Streisand: A Biography*. New York: Rowman & Littlefield, 2016.

Ekholm, Elizabeth. "The Effect of Singing Mode and Seating Arrangement on Choral Blend and Overall Choral Sound." *Journal of Research in Music Education* 48, no. 2 (2000): 123–35.

Ekman, Paul. "Facial Expressions of Emotion: New Findings, New Questions." *Psychological Science* 3 (1992): 34–38.

Ekman, Paul, Richard J. Davidson, and Wallace V. Friesen. "The Duchenne Smile: Emotional Expression and Brain Physiology, II." *Journal of Personality and Social Psychology* 58, no. 2 (1990): 342–53.

Falkenberg, Irina, Mathias Bartels, and Barbara Wild. "Keep Smiling! Facial Reactions to Emotional Stimuli and Their Relationship to Emotional Contagion in Patients with Schizophrenia." *European Archives of Psychiatry and Clinical Neuroscience* 258, no. 4 (2008): 245–53.

Findsen, Brian. *Learning Later*. Malabar, FL: Krieger Publishing, 2005.

Fleming, Renée. *The Inner Voice: The Making of a Singer*. New York: Penguin, 2005.

Foster, David J., Daniel A. Weigand, and Dean Baines. "The Effect of Removing Superstitious Behavior and Introducing a Pre-performance Routine in Basketball Free-Throw Performance." *Journal of Applied Sport Psychology* 18, no. 2 (2006): 167–71.

Gallese, Vittorio, and Alvin Goldman. "Mirror Neurons and the Simulation Theory of Mind-Reading." *Trends in Cognitive Sciences* 2, no. 12 (1998): 493–501.

Garnett, Liz. *Choral Conducting and the Construction of Meaning: Gesture, Voice, Identity*. Farnham, UK: Ashgate Publishing, 2009.

Goodrich, Andrew. "Peer Mentoring in a High School Jazz Ensemble." *Journal of Research in Music Education* 55, no. 2 (2007): 94–114.

Gorelick, Brian, and Charles Leonhard. "The Choral Rehearsal: A Laboratory for Musical Learning and Aesthetic Responsiveness." *Choral Journal* 51, no. 4 (2010): 82–84.

Green, Lucy. *Music, Informal Learning and the School: A New Classroom Pedagogy*. Aldershot, UK: Ashgate Publishing, 2009.

Gregory, Andrew H. "The Role of Music in Society: The Ethnomusicological Perspective." In *The Social Psychology of Music*. Edited by David J. Hargreaves and Adrian C. North, 123–40. Oxford: Oxford University Press, 1997.

Griffiths, Noola K. "'Posh Music Should Equal Posh Dress': An Investigation into the Concert Dress and Physical Appearance of Female Soloists." *Psychology of Music* 38, no. 2 (2010): 159–77.

Hamann, Donald L., and Martha Sobaje. "Anxiety and the College Musician: A Study of Performance Conditions and Subject Variables." *Psychology of Music* 11, no. 1 (1983): 37–50.

Hattie, John, and Helen Timperley. "The Power of Feedback." *Review of Educational Research* 77, no. 1 (2007): 81–112.

Howard, Sandra A. "The Effect of Selected Nonmusical Factors on Adjudicators' Ratings of High School Solo Vocal Performances." *Journal of Research in Music Education* 60, no. 2 (2012): 166–85.

Howe, Michael J. A., Jane W. Davidson, and John A. Sloboda. "Natural Born Talents Undiscovered." *Behavioral and Brain Sciences* 21, no. 3 (1998): 432–37.

Huron, David. "Is Music an Evolutionary Adaptation?" *Annals of the New York Academy of Sciences* 930, no. 1 (2001): 43–61.

Hylton, John Baker. *Comprehensive Choral Music Education*. Englewood Cliffs, NJ: Prentice Hall, 1995.

Jordan, James M. *Evoking Sound: Fundamentals of Choral Conducting and Rehearsing*. Chicago: GIA Publications, 1996.

Kanouse, David E., Peter Gumpert, and Donnah Canavan-Gumpert. "The Semantics of Praise." In *New Directions in Attribution Research*. Edited by William Ickes, Robert F. Kidd, and John H. Harvey, 3:97–115. Mahwah, NJ: Lawrence Erlbaum Associates, 1981.

Kaplan, Abraham. *Choral Conducting.* New York: Norton, 1985.

Kenny, Dianna. *The Psychology of Music Performance Anxiety.* New York: Oxford University Press, 2011.

Kenny, Dianna T., Pamela Davis, and Jenni Oates. "Music Performance Anxiety and Occupational Stress amongst Opera Chorus Artists and Their Relationship with State and Trait Anxiety and Perfectionism." *Journal of Anxiety Disorders* 18, no. 6 (2004): 757–77.

Kenny, Dianna, Tim Driscoll, and Bronwen Ackermann. "Psychological Well-Being in Professional Orchestral Musicians in Australia: A Descriptive Population Study." *Psychology of Music* 42, no. 2 (2014).

Kenny, Dianna T., James M. Fortune, and Bronwen Ackermann. "Predictors of Music Performance Anxiety during Skilled Performance in Tertiary Flute Players." *Psychology of Music* 41, no. 3 (2013): 306–28.

Kirchner, Joann Marie. "The Relationship between Performance Anxiety and Flow." *Medical Problems of Performing Artists* 23, no. 2 (2008): 59–65.

Kreutz, Gunter et al. "Effects of Choir Singing or Listening on Secretory Immunoglobulin A, Cortisol, and Emotional State." *Journal of Behavioral Medicine* 27, no. 6 (2004): 623–35.

Laird, James D. "Self-attribution of Emotion: The Effects of Expressive Behavior on the Quality of Emotional Experience." *Journal of Personality and Social Psychology* 29, no. 4 (1974): 475–86.

Lamont, Alexandra. "The Beat Goes On: Music Education, Identity and Lifelong Learning." *Music Education Research* 13, no. 4 (2011): 369–88.

Lave, Jean, and Etienne Wenger. *Situated Learning: Legitimate Peripheral Participation.* New York: Cambridge University Press, 1991.

Lehrer, Paul M. "A Review of the Approaches to the Management of Tension and Stage Fright in Music Performance." *Journal of Research in Music Education* 35, no. 3 (1987): 143–53.

Levine, Richard J. "Epidemic Faintness and Syncope in a School Marching Band." *JAMA* 238, no. 22 (1977): 2373–76.

Levitin, D. J. *The World in Six Songs: How the Musical Brain Created Human Nature.* London: Penguin, 2008.

Luszczynska, Aleksandra, Benicio Gutiérrez-Doña, and Ralf Schwarzer. "General Self-Efficacy in Various Domains of Human Functioning: Evidence from Five Countries." *International Journal of Psychology* 40, no. 2 (2005): 80–89.

McKinney, James C. *The Diagnosis and Correction of Vocal Faults: A Manual for Teachers of Singing and for Choir* Directors. Revised edition. Nashville, TN: Genevox, 1994.

Mellor, Liz. "An Investigation of Singing and Well-Being as a Group Process." *British Journal of Music Education* 30, no. 2 (2013): 177–205.

Messinger, Daniel S., Alan Fogel, and K. Laurie Dickson. "What's in a Smile?" *Developmental Psychology* 35, no. 3 (1999): 701–8.

Meyer, Wulf-Uwe. "Paradoxical Effects of Praise and Criticism on Perceived Ability." *European Review of Social Psychology* 3, no. 1 (1992): 259–83.

Miller, Richard. *On the Art of Singing.* New York: Oxford University Press, 1996.

Moffatt, M. E. K. "Epidemic Hysteria in a Montreal Train Station." *Pediatrics* 70, no. 2 (1982): 308–10.

Müller, Viktor, and Ulman Lindenberger. "Cardiac and Respiratory Patterns Synchronize between Persons during Choir Singing." *PloS one* 6, no. 9 (2011): e24893.

Murray, Michael, and Alexandra Lamont. "Community Music and Social/Health Psychology: Linking Theoretical and Practical Concerns." *Music, Health and Wellbeing* 76 (2012).

Nadler, David A. "The Effects of Feedback on Task Group Behavior: A Review of the Experimental Research." *Organizational Behavior and Human Performance* 23, no. 3 (1979): 309–38.

Nápoles, Jessica. "The Relationship between Type of Teacher Talk and Student Attentiveness." *Journal of Music Teacher Education* 16, no. 1 (2006): 7–19.

Nápoles, Jessica, and Angel M. Vázquez-Ramos. "Perceptions of Time Spent in Teacher Talk: A Comparison among Self-Estimates, Peer Estimates, and Actual Time." *Journal of Research in Music Education* 60, no. 4 (2013): 452–61.

Olivier, Laurence. *On Acting.* London: Weidenfeld and Nicolson, 1986.

Oxford Dictionary of English. Oxford: Oxford University Press, 2003.

Pacherie, Elisabeth. 2011 "Framing Joint Action." *Review of Philosophy and Psychology* 2, no. 2 (2011): 173–92.

Palmer, Andrew. *Divas in Their Own Words.* Nottingham, UK: Vernon Press, 2000.

Parker, Elizabeth C. "Exploring Student Experiences of Belonging within an Urban High School Choral Ensemble: An Action Research Study." *Music Education Research* 12, no. 4 (2010): 339–52.

Pearce, Eiluned, Jacques Launay, and Robin I. M. Dunbar. "The Ice-Breaker Effect: Singing Mediates Fast Social Bonding." *Open Science* 2, no. 10 (2015): 150–221.

Pitts, Stephanie E. *Valuing Musical Participation.* Aldershot, UK: Ashgate Publishing, 2005.

Porges, Stephen W. "Orienting in a Defensive World: Mammalian Modifications of Our Evolutionary Heritage. A Polyvagal Theory." *Psychophysiology* 32, no. 4 (1995): 301–18. doi:10.1111/j.1469-8986.1995.tb01213.x.

Powell, Trevor J., and Simon J. Enright. *Anxiety and Stress Management.* London: Routledge, 1990.

Price, Harry E., and James L. Byo. "Rehearsing and Conducting." In *The Science and Psychology of Music Performance: Creative Strategies for Teaching and Learning.* Edited by Richard Parncutt and Gary McPherson, 269–83. New York: Oxford University Press, 2002.

Rachman, Stanley J. *Anxiety.* Hove, UK: Psychology Press, 1998.

Reynolds, Gordon. *The Choirmaster in Action.* London: Novello, 1972.

Richman, Bruce. "On the Evolution of Speech: Singing as the Middle Term." *Current Anthropology* 34 (1993): 721–22.

Riskind, John H., and Carolyn C. Gotay. "Physical Posture: Could It Have Regulatory or Feedback Effects on Motivation and Emotion?" *Motivation and Emotion* 6, no. 3 (1982): 273–98.

Rodenburg, Patsy. *Presence: How to Use Positive Energy for Success in Every Situation.* London: Penguin, 2007.

Rodgers, Richard, and Oscar Hammerstein II. *The King and I.* New York: Williamson Music, 1951.

Rogers, Carl R., Harold C. Lyon, and Reinhard Tausch. *On Becoming an Effective Teacher: Person-Centred Teaching, Psychology, Philosophy, and Dialogues with Carl R. Rogers and Harold Lyon.* Abingdon, UK: Routledge, 2013.

Rowe, Paul F. *Choral Music Education.* Second edition. Englewood Cliffs, NJ: Prentice Hall, 1983.

Ryan, Charlene, and Nicolle Andrews. "An Investigation into the Choral Singer's Experience of Music Performance Anxiety." *Journal of Research in Music Education* 57, no. 2 (2009): 108–26.

Salmon, Paul G. "A Psychological Perspective on Musical Performance Anxiety: A Review of the Literature." *Medical Problems of Performing Artists* 5, no. 1 (1990): 2–11.

Salmon, Paul, R. Schrodt, and Jesse Wright. "A Temporal Gradient of Anxiety in a Stressful Performance Context." *Medical Problems of Performing Artists* 4, no. 2 (1989): 77–80.

Sawyer, Keith R. "Group Creativity: Musical Performance and Collaboration." *Psychology of Music* 34, no. 2 (2006): 148–65.

Shibata, Kazuhisa, Yuka Sasaki, Ji Won Bang, Edward G. Walsh, Maro G. Machizawa, Masako Tamaki, Li-Hung Chang, and Takeo Watanabe. "Overlearning Hyperstabilizes a Skill by Rapidly Making Neurochemical Processing Inhibitory-Dominant." *Nature Neuroscience* 20, no. 3 (2017): 470–75.

Slatkin, Leonard. *Conducting Business: Unveiling the Mystery behind the Maestro.* Milwaukee, WI: Amadeus Press, 2012.

Smith, Jonathan A. "Semi-structured Interviewing and Qualitative Analysis." In *Rethinking Methods in Psychology.* Edited by Rom Harr, Luk Van Langenhove, and Jonathan A. Smith, 9–27. London: Sage Publications, 1995.

Smith, Jonathon A., Paul Flowers, and Michael Larkin. *Interpretative Phenomenological Analysis.* London: Sage Publications, 2009.

Solovitch, Sara. *Playing Scared: My Journey through Stage Fright.* London: Bloomsbury Publishing, 2015.

Southcott, Jane E. "And as I Go, I Love to Sing: The Happy Wanderers, Music and Positive Aging." *International Journal of Community Music* 2, nos. 2–3 (2009): 143–56.

Spahn, Claudia, Matthias Echternach, Mark F. Zander, Edgar Voltmer, and Berhard Richter. "Music Performance Anxiety in Opera Singers." *Logopedics Phoniatrics Vocology* 35, no. 4 (2010): 15–182.

Spradling, Robert L. "The Effect of Timeout from Performance on Attentiveness and Attitude of University Band Students." *Journal of Research in Music Education* 33, no. 2 (1985): 123–37.

Stebbins, Robert A. *The Barbershop Singer: Inside the Social World of a Musical Hobby.* Toronto: Toronto Press, 1996.

———. *Between Work and Leisure.* New Brunswick, NJ: Transaction Publishers, 2004.

Stepper, Sabine, and Fritz Strack. "Propriceptive Determinants of Emotional and Nonemotional Feelings." *Journal of Personality and Social Psychology* 64, no. 2 (1993): 211–20.

Steptoe, Andrew. "Negative Emotions in Music Making: The Problem of Performance Anxiety." In *Music and Emotion: Theory and Research.* Edited by Patrik N. Juslin and John A. Sloboda. Oxford: Oxford University Press, 2001.

———. "Performance Anxiety: Recent Developments in Its Analysis and Management." *Musical Times* 123, no. 164 (1982): 537–41.

Stock, C. G. "Effects of Praise and Its Source on Performance." *Perceptual and Motor Skills* 47 (1978): 43–46.

Strack, Fritz, Leonard L. Martin, and Sabine Stepper. "Inhibiting and Facilitating Conditions of the Human Smile: A Nonobtrusive Test of the Facial Feedback Hypothesis." *Journal of Personality and Social Psychology* 54, no. 5 (1988): 768–77.

Sundberg, Johan. *The Science of the Singing Voice.* DeKalb: Northern Illinois University Press, 1987.

Swann, William B., Brett W. Pelham, and Thomas R. Chidester. "Change through Paradox: Using Self-Verification to Alter Beliefs." *Journal of Personality and Social Psychology* 54, no. 2 (1988): 268–73.

Tear, Robert. *Singer Beware: Cautionary Story of the Singing Class.* London: Hodder and Stoughton, 1995.

Ternström, Sten. "Hearing Myself with Others: Sound Levels in Choral Performance Measured with Separation of One's Own Voice from the Rest of the Choir." *Journal of Voice* 8, no. 4 (1994): 293–302.

———. "Preferred Self-to-Other Ratios in Choir Singing." *Journal of the Acoustical Society of America* 15, no. 6 (1999): 3563–74.

Ternström, Sten, and Duane Richard Karna. "Choir." In *The Science and Psychology of Music Performance: Creative Strategies for Teaching and Learning.* Edited by Richard Parncutt and Gary McPherson, 269–83. New York: Oxford University Press, 2002.

Thurman, Leon, and Graham Welch. *Bodymind and Voice: Foundations of Voice Education.* Second edition. Iowa City, IA: National Center for Voice and Speech, 2000.

Valentine, Elizabeth. "Alexander Technique." In *Musical Excellence: Strategies and Techniques to Enhance Performance.* Edited by Aaron Williamon, 179–96. Oxford: Oxford University Press, 2004.

Van Dijk, Dina, and Avraham N. Kluger. "Positive (Negative) Feedback: Encouragement or Discouragement." *The Annual Convention of the Society for Industrial and Organizational Psychology.* New Orleans, Louisiana, 2000.

Van Kemenade, Johannes F. L. M., Maarten J. M. Van Son, and Nicolette C. A. Van Heesch. "Performance Anxiety among Professional Musicians in Symphonic Orchestras: A Self-Report Study." *Psychological Reports* 77, no. 2 (1995): 555–62.

Vealey, Robin S., Megan Garner-Holman, Susan Walter Hayashi, and Peter Giacobbi. "Sources of Sport-Confidence: Conceptualization and Instrument Development." *Journal of Sport and Exercise Psychology* 20, no. 1 (1998): 54–80.

Vickhoff, Björn. *A Perspective Theory of Music Perception and Emotion.* Gothenburg, Germany: University of Gothenburg, 2008.

Villar, Feliciano, Montserrat Celdran, Sacramento Pinazo, and Carme Triado. "The Teacher's Perspective in Older Education: The Experience of Teaching in a University for Older People in Spain." *Educational Gerontology* 36, no. 10 (2010): 951–67.

Wapnick, Joel, Alice Ann Darrow, Jolan Kovacs, and Lucinda Dalrymple. "Effects of Physical Attractiveness on Evaluation of Vocal Performance." *Journal of Research in Music Education* 45, no. 3 (1997): 470–79.

Welch, Graham. "The Genesis of Singing Behaviour." *Proceedings of the Sixth International Conference on Musical Perception and Cognition.* Department of Psychology, University of Keele, UK, 2000.

———. "We Are Musical." *International Journal of Music Education* 23, no. 2 (2005): 117–20.

Wenger, Etienne. *Communities of Practice: A Brief Introduction.* https://scholars-bank.uoregon.edu/xmlui/, 2011.

———. *Communities of Practice: Learning, Meaning and Identity.* Cambridge: Cambridge University Press, 1998.

———. "Communities of Practice and Social Learning Systems." *Organization* 7, no. 2 (2000): 225–46.

———. "Knowledge Management as a Doughnut: Shaping Your Knowledge Strategy through Communities of Practice." *Ivey Business Journal* 68, no. 3 (2004): 2.

Wessely, Simon. "Mass Hysteria: Two Syndromes?" *Psychological Medicine* 17, no. 1 (1987): 109–20.

Wesson, Karen, and Ilona Boniwell. "Flow Theory: Its Application to Coaching Psychology." *International Coaching Psychology Review* 2, no. 1 (2007): 33–44.

Wester, Misse. "Fight, Flight or Freeze: Assumed Reactions of the Public during a Crisis." *Journal of Contingencies and Crisis Management* 19, no. 4 (2011): 207–14.

Wild, Barbara, Michael Erb, Michael Eyb, Mathias Bartels, and Wolfgang Grodd. "Why Are Smiles Contagious? An fMRI Study of the Interaction between Perception of Facial Affect and Facial Movements." *Psychiatry Research: Neuroimaging* 123, no. 1 (2003): 17–36.

Williamon, Aaron. *Musical Excellence: Strategies and Techniques to Enhance Performance.* New York: Oxford University Press, 2004.

Williamson, Marianne. *A Return to Love.* New York: HarperCollins, 1992.

Wilson, Glenn D. "Performance Anxiety." In *The Social Psychology of Music.* Edited by David J. Hargreaves and Adrian C. North, 230. Oxford: Oxford University Press, 1997.

———. *Psychology for Performing Artists: Butterflies and Bouquets.* London: Jessica Kingsley Publishers, 1994.

Wiltermuth, Scott S., and Chip Heath. "Synchrony and Cooperation." *Psychological Science* 20, no. 1 (2009): 1–5.

Withnall, Alexandra. *Improving Learning in Later Life* . Abingdon, UK: Routledge, 2009.

Witt, Anne C. "Use of Class Time and Student Attentiveness in Secondary Instrumental Music Rehearsals." *Journal of Research in Music Education* 34, no. 1 (1986): 34–42.

Womack, Mari. "Why Athletes Need Ritual: A Study of Magic among Professional Athletes." In *Sport and Religion.* Edited by Shirl J. Hoffman, 191–202. Champaign, IL: Human Kinetics, 1992.

Yarbrough, Cornelia, and Harry E. Price. "Prediction of Performer Attentiveness Based on Rehearsal Activity and Teacher Behavior." *Journal of Research in Music Education* 29 (1981): 209–17.

Index

a cappella practice, 42
acoustics. *See* choral acoustics
action stations, 77; choir configuration and, 75–76, 79; choral acoustics in, 75, 77, 79; positions and, 76
adaptation, 73–75
adrenaline increase, 4, 32–33
adult learning, 138
adults, 117
age, 139; destructive criticism and, 129–130, 131; praise and, 117
aggression, 130–131, 146
alarm responses, 31–32
Alexander technique, 28
Alzheimer's Society, xv–xvi
amateur singer groups: benefits for, xv; "careers" in, xvi–xviii, 85; extent of, xv; goals within, 148–149; research on, xvi; schools compared to, 123; types of, xxi
amateur singers, xvii–xviii; interviews with, xix–xx; trained singers compared to, 59, 61, 66, 93
antagonistic behavior, 146
anxiety, 15, 32–33. *See also* musical performance anxiety
appearances: idiosyncrasies in, 48; for men, 47–48; physical comfort and, 48; roles related to, 49; uniforms for, 49, 50; for women, 47, 49
apprentice, choral, 105

Aristotle, 39
arrangements, custom-made, 46–47
artifacts, 110
audience, 54, 55, 114
audience interaction: in communicating confidence, 11; eye contact in, 11
authenticity: body language and, 18–19; in communicating confidence, 17–19; of conductors, 147; empowerment and, 17–18; illusion of, 18
authority, 140
avoidance, 33

"backward chaining", 39
balanced feedback, 120; nonspecificity and, 119–120; respect from, 122, 141; scarcity of, 119
Bandura, Albert, 2, 110–111
Banks, Tyra, 10
Baring Trust, xvi
Beyonce, 21
biochemistry, 19; adrenaline increase in, 4, 32–33; "mirror neuron" system and, 15; oxytocin, 83
body language, 2–5; authenticity and, 18–19; breath-calming exercises in, 6–8; of conductors, 22–23, 25–26, 28, 29; postural exercises in, 5–6; relaxation exercises in, 6–7
bone-conducted sound, 58
boredom, 23

brain, xv–xvi
breath-calming exercises, 6–8
breathing, 6; of conductors, 28; eye contact
    and, 14, 93
brightness, in singing, 10
"busking", 20, 39

call-and-response songs, 14, 44
cancer, xv–xvi
career amateurs, xvii–xviii, 85
chameleon effect, 14–16, 25
charisma, 20
childhood, xvi–xvii, 1
choir configuration, xxiii, 58, 59; action
    stations and, 75–76, 79; exercises on,
    74–75; hearing each other in, 60–61;
    individual placement in, 69–71;
    rehearsal room to venue and, 71–74;
    subjectivity on, 59–60. *See also*
    closeness
choir formation: communication and,
    64–66; inter-singer spacing in, 66, 76;
    sections in, 65–66; in semicircle,
    64–65, 70, 74
choirs, xxiv, 57, 103; as community, 49;
    conflict with other, 102
The Choir with No Name, 82
choral acoustics, xxiii, 57; in action
    stations, 75, 77, 79; closeness and,
    61–64; confidence and, 60–61; familiar
    individual placement and, 70–71,
    72–73; positions and, 58, 61, 67–69;
    venues and, 60
choral apprentice, 105
choral diversity, 138; adult learning and,
    138; rapport in, 139, 141; recognition
    of, 137–138; tips about, 139
choral persona exercises, 21
choral singing types, xx
choral team: activities for, 87;
    collaboration and, 84–87; commitment
    of, 84; empathy within, 90; learning
    within, 90–93; praise within, 88–89;
    pride in, 85–86; responsibility in,
    86–87; security of, 84; support within,
    87–89; trust within, 89–90, 153
churches, 62–63, 67
clapping, 38

closeness, 61–62, 74; churches and, 62–63;
    hearing each other and, 62; isolation
    without, 62; open-air performances and,
    63–64; SOR and, 58, 59, 64; in venue
    positions, 67–68
clothing, 20–21, 54, 55. *See also*
    appearances
cognitive symptoms, 32
collaboration, xxiii, 81, 146; choral team
    and, 84–87; community and, 82–84,
    150–151; conflicts within, 99–102;
    reciprocal peer learning in, 90–93,
    105–106; role models in, 94–95, 150;
    team leaders in, 95–99; trust in, 87–90,
    93
comfort, physical, 48
commentaries, 100
communicating confidence: audience
    interaction in, 11; authenticity in,
    17–19; chameleon effect in, 14–16, 25;
    choral persona exercises in, 21;
    emotions in, 8–10; eye contact
    exercises in, 14; among group singers,
    14–16; power performance exercises in,
    19–20; presence in, 11–13; smiling
    exercises in, 10–11; smiling in, 8, 9–10;
    tips for, 16–17
communication, 64–66; nonverbal, 28, 111
communication style, 129–131, 138;
    significance of, 139–140. *See also*
    criticism; feedback; verbal
    communication
community, 82; bonding with, 82–83;
    choir as, 49; collaboration and, 82–84,
    150–151. *See also* choral team
community of practice (CoP), 105, 109,
    110; definition of, 103–104; description
    of, 104; development of, 109–110;
    emulation in, 104, 105, 107; full
    member of, 106–107; harmony in, 104,
    106; master singer in, 105–106;
    newcomers in, 104–105; pitch in, 104,
    105, 106; position in, 108; reality of,
    106–107; self-efficacy and, 107–108;
    tolerance in, 106, 107
competition, 94
condescension, 129–130
conductor confidence modeling tips, 27–28
conductor empowerment exercises, 26–27

conductors, xvi, xxii, xxiii, xxiv, 101, 146, 147; action stations and, 77; body language of, 22–23, 25–26, 28, 29; breathing of, 28; complexity for, 149; confidence from, 81; distractions and, 154–155; education and, xvi–xvii, 103; emotional contagion from, 22–23; experience of, 22, 140–141; eye contact of, 22–23, 24, 26, 27; facial feedback from, 25, 26, 27, 29; feedback and, 114–116, 120, 142; internal leadership and, 109; listening by, 147, 150; mission statement of, 156; perfectionism and, 126; performance of, 24; power of, 140, 147–148, 151, 155; questions for, 147; reflections of, 155–156; as senior learners, 146–147, 155–156; stereotype of, 113; as teachers, 103, 148; team leaders and, 98–99, 149; terminology from, 91–92, 134; tips for, 98–99, 149–150; training of, 140–141; uniforms for, 50; in venue positions, 68–69; verbal communication and, 113–114. *See also* destructive criticism

confidence, ix, xviii–xix, xxii, 1–2; choral acoustics and, 60–61; from conductors, 81; definitions of, xxii, 1–2; mixed-voice formations and, 66; "overlearning" and, 40–41; of team leaders, 97. *See also* communicating confidence

confidence strategies, xxii–xxiv

configuration exercises, 74–75

conflicts, 99–100, 101; within collaboration, 99–102; from commentaries, 100; from critical peers, 101–102; from distractions, 100; flow and, 100–101; intimidation in, 101–102; management of, 102; with other choirs, 102; from talking, 100

connectivity, 109

consciousness, 36–37

constructive criticism, 123–124, 142; guide for, 125; sensitivity of, 124–125; specificity and, 125, 142; welcome of, 124

CoP. *See* community of practice

coping, with criticism, 135–136

credibility, of feedback, 115–116, 140, 142

critical peers, 101–102

criticism, 124, 135–136; aggression related to, 130–131; condescension with, 129–130; from dictators, 130–131; doubts and, 120–121; excessiveness of, 122, 126; need for, 120–121; praise and, 117; respect related to, 129–131. *See also* constructive criticism; destructive criticism

Csikszentmihalyi, Mihalyi, 36, 153

Cuddy, Amy, 19

cues, 70

cue sharing, 65

Darwin, Charles, 8

destructive criticism, 123–124, 125, 140, 142; age and, 129–130, 131; doubt and, 126, 127; emotions and, 128, 132, 146; of individual singers, 125–126, 131, 142; innocence and, 127; morale and, 127–128; quitting from, 125–126, 130, 131; respect and, 131; of sections, 127; self-efficacy and, 128; tips about, 131–132; victimization and, 126–127

dictators, 130–131, 146

discipline, 132

distractions, 100, 154–155

doubts, 33–34, 120; criticism and, 120–121; destructive criticism and, 126, 127

early life experiences, 128

early onset anxiety, 32–33

Ebbinghaus, Hermann, 40

education, xvi–xvii, xx, 103; from conductors, 103; high school, xvi–xvii; from peer interactions, 147–148

egos, 43

embodied cognition, 9

embodied instrument, 29, 42, 57

embodiment. *See* body language

emotional contagion, 14–16, 94, 154, 155; from conductors, 22–23

emotions, xix, xxi, 6, 9; in communicating confidence, 8–10; destructive criticism and, 128, 132, 146; familiar individual placement and, 108. *See also* confidence

empathy, 8, 90
empowerment, 26–27; authenticity and,
	17–18
emulation, 104, 105, 107
energy, kinetic, 19
enjoyment, 36, 132, 142; of community,
	83–84; from repertoire selection, 45–46
Europa Cantat, xv
exaggeration, 19
exercises: breath-calming, 6–8; on choir
	configuration, 74–75; choral persona,
	21; conductor empowerment, 26–27;
	configuration, 74–75; eye contact, 14;
	"note-bashing", 38–39; postural, 5–6;
	power performance, 19–20; relaxation,
	6–7; smiling, 10–11; for team leaders,
	99; for trust, 93. *See also* tips
exits, 76; in presentation, 51–52, 53, 54
expectations, 134–135, 142; individual
	needs and, 132–135; terminology
	related to, 134, 139
experiences, 4–5, 107–108, 128; of
	conductors, 22, 140–141
extrances, 51–52, 53, 54
eye contact, 16, 35; in audience interaction,
	11; breathing and, 14, 93; of
	conductors, 22–23, 24, 26, 27
eye contact exercises, 14
eyes, 10, 27

faces, 42
facial feedback, 25, 26, 27, 29; smiling in,
	27; vocal tone and, 26
familiar individual placement, 70, 71, 102;
	adaptation and, 73–75; choral acoustics
	and, 70–71, 72–73; configuration
	exercises and, 74–75; emotions and,
	108; last-minute changes and, 71–72.
	See also action stations
family, 114–115
feedback, 113–114, 123, 142; from
	audience, 114; from conductors,
	114–116, 120, 142; credibility of,
	115–116, 140, 142; from family,
	114–115; from friends, 114; individual
	needs and, 135–136; interpretation of,
	135, 138–139; nonspecificity of,
	119–120, 122; positive feedback loop,
	14; praise as, 116–119; rapport and,

142; respect and, 115–116; self-efficacy
	and, 115, 135; source of, 114–116. *See
	also* balanced feedback; criticism;
	facial feedback
first circle performances, 13
Fitzgerald, Ella, xv
flight, fight, or freeze, 31–32
flow, 36, 100–101, 153; consciousness
	related to, 36–37; facilitation of, 154;
	incapacity related to, 154–155; "note-
	bashing" exercises for, 38–39;
	preparation and, 37–38, 56. *See also*
	"overlearning"; repertoire selection
fMRI. *See* functional magnetic resonance
	imaging
folders, music, 50, 54
foreign languages, 44, 91
formal musical education, xx
formation, 64. *See also* choir formation
Francis of Assisi (saint), 31
friends, 114
functional magnetic resonance imaging
	(fMRI), 9

geography, xx
group singers, 14–16. *See also* amateur
	singer groups; choirs

habits, 6
handbooks, choir, 50, 110
harmony, 38–39; in CoP, 104, 106
HCL. *See* human compatible learning
hearing each other, 60–61; closeness and,
	62. *See also* choir formation; choral
	acoustics
heart rate, 83
height, 68, 69
high school, xvi–xvii
homogeneity, 107
human compatible learning (HCL): as
	collaboration, 146; conductors in, 146;
	as person-centered teaching, 148; in
	singer-centered choral conducting,
	145–146, 148
humming, 42, 44
humor, 132

identity, 111, 128
illusion, 18

individual needs, 132, 137, 138, 154; expectations and, 132–135; feedback and, 135–136; humor and, 132; laughter and, 132; rapport as, 137; recognition as, 136–137

individual placement, 108; in choir configuration, 69–71; cues and, 70; in mixed-voice formations, 69–70; team leaders and, 96–97, 99. *See also* configuration exercises; familiar individual placement

individual singers, 125–126, 131, 142

insecurity, 120

inspiration, 94–95

internal leadership, 109

interpretation, 36, 41; of feedback, 135, 138–139; flow and, 37; musical expression immersion and, 35–36; "overlearning" related to, 40–41

inter-singer spacing, 66, 76

interviews, xix–xx, xxi, 141, 145

intimacy, 12–13

isolation, 62

Jagger, Mick, 19

kinetic energy, 19

King and I, 12, 17

languages, 44, 91. *See also* body language; terminology

Lao Tzu, 1, 145

last-minute changes, 71–72

laughter, 132

leader, ix

leadership, internal, 109. *See also* master singers; role models; team leaders

learning, 90–93. *See also* "over-learning"

"legitimate peripheral participation", 104

listening, 24, 147, 150

low self-efficacy, 4

Martin, L. L., 9

"mass anxiety hysteria", 15

master singers: choral apprentices and, 105; situated learning theory and, 105–106; soloists, 67–68, 94. *See also* superstars

membership, 110

memorization, 41–42

men, 47–48

"mirror neuron" system, 15

mixed-voice formations, 65–66, 74; individual placement in, 69–70

modeling, 27–28, 107. *See also* role models

modesty, 96, 97

monitors, 50, 53, 54, 55

morale, 127–128

motivation, 32–34; from praise, 116, 117–118

MPA. *See* musical performance anxiety

musical attainment, 142

musical directors. *See* conductors

musical expression immersion, 32, 34, 56; enjoyment and, 36; eye contact and, 35; interpretation and, 35–36; smiling and, 34. *See also* flow

musical identity development, 128

musical performance anxiety (MPA), xviii, 2, 31, 32; motivation and, 32–34; symptoms of, 32–33

musical terminology. *See* terminology

music folders, 50, 54

names, 82, 137, 150

negative feedback, 135. *See also* destructive criticism

"nerves", 14–15. *See also* anxiety

newcomers, 104–105

Newell, Alex, 20

non-performing choirs, 148

nonspecificity, of feedback, 119–120, 122

nonverbal communication, 28, 111. *See also* body language

note-bashing, 38–39, 41

Olivier, Laurence, 2

open-access community choirs, 5

open-air performances, 63–64

open questions, xxi, 141

opera, xvii

"Our Deepest Fear" (Williamson), 156

"overlearning", 40, 41–42; confidence and, 40–41; interpretation related to, 40–41; practice and, 39–42

oxytocin, 83

Paderewski, I. J., 32, 41
Parliament Choir, xvi
patience, 134–135
peer interactions, 147–148
peer relationships, 110. *See also*
  community of practice
perfectionism, 34, 126
"performance persona", 20–21
performance-relatedness, of praise, 119
performances, 13, 19–20; of conductors,
  24; extra-musical factors and, 55, 56;
  feedback of, 123; open-air, 63–64. *See
  also* musical performance anxiety
person-centered teaching, 148. *See also*
  singer-centered choral conducting
physical comfort, 48
physical symptoms, 32
physiological symptoms, 4
physiological synchronization, 83
physiology, 83
pitch, 104, 105, 106
positions: action stations and, 76; choral
  acoustics and, 58, 61, 67–69; in CoP,
  108; in presentation, 50–53, 56. *See
  also* venue positions
positive feedback loop, 14
postural exercises, 5; bent knees in, 5;
  "bucket carry" as, 5; feet placement in,
  6; sitting in, 6; stance in, 5–6; straight
  spine as, 5–6
posture, 3–4; power, 18–19, 25, 27; stance,
  6, 7–8
power: of conductors, 140, 147–148, 151,
  155; sharing of, 147–148
power performance exercises, 19–20
power postures, 18–19, 25, 27
practice, 33, 34, 41; "overlearning" and,
  39–42; smiling and, 34. *See also*
  community of practice; preparation
praise: age and, 117; within choral team,
  88–89; with constructive criticism, 142;
  criticism and, 117; definition of, 116;
  desire for, 122–123; effectiveness of,
  116–119; as feedback, 116–119;
  influence of, 116–119; motivation
  from, 116, 117–118; need for, 117;
  performance-relatedness of, 119; reality
  of, 118–119; as routine, 118; self-
  esteem and, 116; sincerity of, 118, 119;

specificity of, 117–118, 119, 122–123;
  trust in, 118–119; variability of, 119
preparation, 33; flow and, 37–38, 56; lack
  of, 32–40
presence: in communicating confidence,
  11–13; definition of, 12; second circle,
  12–13; stage, 12, 19
presentation: entries and exits in, 51–52,
  53, 54; positions in, 50–53, 56;
  strategies for, 53–54
pride, 85–86
public singing, 55

qualitative research, xx–xxi, 81
questions, xxi, 141, 147
quitting, 101; from destructive criticism,
  125–126, 130, 131

ranges, 46
rapport, 137, 142; in choral diversity, 139,
  141; goals and, 150; rhythm and, 93
reciprocal peer learning, 90–93, 105–106
recognition, 136–137; of choral diversity,
  137–138
reframing, of physiological symptoms, 4
rehearsal room to venue, choir
  configuration, 71–74
rehearsals, for sections, 99
rehearsal strategies, 41–42
relaxation exercises, 6–7
repertoire selection, 44; choice in, 46–47;
  complexity of, 45–46; custom-made
  arrangements in, 46–47; enjoyment
  from, 45–46
research, xvi, xviii; qualitative, xx–xxi, 81
respect, 115–116, 131; from balanced
  feedback, 122, 141; criticism related to,
  129–131
responsibility, 86–87
rhythm, 87, 91; names and, 137; rapport
  and, 93
rituals, 54, 56
Rodenburg, Patsy, 12–13
Rogers, Carl, 148
role models, 94–95; in collaboration,
  94–95, 150; competition with, 94
rounds, 87
routine, praise as, 118

sales analogies, 37–38

scales, 44

schools, xvi–xvii; amateur singer groups compared to, 123

seating, 54. *See also* familiar individual placement; positions

second circle presence, 12–13

sections, 99; in choir formation, 65–66; destructive criticism of, 127

security, 84; insecurity, 120

self-confidence, 1–2

self-efficacy, 1–2, 4; CoP and, 107–108; destructive criticism and, 128; experiences and, 4–5; feedback and, 115, 135

self-efficacy theory, 107–108

self-esteem, 116

self-perception mechanisms, 9

self-to-other ratio (SOR), 58, 59, 64

semicircle, 64–65, 70, 74

senior learners, 146–147, 155–156

sensitivity, 135–136; of constructive criticism, 124–125

Sidney de Haan Center, xvi

silence, 120–121

sincerity, 118, 119

singer-centered choral conducting: HCL in, 145–146, 148; observations and, 145

singing, xx, 9, 10, 55

"Singing Europe" survey, xv

"Singing for the Brain", xv–xvi

"Sing with Us", xv–xvi

situated learning theory, 103; master singers and, 105–106. *See also* community of practice

smeyes, 10, 27

"smile muscle" (zygomaticus major), 9

smiling, 24, 34, 121; in communicating confidence, 8, 9–10; in facial feedback, 27; musical expression immersion and, 34; while singing, 9

smiling exercises, 10–11

soloists, 67–68, 94

songs, 14, 44, 87

song share, 99

SOR. *See* self-to-other ratio

sound-pressure level (SPL), 58, 59

specificity, 142; constructive criticism and, 125, 142; nonspecificity, 119–120, 122;

of praise, 117–118, 119, 122–123. *See also* nonspecificity

SPL. *See* sound-pressure level

sports, 82–83

stage-fright, 31. *See also* musical performance anxiety

stage presence, 12, 19

stance, 6, 7–8

starting notes, 42, 46

Stebbins, Robert, xvii

Stepper, S., 9

storage, 54

Strack, F., 9

Streisand, Barbra, 31, 33–34

superstars, 21; Streisand as, 31, 33–34

talking, 100

teachers, 103, 148. *See also* master singers; senior learners

team leaders, 150; absence of, 98; in collaboration, 95–99; conductors and, 98–99, 149; confidence of, 97; exercises for, 99; individual placement and, 96–97, 99; modesty of, 96, 97; skills of, 96

Tenovus Cancer Care, xv–xvi

terminology, xxiv, 102; from conductors, 91–92, 134; expectations related to, 134, 139

tessitura, 46

Thurman, Leon, 145–146

tips: about choral diversity, 139; for communicating confidence, 16–17; conductor confidence modeling, 27–28; for conductors, 98–99, 149–150; about destructive criticism, 131–132

tolerance, 106, 107

tradition, 106

trained singers, 61, 66, 93; levels of, 59, 91

training, of conductors, 140–141

transitions, 39

trust: balanced feedback and, 120; within choral team, 89–90, 90, 153; in collaboration, 87–90, 93; exercises for, 93; in praise, 118–119; from verbal communication, 121

uniforms, 49, 50, 110; for conductors, 50

venue positions, 67; closeness in, 67–68; conductor in, 68–69; height in, 68, 69; soloists in, 67–68

venues, 53, 60; rehearsal room to, choir configuration in, 71–74. *See also* action stations

verbal communication: conductors and, 113–114; nonverbal communication, 28, 111; silence and, 120–121; trust from, 121

verbal persuasion, 107–108

victimization, 126–127

vocal confidence life history, xix–xx

vocal tone, 26

voice embodiment, 3; embodied instrument, 29, 42, 57. *See also* body language

Voltaire, 139

volume, 99–100

vowels, 44

vulnerability, 31

walking, 11, 19

warm-up, 27, 99, 135; effectiveness of, 42–43; suggestions for, 44. *See also* body language

Wegner, Etienne, 109

Welch, Graham, 145–146

Williamson, Marianne, 156

women, 47, 49

work songs, 87

zone. *See* flow

zygomaticus major ("smile muscle"), 9

About the Author

Dr. Michael Bonshor is a long-established singing teacher and musical director. He has a background as a professional singer with international contracts, and he enjoys teaching singers of all ages and abilities. He has taught singers from four to ninety-four years old, and his students have ranged from beginners who have previously been told that they are "tone deaf" (not true in the case of any singer that Michael has met so far) to advanced singers who are already performing professionally.

Michael's work as a conductor is equally varied and has encompassed large choral societies, amateur operatic societies, open-access community choirs, small-scale close-harmony groups, chamber choirs, and professional ensembles. As a teacher and conductor, he has felt privileged to work with a diverse population of singers with a wide variety of hopes, aspirations, and musical interests. All singers are welcome in Michael's teaching practice, whether their aims include a professional career or whether they just want to have fun while learning how to use their voices healthily.

As a music psychologist, Michael has special expertise in musical well-being and performance psychology. His MA dissertation examined music performance anxiety (MPA) among adult singers, and his PhD thesis focused on confidence-building for amateur choral singers. He has presented his research at international conferences and throughout the United Kingdom, and he has been awarded fellowships at the University of Sheffield and the Institute of Musical Research, Royal Holloway, University of London. He is also an associate member of the International Center for Community Music at York St. John University as well as a fellow of the Incorporated Society of Musicians.

Michael strongly believes in making meaningful connections between his work in positive psychology and his professional practice. He received a grant from the Institute of Musical Research for his interactive conference *Real World Applications of Choral Research*, and he continues his career as a conductor, teacher, and workshop leader along with his research commitments. In his spare time, he enjoys English Breakfast tea while pondering the intricacies of the *Times* crossword. Weather permitting, he is also a keen dog-walker. His proverbial best friend, Harley, is a Parson Jack Russell who refuses to go outside if it is raining!

Lightning Source UK Ltd.
Milton Keynes UK
UKHW011854010519
341952UK00001B/40/P